FRONTIERS OF BOYHOOD

The
William F. Cody
Series on the History and
Culture of the American West

FRONTIERS OF BOYHOOD

Imagining America, Past and Future

MARTIN WOODSIDE

UNIVERSITY OF OKLAHOMA PRESS : NORMAN

BUFFALO BILL
CENTER
OF THE WEST

Buffalo Bill Center of the West sponsorship of The William F. Cody Series on the History and Culture of the American West is generously funded by the Geraldine W. and Robert J. Dellenback Foundation, Inc.

This book is published with the generous assistance of the McCasland Foundation, Duncan, Oklahoma.

Library of Congress Cataloging-in-Publication Data

Names: Woodside, Martin, author.
Title: Frontiers of boyhood : imagining America, past and future / Martin Woodside.
Description: First. | Norman, OK : University of Oklahoma Press, [2020] | Series: The William F. Cody series on the history and culture of the American West; volume 7 | Includes bibliographical references and index. | Summary: "Revisits these narratives of American boyhood and frontier mythology to show how they worked against and through one another—and how this interaction shaped ideas about national character, identity, and progress"—Provided by publisher.
Identifiers: LCCN 2019041395 | ISBN 978-0-8061-6476-2 (hardcover) ISBN 978-0-8061-9024-2 (paper)
Subjects: LCSH: West (U.S.)—In popular culture. | Frontier and pioneer life—West (U.S.)—Mythology. | Frontier and pioneer life in literature. | Boys—Books and reading—United States. | Boys in literature. | Masculinity in popular culture—United States—History.
Classification: LCC F591 .W864 2020 | DDC 978—dc23
LC record available at https://lccn.loc.gov/2019041395

Frontiers of Boyhood: Imagining America, Past and Future is volume 7 in The William F. Cody Series on the History and Culture of the American West.

The paper in this book meets the guidelines for permanence and durability of the Committee on Production Guidelines for Book Longevity of the Council on Library Resources, Inc. ∞

CONTENTS

SERIES EDITORS' PREFACE

The 1879 autobiography *The Life of Hon. William F. Cody* contains a series of illustrations that capture in simple line drawings the most dramatic moments in Cody's life story. The images in the early chapters, focused on Cody's childhood, offer a tableau of a boy's life on the American frontier. They include a triptych of young Bill's adventures hunting small animals, falling off a horse, and getting chased by a dog. Any reader familiar with American literature of this period might be excused for seeing Tom Sawyer in this portrait. The fact that *The Adventures of Tom Sawyer,* published three years before *The Life,* in 1876, had the same illustrator, True Williams, only reinforces the convergence of these two narratives. In both volumes, Williams celebrates a romantic image of frontier boyhood that would serve as the template for countless other works of popular fiction in the final decades of the nineteenth century. The imaginative connection to Twain's novel also foregrounds the place of boys in the story of the West, as both the protagonists and the consumers—readers and audience members—for whom Twain, Cody, and other culture makers crafted their narratives.

The William F. Cody Series on the History and Culture of the American West supports history, biography, and cultural studies that place Buffalo Bill and the Wild West exhibition in the context of their times. These studies also illuminate the legacy of Cody's efforts, as well as the social and economic forces that inspired them in the first place. Collectively, the range of works appearing here offer a richly diverse account of how culture makes nations and how individuals come to symbolize foundational social values.

In *Frontiers of Boyhood: Imagining America, Past and Future,* Martin Woodside extends the purview of this series to the interdisciplinary space of childhood studies. Addressing the history, sociology, and culture of boyhood as it was transformed over the second half of the nineteenth century, Woodside examines how the literal and imagined landscapes of the American West informed the modern concept of boyhood. Each chapter places popular expressions of frontier life, such as Buffalo Bill's Wild West, alongside other literary and cultural forms, including the western adventures of Mark Twain's novels and Hamlin Garland's tales of the farmstead. In the process, Woodside shows how these works complemented a broader narrative of masculine social development.

The figure of Buffalo Bill serves as a focal point of this study in that it usefully concentrates the main historical strands in a single iconography. The frontier as both Americanizing and masculinizing was a primary theme of the Wild West exhibition. The Buffalo Bill mythology begins with the eleven-year-old Cody making his own way in frontier Kansas and expands to countless young male readers and viewers finding a future version of themselves in the story of the Wild West as told by the dime novel hero and the arena performer. Woodside's study situates this history among the contexts that best reveal its impact on generations of Americans.

Jeremy Johnston
Frank Christianson
Douglas Seefeldt

ACKNOWLEDGMENTS

I am the author of this book, but the book itself would not be possible without the help of a great many people. This book grew out of my dissertation, and I remain indebted to my committee members, Holly Blackford, Robin Bernstein, Dan Cook, and Susan Miller, for the careful attention they paid to my work. I owe a special debt to Lynne Vallone, who chaired my committee and has provided invaluable assistance every step of the way. I am very thankful for much-needed help received from the staff at the Buffalo Bill Museum and Grave, the Denver Public Library, the Beinecke Rare Book and Manuscript Library, and the University of Delaware Library, who helped guide my research. I am especially thankful to the good folks at the Buffalo Bill Center of the West, including Jeremy Johnston, Linda Clark, John Rumm, Mary Robinson, and everyone else who made my time at the McCracken Research Library successful, providing my first inklings of what this book could be. I am deeply grateful to Jeremy, Frank Christianson, and Douglas Seefeldt for including this book in the William F. Cody Series on the History and Culture of the American West, and equally grateful for Adam Kane and the rest of the staff at the University of Oklahoma Press for guiding me through the editorial process. The readers chosen by the press to review early versions of this material provided insightful feedback that made revisions a lot easier. I want to thank my friends, colleagues, and family for all that they do, especially my wife, Lois, who exhibited considerable patience with me as I rambled on about dime novels and Wild West shows and supported me as I abandoned her with two small children to fly across the country and rummage through various archives. Elizabeth and Clara, the small children in question, make me smile every day—and that helps.

Some of the material in this book has been published in alternate forms. Parts of chapter 1 were published as "The Nineteenth-Century Dime Western, and Empowered Adolescence" in *Boyhood Studies* (9.2) in 2016, and parts of chapter 4 were published as "Wild West Children: Performing the Frontier" in the *Journal of the History of Childhood and Youth*

(10.1) in 2017. I am indebted to those publications for providing me with an outlet for this work and helping me to develop it further.

Finally, I dedicate this book to my father, John Martin Woodside, III. I regret that he did not live long enough to hold these pages in his hands but am comforted by the knowledge that his life force breathes through every word I write.

Martin Woodside
February 2020

FRONTIERS OF BOYHOOD

INTRODUCTION

"Go West, young man, and grow up with the country."

On July 13, 1865, Horace Greeley published these famous words in a *New York Tribune* editorial. Like much in the history of the American West, the authorship of the credo remains in dispute, and also like much of that history, this dispute hardly seems to matter. As reporter Maxwell Scott says at the end of *The Man Who Shot Liberty Valance*, a film that offers as persuasive an analysis as any of the relationship between the myth and the history of the American frontier, "This is the West, sir. When legend becomes fact, print the legend." Greeley's legendary utterance is now fact, and since the publication of that *Tribune* editorial, the motto has served as the title for three feature films, a Bing Crosby album, and countless headlines.[1]

The quotation also serves as a useful frame for this project. In the second half of the nineteenth century, Americans completed the final stages of westward migration, fulfilling the call of Manifest Destiny, and began to come to terms with the notion that the frontier was closed and, with it, a defining chapter in US history. As Greeley's words suggest, that frontier has become synonymous with a distinctive type of idealized American masculinity, often represented as synonymous with the American national character. The iconography of American frontier manhood is pervasive and long-standing, bridging the centuries and including larger-than-life figures such as John Wayne, the Marlboro Man, and a series of cowboy presidents starting with Teddy Roosevelt. Wedding strong character to feisty individualism, these men have come to signify a persuasive and aggrandized vision of the American ethos formed, like the nation itself, through exposure to the open—and wild—West.[2]

Ideas of youth play a prominent role in this mythologizing of the West, a role current scholarship has largely failed to account for. Greeley's

statement exhorts "young men" to head west and, importantly, frames
that journey with the language of development. Imagining the West as
a literal and metaphorical space for development and progress, many
nineteenth-century writers and thinkers drew on distinctive ideologies
of age, race, and gender. As "civilization" spread westward, the influence
of white, masculine hegemony intensified through the occupation of the
"open" frontier. Greeley's words tell a story about that process, one that
became increasingly influential after 1850.

The exhortation also tells a story about changing ideas of American
boyhood. In the same time frame, ideals of American childhood were
dynamic, and the development of the child, particularly the boy, became
an increasingly fraught social concern. For many educators, politicians,
and parents, developing boys the right way seemed a pivotal step in
securing the growing nation's idealized future. This book revisits these
powerful narratives of American progress, examining how disparate
constructions and conversations about American boyhood and frontier
mythology worked through and against each other and how this relationship shaped late-nineteenth-century ideas about national character,
identity, and progress. The relationship between these varied ideas about
boyhood and the frontier was complex and multifaceted, but it was dominated by one arresting notion: in the space of the West, boys would grow
into men, and the fledgling nation would grow to fulfill its promise.

Notions of youth and the frontier have long commingled in the
American imagination. In the Federalist Era, descriptions of the incipient nation were often couched in the language of childhood, even as
prominent thinkers and leaders began to conceive of the United States
in terms of westward expansion. This ideological braiding culminated
in Frederick Jackson Turner's 1893 essay "The Significance of the Frontier in American History," which enshrined the idea of the frontier as
the defining feature of the American ethos. For Turner, this "perennial
rebirth, this fluidity of American life, this expansion westward with its
new opportunities, its continuous touch with the simplicity of primitive
society, furnish the forces dominating American character."[3]

With his frontier thesis, Turner cemented the doctrine of Manifest
Destiny as a credible historical narrative. While historians since then
have effectively discredited that narrative, Turner's thesis has endured,

articulating what D. H. Lawrence describes as "the true myth of America." As Lawrence discerned, that myth is closely bound up with conceptions of youth. America "starts old, old, wrinkled and writhing in an old skin. And there is a gradual sloughing of the old skin towards a new youth."[4] This notion of America growing backward, evolving *toward* youth, establishes the frontier as a quite literal space of and for youth, a space that idealizes youth—fetishizing a vision of childhood wherein the body grows young and the mind accumulates wisdom and experience.

Aligning the space of the frontier with "youth," Turner made notions of childhood critical to his story of American progress and triumph. And, of course, Turner's narrative provided more than a reckoning of American history; it offered a road map for developing and securing the nation's future. In the final decades of the nineteenth century, many projected that future through the reformulation of dominant American masculinity—that is, a formulation wherein white cultural elites sought to remain dominant. From James Fenimore Cooper's romances to Turner's thesis, the western pioneer was persistently offered as a white masculine icon, and the frontier gained credence as a potent space for developing this distinctive vision of American manhood.

The mythology wrought from Turner's frontier history has demonstrated astonishing staying power. Likewise, the figure of the white male pioneer maintains a stubborn centrality at the core of this mythology. R. W. B. Lewis articulated an early and influential explanation of the white male hero's symbolic importance. Lewis argues that nineteenth-century thought was dominated by the Edenic garden, a mythic place beyond time and space where a new, *better* kind of "first man" is born—the American man. Focusing on the years 1820–60, he describes this American Adam as "an individual standing alone, self-reliant and self-propelling, ready to confront whatever awaited him with the aid of his own unique and inherent resources."[5] Tracing the American Adam through the nineteenth century, Lewis points to Cooper as the author who managed to present "a fictional Adamic hero unambiguously treated" (5). He argues that Cooper's frontier fiction established the prototype for the white male pioneer that later anchored Turner's narrative of American development.

Following Cooper's lead, countless writers of American frontier fiction presented the white male pioneer as an embodiment of heroism and individuality. In Cooper's novels, the Indian scout Natty Bumppo represents the ideal frontier hero and a harbinger of American prosperity and progress. Bumppo is "a self-reliant young man," as Lewis puts it, "who does seem to have sprung from nowhere" (91). Modeled after real-life scouts like Daniel Boone, Bumppo signified a heroic figure manifested through a coterie of real or fictional (or sometimes both) frontier icons, including Kit Carson, William "Buffalo Bill" Cody, and the stoic outsider in Owen Wister's *The Virginian*.

This romantic vision of the frontier may seem monolithic, even in the nineteenth century, but it did not go unchallenged. Many critics and authors, perhaps most prominently Mark Twain, dismissed Cooper's imagined frontier as storybook romance. At the same time, writers like Caroline Kirkland, who moved with her husband, William, to Michigan in 1835, strove to present more realistic depictions of western settlement. Black cowboys like Nat Love and Oscar Micheaux traveled west, prospered, and authored books that challenged the aggressive and inaccurate "whiting" of the American pioneer.[6]

As the nineteenth century progressed, a group of writers more steeped in literary realism moved decisively away from any kind of Edenic view of the American West. Settlers pushed on into the trans-Mississippi region, into the Great Plains and beyond, and idyllic notions of the "virgin land" increasingly became complicated by the harsh realities of claiming and cultivating that land. After the Civil War, the United States turned its full attention to the bloody business of the Indian wars, and farmers pushing west confronted long droughts and hostile natives, while finding themselves increasingly under the thumb of bankers and railroad agents. In 1884, Hamlin Garland boldly claimed that "for nearly a century free land has been a myth. Every foot of it," he argued, "was bought with blood and sweat and tears."[7]

Modern scholars have worked hard to confront both the myth of the frontier and the white male hero it celebrates. For instance, Denise Mary MacNeil points out that the tradition of the frontier hero actually extends back to the seventeenth-century captivity narratives of Mary Rowlandson and others. Failing to acknowledge the diverse strands of this American frontier mythology, MacNeil claims, "interferes with our efforts to move past a gender-bifurcated society and culture."[8] An influential myth, she explains, "has the power to obscure and confuse the drives of competing realities into one apparently unified whole. Being ignorant of one's myths results in being unaware of this power" (68–69). Attempting to reconcile these competing realities, MacNeil holds Rowlandson up as the true prototype of the American hero, noting that her narrative demonstrates all the qualities of the frontier hero described by Lewis and others. Despite these efforts, American frontier mythology has proven remarkably resilient, and the solitary figure of the white male frontier hero remains fixed in the popular imagination.

In the late nineteenth century, Buffalo Bill played a significant role in this process, emerging as the most compelling symbol of American frontier masculinity. Like Natty Bumppo, most of the heroes in nineteenth-century frontier narratives were cultural outsiders; socially isolated, they straddled the line between wild and civilized. Like Bumppo, many of these figures were martyrs, leading the way to a developed West they could never be part of. William Cody offered something different, presenting Buffalo Bill both as "wild" scout and ideal citizen. He roamed the peripheries of the civilized world, as his predecessors did, raised and developed into a paragon of manhood on the wild frontier. At the same time, he was a show business impresario, performing his exploits in various mediums and formats and serving as an ambassador of the American frontier experience to the nation and, later, the world. Setting the stage for countless twentieth-century Western films, TV shows, and radio programs, Buffalo Bill continued the established tradition of the white male frontier hero while revolutionizing the way that ideal could be represented and performed.

Buffalo Bill takes center stage in the organization of this project, serving as a critical framing device for my analysis of the connections between frontier myth and American boyhood in the late nineteenth and early twentieth centuries. Describing Buffalo Bill and the cultural context that helped birth him, Henry Nash Smith explains how "the persona" created by decades of frontier fiction authors "was so accurate an expression of the popular imagination that it proved powerful enough to shape an actual man in its own image."[9] This book explores less the "actual man" than the icon he became. More than any other figure, Buffalo Bill focalizes the dynamic relationship between discourses of boyhood and the frontier narrative in an array of cultural products, traditions, and performances.

Cody's career—like Turner's thesis—came to prominence at a time when dominant social constructions of masculinity were being challenged. Gail Bederman describes the second half of the nineteenth century as a time when American notions of manhood were broadly contested and thoroughly reimagined through a number of cultural projects and movements, some complementary and others conflicting, but all working together to mark the boundaries of a "new" American masculinity. In these years, she argues, entrenched patriarchal forces sought new ways to describe white male potency and legitimize their own position atop the social hierarchy. Late-nineteenth-century frontier narratives, Bederman points out, helped contribute to a powerful reformulation of hegemonic masculinity. At the same time, these frontier narratives contributed just as powerfully to late-nineteenth-century negotiations of American boyhood, negotiations in which anxiety about white male dominance played a prominent role.[10]

American ideas of childhood underwent significant changes in the nineteenth century. Swedish educator Ellen Key published *The Century of the Child* in 1900, and the book's title became an unofficial credo for Progressive Era efforts that helped usher in modern ideas of the Western child. Of course, that Key (rightly) imagined the twentieth century as a period devoted to new ideas of childhood and new protections for children suggests that these ideas had already been present in many Western societies in the previous century. This was certainly the case in the United States, where in the early nineteenth century, as Steven Mintz describes it, "modern childhood was invented."[11]

These modern American ideas of childhood can be traced back to early articulations of the Romantic Child most scholars associate with the Enlightenment in Europe. Drawing on diverse sources, including the poetry of William Wordsworth, the fairy tales of Charles Perrault, the paintings of Joshua Reynolds, and the writings of Jean-Jacques Rousseau and John Locke, scholars often locate the first glimmerings of Romantic Childhood in the seventeenth century. There is no clean line running through this collection of thinkers and writers to contemporary ideas of Western childhood. Still, as Anne Higonnet describes it, most historical accounts agree on a general timeline governing the transition from the idea of children as "faulty small adults in need of correction and discipline" into the sacralized "concept of an ideally innocent childhood."[12] The distinction between childhood and children is critical, as scholars of the contemporary rhetoric of Western childhood bemoan how Western constructions of ideal childhood often obscure and even diminish the lives of actual children.[13]

The spread of Romantic Childhood in American society during the nineteenth century drew on the ideas of European thinkers and artists, but also on the growing influence of the American middle class. Scholars have argued that the appeal of Romantic Childhood can be clearly pegged to economic factors. In her examination of American child labor debates during the late nineteenth and early twentieth centuries, Viviana Zelizer describes two competing ideals of childhood, the "useful child" and the "useless child." The former was valued as a vital contributor to the household economy and stood as a paragon of American values that prized hard work and utility. The latter was valued not for the ability to contribute to the household in the present—that is, by performing labor and earning money—but as a symbol of futurity. Advocates of what Zelizer calls the "useless child" argued that the child should be removed from the demands of the market and prized for potential rather than utility. As Zelizer notes, these categories revealed deep conflicts rooted in social class. The idea of the "useless child" originated in more affluent middle-class families that could afford to sever the link between the child and the marketplace. Many working-class families could not get by without the working child's income.[14]

Cultural beliefs about gender also had a pronounced effect on shifting nineteenth-century ideas of childhood. Mintz argues that the American middle-class home was governed by "a host of gender-specific assumptions about behavior, attitudes, emotional sensibilities, and aspirations."[15] E. Anthony Rotundo, in describing white middle-class boy and youth cultures during the nineteenth century, argues that these boys were "shaped for manhood" as a result of a "father [who was] no longer dominant and with the mother a powerful and effective tutor in virtue."[16] At a young age, these boys were set loose, and their autonomous play stood in stark contrast to sisters and mothers still fettered to the home. Rotundo describes the play of these boys as aggressive and violent, claiming that the free rein they were granted united boys against the femininity of home and outside adult structures, often male, that sought to control their behavior. Forced to live both in and against these structures, the American boy, Rotundo notes, "learned to live in a world . . . with divided loyalties and a divided heart," a process that prepared him for the conflicted nature of middle-class manhood (43).

Of course, American boys grew up in diverse circumstances; many of them experienced boyhood much differently than Rotundo describes. In *Building Character in the American Boy*, David Macleod relies on autobiographical sources from well-known writers like Hamlin Garland and less celebrated ones such as Leonard Covello to demonstrate that boyhood experiences varied dramatically in the nineteenth century, from rural to urban, from the immigrant working class to the protestant middle class. In *Growing Up with the Country*, Elliott West highlights the distinctive experiences of the children who went west as settlers. These differences are what make questions about nineteenth-century boyhood so complex and so compelling. Just as the second half of the nineteenth century witnessed a crisis of masculinity, it witnessed a crisis of boyhood as well. Both crises reflected a splintering of traditional ideals and a challenge to hegemony. Both crises were also deeply implicated with the mythology of the frontier. Building on Bederman's analysis of American masculinity, this book fleshes out how shifting ideas of boyhood and the frontier influenced broader social and cultural debates in the nineteenth and early twentieth centuries.

In its presentation of the dominant white male hero, Turner's essay describes the frontier as an ever-shifting contact zone, wherein inhospitable conditions helped foster the American's "domineering individualism." For Turner, westward movement is a (pro)creative act. Pioneering takes the European and, through exposure to the land, births the "American." As Turner famously describes it, the American character is actualized through "the existence of an area of free land, its continuous recession, and the advance of American settlement westward." While the existence—or rather the idea—of this "free land" proves a crucial part of Turner's thesis, the dynamic nature of the frontier is just as critical.

The most important part of the settlement process remains the process itself, with the frontier serving as "the outer edge of the wave—the meeting point between savagery and civilization." The land is not simply there to be acted on by the pioneer; rather, the two develop through exposure to each other, enacting a model deeply steeped in evolutionary theory. Turner describes this process in some detail:

> The wilderness masters the colonist. It finds him a European in dress, industries, tools, modes of travel, and thought. It takes him from the railroad car and puts him in the birch canoe. It strips off the garments of civilization and arrays him in the hunting shirt and the moccasin. It puts him in the log cabin of the Cherokee and Iroquois and runs an Indian palisade around him. Before long he has gone to planting Indian corn and plowing with a sharp stick, he shouts the war cry and takes the scalp in orthodox Indian fashion. In short, at the frontier the environment is at first too strong for the man. He must accept the conditions which it furnishes, or perish, and so he fits himself into the Indian clearings and follows the Indian trails. Little by little he transforms the wilderness, but the outcome is not the old Europe, not simply the development of Germanic germs, any more than the first phenomenon was a case of reversion to the Germanic mark. The fact is, that here is a new product that is American.[17]

Strong thematic connections between the emerging rhetoric of child development and ideations of the frontier resonate in Turner's thesis. The myth of escape that dominates Turner's essay also serves as creation myth. That myth presents the rebirth of the European as the American, the eastern urbanite as the western pioneer, and most prominently, the old as the young. Turner makes powerful claims about American identity and the distinctive qualities of the American character, qualities born not out of "Germanic germs" but rather through the process of mastering the New World wilderness. As Turner explains, "American development has exhibited not merely advance along a single line but a return to primitive conditions on a continually advancing frontier line, and a new development for that area." In this construction, the frontier hero works both as an impossible ideal and a vital evolutionary link.

As concerned with the past as with the future, Turner's thesis follows Herbert Spencer's evolutionary model of movement from homogeneity to heterogeneity, ideas initially laid out in the first volume of Spencer's *A System of Synthetic Philosophy* (1862). According to Turner, the nation develops through "the steady growth of a complex nervous system from the originally simple, inert continent," and the figure of the male pioneer serves as both author and product of this transformative process, the stimulating agent that brings the "inert continent" to life. Turner's pioneer is "all but omnicompetent, an almost monstrous archetype of aggressive masculinity," as Richard Hofstadter describes him. This figure is masterful, independent, and unrefined, perfectly suited to thrive in "a Darwinian battleground, an arena of rigorous and demanding competition."[18] First, he is mastered by the wild, then regenerated through contact with—and conquest of—the primitive. Relying on Spencer's evolutionary paradigm, Turner codes the frontier as a male space and, more precisely, a space where young manhood is developed and thrives.

Spencer's theories of development were heavily gendered. Boys and girls, he argued, went through radically different cycles of development. While girls developed faster, they also peaked much earlier. As Crista DeLuzio explains, Spencer and his followers, including American psychologists Edward Clarke and G. Stanley Hall, used this logic to explain how female development prepared girls for reproduction and marked women as inferior to men. The boy developed more slowly, but his growth also held greater possibilities. Prolonged development may have rendered the boy more awkward and immature as a youth, DeLuzio notes, but that slow growth "was nonetheless both cause and effect of his superior evolutionary development."[19] Spencer's theories, which provided the foundation for social Darwinism, had a clear racial component as well. In his evolutionary model, "individual evolution" replicated the evolution of the species. In this way, the boy had a higher developmental ceiling than the girl, and the civilized—namely, white—boy had the highest ceiling of all. Exposed to the frontier, this white boy was positioned to grow into Turner's triumphant American pioneer—just as Cody grew from a poor boy on the Kansas plains into America's most famous Indian scout.

Driven by new—and still unrefined—theories of evolution and the flawed science of Lamarckian genetics, Child Study pedagogues like Hall

advanced a model of child development that built on the same ideological foundation as Turner's thesis. The education and supervision of boys
was a burgeoning cultural concern in late-nineteenth-century America.
Hall's *Adolescence* (1904) stands as a key text for this cultural moment.
While cross-cultural discussion of puberty and adolescence can be
traced back much earlier, Hall's massive two-volume book crystallized
a philosophy of child study that became a dominant American narrative. The overwhelming focus of *Adolescence* is on the education of white
middle-class boys whom Hall sought to immunize from the effeminizing
tendencies of modern civilization. Through the doctrine of racial recapitulation, Hall and other pedagogues imagined boyhood as a site for
revitalizing white middle-class manhood.[20]

For Hall and others, this revitalization involved giving shape to the
inner wildness of the boy. Adolescence, as Hall famously described it,
is "a new birth," a time when "the higher and more completely human
traits are now born." For adolescence to be successful, though, childhood
must be recognized as "a wild undomesticated stage." In this stage, Hall
notes, the boy is not merely "a product of nature, but a candidate for
a highly developed humanity," a humanity born out of preserving and
harnessing the boy's primitive nature.[21]

Numerous important nineteenth-century cultural projects followed
Hall's evolutionary logic in projecting boyhood through the space of
the frontier. Frontier themes appealed to all manner of late-nineteenth-
century cultural producers, including theater managers, photographers,
cartoonists, and, of course, writers. Some, such as Garland and Cody,
actually lived as boys on the frontier, while others imagined the frontier
as a space for idealized boyhood. While adopting different approaches
and attempting to reach different audiences, their work drew implicitly
on the powerful relationship between the space of the frontier and the
cultures and ideologies of boyhood.

This book surveys a range of influential nineteenth-century writers,
performers, and educators. My analysis of the relationship between
boyhood and frontier mythology is organized around three central
themes. First, this book examines how nineteenth-century frontier narratives position the West as a space where white American boys grow into
hyper-masculinized American men. In the second half of the nineteenth

century, this process was manifested in competing narratives of progress. Rooted in the long-standing tradition of the American pastoral, men like Turner celebrated the pioneer as a farmer. Other writers and entertainers, such as Buffalo Bill, touted a much more violent vision of the American pioneer, one that claimed that American history was made with the gun rather than the plow. The competing narratives of the gun and the plow play an integral part in broader cultural negotiations of American boyhood and its relationship to the frontier myth.

In both narratives, these American creation myths play out from east to west rather than from north to south. In his biography of celebrated Civil War veteran James Tanner, James Marten explores this development. In explaining why Tanner's fame was so fleeting in contrast to that of his contemporary Buffalo Bill, Marten concludes that Tanner's story was rooted in the legacy of the war. It "asked—indeed, demanded—that Americans look back to a tragic if glorious time; to dwell on obligations rather than opportunities; to acknowledge that they could never recognize or reward veterans enough." Buffalo Bill, on the other hand, offered a more palatable story of American progress, recalling a more recent past that many Americans recognized and, in fact, celebrated. While the Civil War became increasingly "irrelevant" in American popular culture, Buffalo Bill represented a vision of the West that "became a metaphor for the American spirit, of which everyone had at least a little."[22]

Second, this book focuses on the ways in which frontier mythology mediates notions of boyhood through the rhetoric of peril and promise. In the imagined West, boys can become outlaws or heroes, delinquents or homesteaders. As ideas of adolescence crystalized in the second half of the nineteenth century, fears of juvenile delinquency began to swell. These developments were not unrelated. The boy crisis of the late nineteenth century was predicated on both the potential for developing boys properly and the threat those boys posed if left to their own devices. The delineation of proper and improper boyhoods did much to define the relationship between frontier mythology and the varied rhetoric of boyhood. In assessing a range of books, performances, organizations, and objects, I analyze these rough categories of proper and improper and investigate how they connect to broader social and cultural conversations about race, gender, and social class.

Finally, this book explores the experiences of children and not just discourses of childhood. That is, I am interested in how different elements of American frontier mythology shaped ideas about what boyhood should be and also how children engaged with and responded to these ideas. Children's voices are often buried in the historical record, and this book is dedicated to digging them out. For instance, middle-class adults worried considerably about boys running away to the frontier in the nineteenth century. For many, the unpredictability of the unsettled West was a threat to the growing boy and the sanctity of the family unit. For many boys, however, those same features promised autonomy and adventure. In this book, I balance both perspectives, examining how ideas of boyhood were constructed while considering the impact of those constructions on boys themselves.

My first chapter, "Boy Life on the Prairie: Garland, Twain, Cody, and Ideal Boyhood," investigates connections between the American Boy Book and the imagined frontier, with a focus on texts by Garland, Twain, and Cody. Boy Books played a pivotal role in articulating and distributing middle-class ideals of boyhood and helped negotiate ideologies of proper and improper boyhood in late-nineteenth-century America. Transposing the Boy Book to the frontier, these three authors entertained new possibilities for developing the right kind of American boy.

Twain's boyhood novels were deeply invested in the idealization of American boyhood, a process that became increasingly problematic in his imagining of the West. The author devoted considerable energy to following Huck to the frontier, commencing *Huck Finn and Tom Sawyer among the Indians* immediately after he finished *Adventures of Huckleberry Finn*. His inability to finish the book reflects a struggle to locate a space for proper boyhood to flourish, a struggle that works to interrogate notions of idealized American boyhood. Nearly twenty years later, in 1899, Garland's *Boy Life on the Prairie* continued to mark the frontier as a site of and for idealized boyhood. When twelve-year-old protagonist Lincoln Stewart first sees his new frontier home, he's seized by an intense "longing to know it—all of it, east, west, north, and south." Lincoln has no desire to return home: "the horseman had become his ideal, the prairie his domain."[23]

Cody's *The Life and Adventures of Buffalo Bill* (1879) is the harbinger of a different kind of frontier narrative. Setting the stage for his successful career as a performer, Cody establishes "Buffalo Bill" as a manly hero developed from frontier boyhood. Carefully bridging the gap between proper and improper boyhoods, Buffalo Bill presents the frontier as a space for performing idealized boyhood, simultaneously mourning the disappearance of both frontier and boyhood alike.

The second chapter, "Dangerous Adolescence and the Dime Western," considers how dime novel Westerns prefigured emerging ideas of adolescence to inform cultural constructions of American boyhood. Nineteenth-century dime novels mediated prevailing notions of proper and improper boyhood by imagining the frontier as a space of and for youth. In the late nineteenth century, dime novel Westerns were seen as "dangerous reading" for both middle-class and lower-class boys, though dangerous in notably different ways. These texts demonstrate how the frontier was configured variously as a place of ideal boyhood and a breeding ground for juvenile delinquency.

This chapter focuses mostly on novels published by Beadle & Adams, specifically the Half Dime Library and the controversial figure of Deadwood Dick. One of many adolescent protagonists roaming the pages of the titles in the half-dime library, Deadwood Dick agitated moral guardians who were increasingly worried that American adolescents needed clearer guidance and more careful supervision. Deadwood Dick provided young readers a rare glimpse at a truly independent teen hero, one who acted on his own desires and openly resisted adult authority. In reading dime Westerns against more didactic works by Horatio Alger and Oliver Optic, along with frontier dime novels featuring Buffalo Bill, this chapter argues that the rhetorics of boyhood and the frontier worked together in complex ways to inform as well as enforce burgeoning notions of American adolescence and national progress.

My third chapter, "The Wild West: Making History and American Boyhood" focuses on the creators of Buffalo Bill's Wild West and the different ways the show shaped its dominant narrative of white American progress to appeal to child spectators and reflect specific ideas of childhood. Tracing Buffalo Bill as a performer from his theater days to his final appearance in the Wild West arena, this chapter makes powerful connections between the mutable aspects of Buffalo Bill and his Wild West in performance and changing ideas of boyhood in the late nineteenth and early twentieth centuries.

Buffalo Bill's Wild West was built on Buffalo Bill's reputation as a dime novel hero, a reputation signifying his appeal to a large boyhood audience. Cody and his partners were well aware of Buffalo Bill's connections to American boyhood, and throughout the show's tenure they developed a dynamic model of the frontier narrative designed to appeal to child—notably boy—spectators. This chapter further explores the ongoing negotiation of proper and improper boyhoods, as Cody and his partners mediated perceptions of propriety and social class in their framing of the frontier narrative. This chapter also surveys broader cultural hopes and concerns about American boys and the settlement of the frontier. Deftly navigating these hopes and concerns, Cody and his partners turned Buffalo Bill into a potent symbol of America's past and future. Targeting the young boys in the audience, Buffalo Bill's Wild West was increasingly promoted not only as entertainment but also as a crucial educational tool and a valuable link to the "vanishing" frontier.

My fourth chapter, "Children, Spectacle, and Agency in Wild West Performance," focuses on the children in and around Buffalo Bill's Wild West, from those in the arena to those in the crowd, arguing that the performers adapted the show's central narratives for their own purposes to a greater extent than they have been given credit for. Special attention is paid to issues of race and gender, with extended considerations of female sharpshooters and American Indian children who performed in the show. While my emphasis will remain on American boyhood, this chapter contextualizes Buffalo Bill's Wild West in a broader consideration of childhood.

The form of Buffalo Bill's Wild West facilitated an innovative mode of performance, taking place both in the arena and in the encampments around the show, where many performers, notably indigenous performers, lived. These spaces blurred the line between performer and spectator, providing child performers with rare opportunities for agency. Seizing these opportunities, young performers complicated the frontier narratives produced by Buffalo Bill's Wild West, notably the show's distinct narratives of white hegemony and proper and improper boyhood.

My fifth and final chapter, "Work and Play: Building Character on the Imagined Frontier," looks at organizational boy work and the children's toy box in the early twentieth century through the lens of frontier mythology. The first half of the chapter examines Cody's contributions to early-twentieth-century scouting organizations, most famous among them the Boy Scouts of America. The second half focuses on toy guns and other objects for and ways of playing Buffalo Bill. The rifle, as symbol and material object, plays a critical role in both parts of the analysis.

This chapter focuses on class and gender while raising theoretical questions about agency, play, and childhood itself. It is abundantly clear that Cody, in all of his various guises as Buffalo Bill, made a lasting impact both on how American adults imagined childhood in the early twentieth century and on how American children performed diffuse accountings of the past and the present through the act of play. I argue that the latter, more than anything, stands as Buffalo Bill's most lasting impact on American ideas of childhood and children as they developed in the first half of the twentieth century.

In the broadest sense this book works as a type of American social and cultural history. My approach to this material draws on various disciplines and methodologies, including literary studies, western history, performance studies, and media studies, but is notably influenced by the burgeoning field of childhood studies. This emerging field focuses both on how ideas of childhood are variously imagined and enforced and on how actual children experience the world, themes that I emphasize in this book. In completing this work, I have benefited from fine scholarship on both childhood and the American frontier. In particular, my analysis follows the example set by a group of scholars who have successfully theorized childhood as a potent tool for negotiating American notions of race, gender, and social class. Robin Bernstein's *Racial Innocence: Performing American Childhood from Slavery to Civil Rights*, Karen Sánchez-Eppler's *Dependent States: The Child's Part in Nineteenth Century American Culture,* and Kenneth Kidd's *Making American Boys: Boyology and the Feral Tale* all serve as models for my work in this regard.

While the rich ideological categories of boyhood and frontier mythology contributed significantly to narratives of race, class, gender, and nationality during the second half of the nineteenth century, this is only the beginning of the story. The relationship between boyhood and the American frontier continued to grow throughout the twentieth century, as the increasing visibility of the cowboy in American culture clearly demonstrates. However, with the rapid escalation of mass culture, especially the prominence of film and, later, television, and the intensifying—and more intensely focused—commodification of childhood in these years, the contours of that relationship shifted rather markedly. Frontier mythology, while enduring, drew on the power of nostalgia, as many facets of childhood and children's culture became increasingly separated from adulthood. My conclusion sketches out the rough parameters of this nostalgia at work in the twentieth century, but there is plenty more for future scholarship to explore on this front.

This book's focus remains the second half of the nineteenth century and the first decades of the twentieth. In these years, American mass culture was in its early stages, as mass-produced literature, such as dime novels, and spectacle, such as Buffalo Bill's Wild West, were able to reach national and international audiences for the first time. As such, these years present a unique opportunity to study early attempts by cultural producers at reconciling conflicting ideologies of both frontier mythology and notions of boyhood in popular movements, such as the scouting movement, and entertainments such as the dime novel. Through diverse cultural venues, a host of contested meanings arose, meanings that helped shape a broader understanding of the American frontier and the American boy. The symbolic language brought forth in these interactions played a prominent role in describing American cultural identity, both in these years and in the years to come.

1

BOY LIFE ON THE PRAIRIE
Garland, Twain, Cody, and Ideal Boyhood

During the second half of the nineteenth century, discourses of boyhood were negotiated through—and shaped by—different types of frontier literature. In the 1830s, James Fenimore Cooper's Leatherstocking Tales enshrined the myth of the frontier in the culture of American boyhood. After the Civil War, Cooper's Natty Bumppo began to be supplanted by dime novel heroes like Jesse James and Buffalo Bill. Starting in the 1870s, the American Boy Book came to prominence, and its authors also incorporated frontier themes in their work. This chapter uses the American Boy Book as an analytical frame, examining how a diverse trio of authors used this literary genre to articulate the dynamic relationship between the civilizing of the frontier and development of the ideal American boy.[1]

Thomas Bailey Aldrich's *The Story of a Bad Boy* famously begins with the author's sly admission that "this was the story of a bad boy. Well not such a very bad boy but a pretty bad boy; and I ought to know, for I am, or rather I was that boy himself."[2] These introductory words sketched out the parameters for what came to be known as the American Boy Book. First serialized in *Our Young Folks* in 1869, *The Story of a Bad Boy* helped give shape to the genre, offering an adult recollection of childhood "badness" that was celebrated rather than regretted. For the adult authors of the Boy Book, and presumably its adult readers as well, boyish misdeeds paved the way for successful adulthood. In the decades that followed, this became a narrative convention, and the figure of the bad boy became a trope. In fact, the preponderance of Boy Book fiction throughout the second half of the century reflected broader cultural trends in imagining American boyhood. Character-building movements such as camping, scouting, and team sports all grew out of escalating anxieties about managing the boy's "natural" and abundant vitality so, as in the

Boy Book, the unruly protagonist grew from Anglo-Saxon boyhood into responsible American manhood. In confronting these anxieties, adults increasingly came to embrace what David Macleod describes as the "artificial cult of the bad boy."[3]

Aldrich's book also gestures to the importance of frontier themes in the cultures of American boyhood. In his second chapter, the author describes being born in the northeastern town of Rivermouth, New Hampshire, but moving south to New Orleans at eighteen months of age. He confesses to having "no recollection of New England" and becomes incensed when his father informs him "some years later" that the family will be moving back north. The young Aldrich lashes out in anger that, as he explains later, stems from his ignorance of life in the North where, as he imagines it, "the inhabitants were divided into two classes—Indians and white people." In this world, bearing more than a passing resemblance to the world of the Leatherstocking Tales, "the Indians occasionally dashed down on New York and scalped any woman or child (giving the preference to children) whom they caught lingering in the outskirts after nightfall."[4]

Beyond being a nod to Cooper, this passage speaks both to the publication date of *The Story of a Bad Boy* and to the author's boyhood experiences some thirty years earlier. Aldrich highlights powerful disjunctions, reminding his adult readers of the considerable distance between the America they lived in and the country they had "grown up" with. Describing New York as an Indian war zone, which it certainly was not in 1869, Aldrich frames the notion of a vanishing frontier with the continuing—even growing—prominence of frontier mythology in the American imagination, particularly in the imagination of the American boy.

In the wake of the Civil War, frontier mythologizing played an increasingly prominent role in American identity projects. The imagined frontier became a powerful tool for organizing the young nation's past and predicting its future, a process that was hardly monolithic. Nineteenth-century histories of the West contained competing narratives, as showcased vividly by the different accounts offered by Frederick Jackson Turner and William "Buffalo Bill" Cody. Scholars have delighted in the near meeting of these two powerful mythmakers at the 1893 World's Columbian Exposition in Chicago, noting that just as Turner delivered his lecture to the American Historical Association in the exposition's White City, Cody was performing his Wild West show over on the midway. Both men presented the American frontier as the dominant theme in the nation's history, and both men became symbols for different interpretations of that history. Turner's pioneer was a Midwestern farmer, and his story of American progress was the story of the cultivation of the land. Cody extolled a different kind of Western hero. As the programs for his Buffalo Bill's Wild West boldly announced, the bullet was "the pioneer of civilization," with Buffalo Bill roaming an imagined frontier that was both timeless and endless.[5]

Notably, the narratives offered by Cody and Turner pivoted on different valuations of violence. Richard Slotkin points out that "Turner's work is remarkable for the degree to which it marginalizes the role of violence in the development of the Frontier."[6] At its heart, as Richard White argues, "Turner took as his theme the conquest of nature; he considered savagery incidental." In stark contradistinction, "Buffalo Bill made the conquest of savages central; the conquest of nature was incidental."[7] A similar set of oppositions operates in frontier literature pitched to child readers, separating, for instance, dime novel Westerns from more genteel literatures of boyhood. In Aldrich's *The Story of a Bad Boy*, notions of Indian warfare are merely products of the boy's overactive imagination. In dime Westerns, as we shall see in chapter 2, Indian-hating—and killing—are central narrative themes.[8]

The analysis that follows traces these divisions through the writing of Hamlin Garland, Mark Twain, and William Cody. In the last few decades of the nineteenth century, all three authors engaged with the "cult of the bad boy," while ultimately creating texts that move beyond the constraints of the Boy Book genre. Working loosely within that genre, these authors tapped into the mythology of the frontier, wrestling with the violence permeating this myth while seeking to establish the frontier as a site of nostalgia and space for development. These efforts demonstrate how strongly ideas of the developing boy and developing frontier were linked in the American imagination during the second half of the century. For many, the future of the nation depended on a new generation of men, paragons of American manhood forged from the raw materials of Anglo-Saxon boyhood in the contact zone of the frontier.

TAKING THE BOY BOOK OUT WEST

Starting with Aldrich's *The Story of a Bad Boy*, the paradoxical process of simultaneously looking forward and back becomes a defining feature of the American Boy Book genre. According to Marcia Jacobson, the Boy Book "was steeped in nostalgia, [and] it idealized the past," while "it also presented a view of boyhood that could be used for the present."[9] Boy Book authors drew on idealized childhood to envision a boyhood that constructed, as David Macleod describes it, "the model of normativity" for adult pedagogues and caretakers who sought to form the right kind of American men.[10]

In refining this model, the Boy Book narrowed its range considerably by geography and, correspondingly, by race and class. Like Aldrich, many prominent Boy Book authors—including Charles Dudley Warner, William Dean Howells, and even Mark Twain—lived in and/or wrote of the rural small town, and the genre promoted, as Kenneth Kidd puts it, "a language of delinquency that separated middle-class white kids from the criminal classes."[11] Through that "language," Boy Book authors often invoked rhetoric akin to Child Study expert G. Stanley Hall's who, like many other late-nineteenth-century Child Study pedagogues, imagined boyhood as a site for revitalizing Anglo-Saxon or white middle-class manhood. Hall theorized that boys had unique access to the primitive, so that through "savage play" the white middle-class boy could maximize his potential as a civilized white middle-class man. For white middle-class boys in the idealized small town, acts of mischief fit the script of "savage play" advocated by Hall and others. On the other hand, for immigrant and other lower-class boys, white or otherwise, acting "bad" connoted juvenile delinquency and served as a threatening harbinger of future criminal behavior.[12]

With its emphasis on successful middle-class manhood, the Boy Book was written as much, if not more, for adults than for boys. In this regard, these narratives not only served the purposes of reminiscence and nostalgia but also something more practical. At a time when the American domestic sphere seemed increasingly fragile, these books offered a model for locating the wildness and autonomy of the middle-class boy safely within idealized notions of the family. In doing so, Aldrich and others offered not only a work of fiction but also a (pseudo)scientific study of the American boy. Unsurprisingly then, Frank Norris, writing at the turn of the century, couches his description of the genre in terms that closely echo the evolutionary rhetoric of Turner and Hall. Norris describes Boy Books as targeting "the average American businessman" by appealing to his "early phases of primitive growth." In dredging up those long-lost days, Norris explains, the Boy Book provides a value that is "vaguely scientific," offering "the study of an extinct species." The boy's value, then, comes from his ability to facilitate the development of the adult man, and ultimately he is celebrated not for his presence as a boy in the everyday world but for his presence as memory, his status as an "extinct species" to be excavated through adult reminiscence.[13]

At first glance, Hamlin Garland's 1899 novel *Boy Life on the Prairie* reads like a standard exercise in this kind of boyhood reminiscence. Jacobson traces *Boy Life on the Prairie* to a creative lull in Garland's career. After publishing steadily throughout the 1870s and 1880s, Garland floundered a bit, according to Jacobson, prompting a trip west for inspiration. Drawing from his observations on that trip, essays first published in *American* magazine in 1887, and poems from his 1893 collection *Prairie Songs*, Garland cobbled together *Boy Life on the Prairie*. The book was not offered as straight autobiography—Garland went on to publish *A Son of the Middle Border* for that purpose in 1917—but it certainly fulfilled a number of criteria for the Boy Book genre, including its celebration of unfettered (middle-class) boys at play and, most importantly, its privileging of boyhood, as Jacobson describes it, as a "condition of being that is truly vanished forever."[14]

However, Garland's Boy Book extends the timeless space of boyhood beyond the borders of the American Northeast; the story is set in Iowa in 1868. While Aldrich used the West as a reflection of a boy's imagination, Garland filters nostalgia through the lens of Turner's pastoral frontier, presenting the untamed West as both a literal and figurative space of youth. In doing so, *Boy Life on the Prairie* projects American boyhood through the chimerical frontier, creating the prototype for a form of the Boy Book that idealizes boyhood through that frontier, while simultaneously mourning the disappearance of both the frontier and boyhood alike.

At the start of the novel, twelve-year-old Lincoln Stewart moves west to Sun Prairie, Iowa, to confront a childhood defined by punishing work and hardscrabble living. Despite these conditions, Garland romanticizes the prairie as a pure space of natural boyhood. In doing so, he stresses Lincoln's deep and abiding connection to the land, with the child's development from boy to man closely paralleling the land's development from wild prairie to domesticated farm. That Lincoln eventually outgrows both spaces and returns east is inevitable; he is no longer a boy, and the open land is no longer open. The loss of boyhood is, in fact, synonymous with the loss of the frontier, and it works for Garland as a powerful engine of memory, a space enshrined in nostalgia and always just out of reach.

Garland's novel follows the Boy Book script quite closely. Lincoln moves exclusively in the world of boys and men—in this way, his days and nights cohere closely to the vision of late-nineteenth-century boyhood culture that E. Anthony Rotundo describes, wherein boys immersed themselves in "backyards, streets, parks, playgrounds, and vacant lots" and largely governed their own play.[15] Throughout the novel, Lincoln remains deeply immersed in the homosocial world of boy's play, and the absence of any significant characters beyond his boyhood circle of friends is striking. Mothers, sisters, and girls from town garner only occasional reference. American Indians are evoked but never present. Likewise, the migration flows that sustained prairie life, and later served as dominant themes for Willa Cather and other authors of prairie fiction, are completely absent. In short, *Boy Life on the Prairie* is very much about white middle-class boyhood, and Garland, like Turner, positions the rural farm as an ideal place for a boy to grow into the right kind of a man. Outside of the boy and that space, nothing else seems to matter.

At the same time, *Boy Life on the Prairie* juxtaposes this sacred space of boyhood with the specific geography of Garland's recollected youth. Unlike the boys Rotundo describes, Lincoln plays in fields and rivers rather than streets and vacant lots. More importantly, Lincoln does not enjoy the same freedom from adult responsibility that his (fictional) eastern counterparts so thoroughly do. Macleod notes that the typical Boy Book reveres the rural as an ideal space of middle-class boyhood while recognizing actual farm life as far from the boy's lived experience. In the early part of the nineteenth century, he argues, farm fathers "demanded that their sons work hard from an early age," though by century's midpoint, the growing emphasis on public schools and the rise of the small town had "opened up a more leisured boyhood."[16] Garland's Lincoln does not enjoy such liberties. Rather than training to be Frank Norris's "average American businessman," he trains to be an actual farmer.

This distinction hints at a significant theme of genteel literary boyhood in the second half of the nineteenth century—a theme further emphasized by imagining boyhood through the lens of the American frontier. Kidd points out that Hall's own "memoir of boy life participates in a larger late-nineteenth-century narrative closing of the frontier farm," the same narrative that culminates in Turner's frontier thesis.[17] In this way, Turner's story of the West serves as a full articulation of the American agrarian myth promoted by Hall and many Boy Book authors alike. In moving the Boy Book to the frontier, Garland attempted to sustain this mythology, marking both the frontier and boyhood alike as timeless and perpetual resources to fuel the narrative of American progress.

Boy Life on the Prairie is something of a throwback, then: a return to the virtuous farm-life boy that other Boy Book authors realized mostly through reverie. It also offers a realistic depiction of the work required of settler children. In the second half of the nineteenth century, modern ideas of childhood as a separate space from adulthood, one set aside for play rather than work, were starting to gain influence in middle-class families, especially in the American Northeast. However, settler families such as Lincoln's were in no rush to adopt this model of childhood. As Elliott West points out, their work was needed to keep the farm running and most "families could not afford idle children."[18] Correspondingly, Lincoln engages in far more work than play, and his growth closely parallels the planting and harvesting seasons for the family's corn crop.

Understandably then, Lincoln attests to being "fond of school," which represented "a chance to get clear of farm work and also it afforded him an opportunity to meet his fellows."[19] The very presence of the school marks Sun Prairie as a western space in transition, an established farm community rather than a frontier outpost. These communities, as West notes, had higher concentrations of women and children and were more likely to have "schools, churches, and other elements of good society."[20]

Nonetheless, school is a rare luxury, as the needs of the family farm come first. In their first year on the farm, the family cannot afford to hire out for plowing, so ten-year-old Lincoln takes on the backbreaking labor himself. The boy's work on the farm proves long, demanding, and even painful; the work is also rewarding, as Garland describes in his account of seeding time: "Day by day, the boys walked their monotonous rounds upon the ever-mellowing soil. They saw the geese pass on to the north, and the green grass come into the sunny slopes. They answered the splendid challenge of the solitary crane, and watched the ground sparrow build her lowly nest. Their muscles grew firm and their toil tired them less."[21]

As the boys cultivate the land, the land cultivates them. In fact, this symbiotic relationship between Lincoln and the land strongly echoes the confrontation between civilized pioneer and untrammeled nature informing the process of American identity formation promoted by Turner and Hall. The ideological core of this rhetoric imagines the frontier as a collision of the savage and civilized, a sort of incubator where the distinct American character is forged by the interaction between settler and primitive. We see this manifested in Lincoln's cultivation of the land and in the savage play Hall promoted. Lincoln and his friends ride the range, camp out, hunt, and even stage a cockfight. Gathered together at an Easter picnic, the boys cook their eggs, and something "primeval and poetic clustered about this vernal camp-fire. . . . [T]hey had returned to the primitive, to the freedom of the savage" (8–9).

Still, if Boy Life on the Prairie positions the Midwestern farm as a space of natural boyhood, it fails to envision it as a tenable space for future generations of American boys. As Lincoln gets older, he grows increasingly tired of the monotonous toil of farming: "After a Sunday of riding about on their ponies, with their friends," he and his friends find it "very hard to return to the stern toil of Monday morning" (69). As these tensions escalate, Lincoln yearns to escape the increasing drudgery of farm work. He cannot wait to leave, to go back east for school. This discontinuity, as Jacobson describes it, emerges as the driving force of Garland's Boy Book, a "sharp sense of the contrast between the beauty of the rural past and the bleakness of industrialized contemporary life."[22] Confronting the bleakness of the present, of contemporary rural life, Lincoln loses his connection to the land—to the space of boyhood itself. On the preci-pice of adulthood, Lincoln turns away from the West; Garland's utopian vision of the agrarian West crumbles as the boy becomes a man.

If the path to successful middle-class adulthood pulls north and east, as Aldrich and others had clearly established, Garland stubbornly at-tempts to preserve the western landscape as a site for nostalgic recovery, a powerful space where memory simultaneously creates and erases. At the end of *Boy Life on the Prairie*, Lincoln returns to Sun Prairie. He is an adult now and finds "a changed world in 1884, a land of lanes and fields and groves of trees. . . . No prairie sod could be found. Every quarter-section, every acre was ploughed. The wild flowers were gone. . . . The very air seemed tamed and set to work at windmills whose towers rose high above every barn, like great sunflowers."[23] As Garland writes in his introduction, he is describing "a vanished world—that of the prairie—much more deeply buried than my words at the ending of this book would indicate." As a "historian of homely Middle Border family life," Garland struggles to preserve that absent world, enmeshed as it is with the idealized space of boyhood (vii–viii).

As Jacobson suggests, the successful Boy Book offers more than just nostalgia. Importantly, the genre offers the adult reader critical tools for use in the present and future. In the book's final chapters, Garland sug-gests that if the physical space of boyhood appears lost, it still lives within the adult narrator, providing him with a kind of double consciousness, an ability to perceive the world as both boy and man. In the last chapter, Lincoln confronts a young woman named Agnes. As Garland describes it, she "seemed two persons to Lincoln. At one moment he saw her with the eyes of awestruck boyhood, and the next, to him, she was a pale young woman, painfully shy in his presence" (316). Being able to see through the "eyes of awestruck boyhood," Lincoln sees more as a man than he could as a boy, this double vision marking a triumphant arc of devel-opment. Much like Turner's pioneer, Lincoln has not only survived his encounter with the primitive but thrived on account of it, emerging from the boyhood zone of the frontier as a powerful model of white American manhood. Sharing Turner's vision, Garland's *Boy Life on the Prairie* cele-brates the triumph of the American farmer and trumpets the space of the farm as a place for developing boys into the right kind of men.

Garland's insistence on the sustaining power of this agrarian myth is remarkable considering his full body of work. In 1899, he published the scene of Lincoln's return home in 1884. Twelve years earlier, in 1887, the author had spoken forcefully to a Boston audience about the failed promise of westward migration. Declaring that "free land is a myth," Garland argues that for the ambitious girl or boy, the western farm "is a living grave, a solitude that eats out the life and hope and joy of life.[24] Known as a staunch defender of literary realism, Garland set out to expose the ugly truth of frontier farm life, motivated by, as Donald Pizer describes it, "a conscious rejection of the conventional myth of the West."[25]

The stark realities of rural life are not completely absent from *Boy Life on the Prairie*, especially through depictions of the hard labor that seems to grind Lincoln Stewart down, both mentally and physically. Ultimately, though, Garland does everything he can to cloak *Boy Life on the Prairie* in saccharine nostalgia. Struggling to establish the West as a cultural bulwark against the East, he drifts from reverie to despair over the vanishing frontier farm. Open western spaces become crowded; the wild becomes cultivated. The prairie is lined with fences as individual family farms are inevitably absorbed into small-town communities. Lincoln returns home to a frontier farm that is always disappearing from view, a vision Garland looks to for regeneration even as he struggles to reconcile it with the stark realities of western farm life.

SAVAGERY, DELINQUENCY, AND IDEAL BOYHOOD

Other Boy Book authors imagined the American boy not through Turner's rural Midwest, the primitive land worked over by the civilized farmer, but through dramatic representations of the "primitives" that inhabited the imagined frontier. Most notable among these is Mark Twain. Critics often include both *The Adventures of Tom Sawyer* and *Adventures of Huckleberry Finn* in assessments of the nineteenth-century Boy Book, though the two novels differ prominently in terms of form. *The Adventures of Tom Sawyer*, like Aldrich's *The Story of a Bad Boy* or Garland's *Boy Life on the Prairie*, takes shape from the author's life projected backward. Following Aldrich's model, Tom Sawyer's story makes use of the past for the author's use in the present. If, as William Dean Howells famously claimed, Twain's novel creates an ideal "study of the boy-mind," that study is not so much about how the boy lives but how the man remembers. In this way, *The Adventures of Tom Sawyer* follows the Boy Book template, even if Twain initially resisted that label. After all, it was only after significant cajoling from both his wife and Howells, who insisted to Twain that he "he ought to treat it explicitly *as* a boy's story," that Twain declared the novel "a book for boys, pure & simple."[26]

Twain's relationship to the Boy Book was tenuous from the start, then, and in *Adventures of Huckleberry Finn*, he breaks with the genre's tradition and turns to Huck as his narrator. The ramifications of this shift in point of view have received no lack of critical scrutiny, and the author's decision to adopt Huck's perspective is at least partially responsible for elevating *Adventures of Huckleberry Finn* beyond genre exercise to the realm of American masterpiece. At the same time, the transition from *The Adventures of Tom Sawyer* to *Adventures of Huckleberry Finn* is all about boyhood, namely Twain's efforts to imagine the ideal American boy. In that regard, Twain's decision to focus on Huck signifies the shift from Aldrich's model of the "good bad boy" to a fractious vision of the boy-savage, with constructions of the American frontier playing a prominent role in the process.

To this day, Huck Finn remains an iconic figure of boyhood, and *Adventures of Huckleberry Finn*'s famous last lines endure as a potent signifier for the familiar metaphor of escape that dominated the golden age of children's literature and Turner's frontier thesis alike. Of course, heading out to the "territory" represents more than escape for both Huck and his creator. Richard Slotkin argues that while Huck ultimately rejects both the grim realities and "the world of romantic illusion" offered him at the novel's conclusion, he "has still not abandoned the hope of finding his way to the mythic frontier."[27] In fact, Twain meant to pursue just this narrative line in *Huck Finn and Tom Sawyer among the Indians*, a sequel taken up immediately after he finished *Adventures of Huckleberry Finn* in 1884.

Twain's unfinished novel has drawn tepid interest from scholars. Typically, the manuscript gets lumped together with other minor works from Twain featuring both Tom and Huck, notably *Tom Sawyer Abroad* (1894) and *Tom Sawyer, Detective* (1896). However, this assessment fails to account for the close relationship *Huck Finn and Tom Sawyer among the Indians* enjoys to its immediate predecessor. The other Tom and Huck novels, the first of which was released a decade after *Adventures of Huckleberry Finn*, are both lighthearted burlesques. More importantly, both novels serve more as a redirection than a continuation of narrative themes dominant in *Adventures of Huckleberry Finn*. While both later novels employ Huck as a narrator, they also—as the titles imply—relegate him to the sidekick status he enjoyed in *The Adventures of Tom Sawyer*. What's more, the two books pick up right after *Adventures of Huckleberry Finn*, effectively erasing Tom and Huck's trip to the frontier from the record. In the end, only Twain's first attempted sequel develops the vision of boyhood sketched out in *Adventures of Huckleberry Finn*, and in this abandoned project, and its subsequent erasure from the "official" chronology of Tom and Huck, we see the failure to realize that vision, of Twain's inability to move away from a "study" of the "boy-mind" and toward a grander project constructing a model of American boyhood through frontier savagery.

Twain, unlike Garland, did not grow up on a western farm, but his impulse to situate the boy out west is not surprising. Throughout his career, Twain maintained a strong connection to the American West. In 1861, at the age of twenty-six and before establishing himself as a writer, he headed to Nevada, where he remained for the better part of the decade. Twain mined these experiences for his 1872 travel narrative *Roughing It*, and the West remained a point of fascination for Twain long after he became a fixture in Hartford, Connecticut, literary circles. In the wake of *Adventures of Huckleberry Finn*, Twain's fascination with the West became a frame for the author's vision of ideal boyhood.

That Twain ultimately abandoned this sequel is as telling as the fact that he conceived it. As Dahlia Armon and Walter Blair explain, Twain intended *Huck Finn and Tom Sawyer among the Indians* as an open refutation of Cooper's fiction—most notably the figure of the noble Indian—in favor of a more realistic portrayal of frontier conditions. In preparing the manuscript, he read widely among the memoirs of army officers, most prominently Richard Irving Dodge's *Our Wild Indians* (1883), alongside works by Francis Parkman and De Benneville Randolph Keim. In Armon and Blair's account, Twain achieved his goal too well, rendering a scenario too realistic to see through to its grisly finish; that scenario involved the kidnapping of a young white woman by a band of Indians, with Tom and Huck in hot pursuit. Based on the "authorities" Twain had turned to, the only outcome for the girl was rape; as such, Armon and Blair speculate, Twain could not continue with the story.[28]

The notion that *Huck Finn and Tom Sawyer among the Indians* became too violent for Twain's liking seems curious. After all, Twain's published writings had long associated violence with the American West. Brooding hostility permeates the action in *Roughing It*, whether through the narrative's frequent exchanges of gunfire or the inevitable carnage brought about when civic structures are imposed on a volatile, often hostile environment. Sydney Krause describes the West invoked in *Roughing It* as one where "the ritual of violence not only characterizes a region; it articulates an impatient population, and materializes an American myth that problems must yield to force."[29] Joseph Coulombe reads the book's violence less as regional and more as indicative of the author's brash attempts at self-stylization. Through manipulating the tone and language in the book, Coulombe argues, Twain draws upon "a new set of gender ideals for men," pitting western and eastern stereotypes of masculinity against each other and presenting "himself as a violent outlaw whose weapon of choice was a pen."[30]

Roughing It is hardly a book for children. Still, Twain's famous Boy Books contain liberal doses of violence in their own right; *Adventures of Huckleberry Finn* is notable in this regard. From the start—in fact, before the novel starts—Huck is surrounded by violence. The son of the town drunk, he lives under the constant threat of abuse so powerful it initiates his flight to Jackson Island and marks the beginning of his trip down the river. In the course of his journey, Huck encounters the feuding Grangerfords, quickly befriending young Buck Grangerford only to watch him and a nineteen-year-old cousin promptly get mowed down in a gunfight. Later, he witnesses Colonel Sherburn murder a drunk in the middle of the street and in front of his daughter, and then stare down the lynch mob that forms to seek retribution. And of course, the swindling Duke and the King, who commandeer Huck's raft for a time and ultimately sell Jim back into slavery, are last seen in the novel being tarred and feathered. In many instances, the violence is "playful," as with the series of indignities (or tortures) Tom Sawyer devises for Jim in the novel's bewildering endgame; nonetheless, Huck Finn's journey down river is rife with violence from beginning to end. In that light, and considering Twain's long-standing association of the West with violence, the notion that *Huck Finn and Tom Sawyer among the Indians* became too violent for the author seems unlikely.

Twain's failure to complete the manuscript is also intriguing when considering the strong connection between *Huck Finn and Tom Sawyer among the Indians* and its predecessor. As Armon and Blair point out, Twain dove into the story in July 1884 while looking over the galleys for *Adventures of Huckleberry Finn*, reinforcing the strong sense of continuity between the two books.[31] If the famous ending of *Adventures of Huckleberry Finn* suggests an uncertain future for the novel's narrator and protagonist, Twain's failure to complete the sequel only emphasizes that uncertainty. Ultimately, his failure to continue Huck's journey westward reveals the unresolved tensions undermining *Adventures of Huckleberry Finn*'s construction of ideal boyhood.

In the course of that novel, Huck replaces Tom Sawyer as Twain's ideal American boy. With that move, the author rejects the Romanticism of Sir Walter Scott and Cooper in favor of a stalwart vision of G. Stanley Hall's boy-savage. Throughout *Adventures of Huckleberry Finn*, Twain uses Huck's character as a corrective to Tom and, with the book's focus on the first-person experience of the boy in the present, to the conventions of the Boy Book itself. But Huck is also a corrective to the prototype of authentic boy-savagery. Hall wanted educators to realize that, for the growing boy, "books and reading are distasteful, for the very soul and body cry out for a more active, objective life, and to know nature and man first hand,"[32] and Huck embodies this doctrine. His plainspoken narrative repudiates Tom's sentimental storybook vernacular, while his escape down the river with Jim reveals Tom's adventures with his gang of robbers to be no more than playacting. Huck says as much early in the book, before he begins his journey down river, dismissing Tom's story of Aladdin's lamp as "just one of Tom Sawyer's lies." While Tom may have "believed in the A-rabs and the elephants," Huck states firmly he does not. For him, such tall tales "have all the marks of a Sunday school."[33]

Turning to Huck also signifies an important geographical shift for Twain. Reviewing *The Adventures of Tom Sawyer*, Howells points out that Twain "has taken the boy of the Southwest for the hero," providing "the best picture of life in that region as yet known to fiction." The inhabitant of a "shabby little Mississippi River town," Tom Sawyer still "belongs to the better sort of people in it," and Howells singles him out as a clear corollary to Aldrich's Tom Bailey, a paragon of the good bad boy.[34] Notably, both Toms have the kind of good breeding that ensures they will grow from mischievous boys into exemplars of Anglo-Saxon manhood.

Huck Finn, on the other hand, is, as Howells describes him, a "worthless vagabond" (22). He does not belong to the better class of people in the town—for that matter, he occupies no clear position in the social world of the town at all. Correspondingly, in *Adventures of Huckleberry Finn*, it is the structure of the town itself, with its smugness, insularity, and hypocrisy, that suppresses Huck. In response, Twain pushed the novel's action out into untamed nature, configuring it, much as Garland did with *Boy Life on the Prairie*, as a space of idealized boyhood.

These narrative moves distance the reader from Tom, who, as Leslie Fielder points out, yearns for a "'higher' level of civilization," while placing the spotlight on Huck, who wants no civilization at all. Huck aspires to the "deeper level of the primitive" in Jim, and it is only in moments of weakness that he turns away from Jim and "the instinctive life" to join Tom in "the world of make-believe, which is also a prison."[35] Of course, *Adventures of Huckleberry Finn* contains so many of those moments of weakness that Twain's intentions regarding Huck eventually become muddled, an effect felt most prominently in the novel's final section, where the boys take on the elaborate "rescue" of Jim.

Earlier in the book, there are moments when life on the river sustains Twain's vision of ideal boy-savagery. Through Jim's stewardship, simply being in nature becomes adventure enough for Huck, who savors the time with his primitive guide, simply "lazying down the river, listening to the stillness." While once his simple clothing marked a contrast with Tom, now Huck abandons clothing altogether: "we was always naked, day and night, whenever the mosquitoes would let us." When he comes into a set of new clothes, Huck quickly rejects them as "too good to be comfortable, and besides, I didn't go much on clothes, nohow." All things considered, Huck concludes, "It's lovely to live on a raft."[36] However, the loveliness of life on the river is constantly disrupted. It is disrupted when they are forced to leave the raft for shore, as when Huck lands with the

Grangerfords and gets caught in the middle of their brutal feud. It is disrupted when the shore comes to them, as well, notably in the personages of the Duke and the King, whose duplicitous behavior proves "enough to make a body ashamed of the human race." (176). Such disruptions are needed, of course, to move the novel along, but they reveal cracks forming in Twain's idealized vision of savage boyhood, as Huck vacillates uneasily from the purity of life on the river to the degraded civilization flourishing on its shores.

In large part these cracks reflect the powerful class tensions simmering beneath the novel's surface. In rejecting Tom Sawyer, Twain rejects the safety net of middle-class domesticity, a decision that becomes increasingly problematic toward the novel's end. As Kidd explains, the typical bad boy's mischievous antics are tempered by his inability to lapse into serious delinquency. Tom Bailey and Tom Sawyer idealize incipient Anglo-Saxon manhood. As Kidd puts it, they are "middle-class white boys" configured as "gentle and temporary savages."[37] Huck, however, is not a middle-class white boy and the line between him and delinquency is razor thin. Appraising the novel's final chapters, Kidd argues that "Huck's rebirth as Tom, and his acquiescence in Tom's wild schemes, suggests a merger of the social outcast with the socially sanctioned Bad Boy" (88). This rebirth can be read not as a merger of the two but a reappraisal of the latter and, by extension, a fraught interrogation of the viability of boy-savagery. In these contentious final chapters, Twain seems stuck between two imperfect possibilities: the middle-class boy, corrupted by his inability to access the truly savage, and the lower-class boy corrupted by his ability to access the same.

These class tensions come to the surface when Huck steals a watermelon. He calls it borrowing, though Tom insists that "it warn't borrowing, it was stealing," and he compels Huck to leave a dime in place of the missing fruit.[38] Huck, as ever, proves the more practical of the two, and arguably comes closer to the truth, insisting that when the time comes "to steal a nigger, or a watermelon, or a Sunday school book, I ain't no ways particular how it's done, so it's done" (254). Clearly, though, this kind of truth is not esteemed in the value system promoted by pedagogues like Hall—precisely the value system in which Tom Sawyer has been raised. For a lower-class boy like Huck, a bit of minor thievery is more likely to be read as juvenile delinquency than Bad Boy mischief; by the time his characters arrive at the Phelps plantation, Twain seems painfully aware of this problem. The theft of watermelons reveals Huck fulfilling his angry promise "to take up wickedness again, which was in my line, being brung up to it." (223).[39]

These cracks stand out as deep fissures by the end of *Adventures of Huckleberry Finn*, and Twain seems at a loss for what to do with Huck. Importantly, like Garland's Lincoln, both boys engage with, react against, and grow through their exposure to the primitive. Unlike Huck, though, Lincoln enjoys the safety of family and a powerful connection to the land; the virtue of work contributes both to his growth and demonstrates the resilience of the settler family. In Garland's vision—much like Hall's farm memoir—the redemptive character of labor develops the boy into the man. Lincoln's struggles are represented directly by his cultivation of the wild into the domestic. Ultimately, Huck is wedded to his liminality, equally distanced from civilized and uncivilized alike. A few critics have suggested that Twain's focus on nascent fears of juvenile delinquency, and not race, resonated most with contemporary readers of *Adventures of Huckleberry Finn*. Certainly, Twain's vacillating projections of Huck highlight the specter of delinquency haunting both *Adventures of Huckleberry Finn* and its abandoned sequel.[40]

Unsurprisingly then, Twain struggles to mediate conflicting notions of boy-savagery in the completed portion of *Huck Finn and Tom Sawyer among the Indians*. In that novel, Huck once again takes on the role of narrator, but Jim is dispensed with as the savage "other." In fact, by the book's third chapter, Jim is gone, kidnapped by Indians along with the Mills girls, Peggy and Flaxy, seventeen and seven years old respectively. Tom, Huck, and Jim fall in with the Mills family on a wagon road, and Huck declares them "the simple-heartedest good-naturedest country folks in the world." Unfortunately, the family "didn't know hardly anything," and the father, mother, and sons are tricked and then butchered by duplicitous Indians who make off with Jim and the girls.[41]

In this new environment neither Tom nor Huck knows much either. After the Indian party absconds with Jim and the surviving Mills girls, the boys pledge to rescue them. They prove unable to do so on their own, however, and are forced to wait for help to arrive. Sitting in the tall grass,

they grow hungry without food, and Huck takes stock of their surroundings, describing "the biggest, widest, levelest world—and all dead; dead
and still and not a sound. The lonesomest place that ever was; enough to
break a body's heart just to listen to the awful stillness of it." (49).

LIGHTING OUT: FROM PLOW TO GUN

Marooned in the prairie grass in the wake of the Mills family massacre,
Huck finds himself far from the idyllic river he floated down with Jim
and completely unable to read the landscape. In place of Huck's primitive spirit guide, we have the savage Indian, a figure Twain regarded with
great skepticism—if not outright disdain. The bloodthirsty Indians in
Huck Finn and Tom Sawyer among the Indians are meant to debunk the very
notion of the noble savage—to show the "real" nature of the Plains Indians—an intention revealed through Tom Sawyer's commentary. Early
on, while trying to persuade Jim and Huck of the virtues of westward
exploration, Tom describes the Indians "as the noblest human beings
that's ever been in the world" (35). Later, while stuck in that tall grass,
Huck asks Tom, "where did you learn about Injuns—how noble they was,
and all that?" Huck quickly sees that he has hit his friend "hard, very
hard," and Tom looks away. Finally, "he said 'Cooper's novels,' and didn't
say anything more" (50).

Critics continue to debate Twain's true opinion of American Indians,
but his published writings often offer harsh portrayals of them. Helen
Harris convincingly argues that, for much of his career, the author portrayed American Indians as "more ludicrously degraded than the usual
stereotype, disparaging them mostly for their poverty, diet and culture."
Harris points out that real-life settler children were often raised on such
stereotypes, surround by tales of Indian "savagery." In one young girl's
recollection, cited by Harris, "A dreadful fear of the Indians was born
and grown into me," so that, years later, she dreamed of "running from
them til my feel rose from the ground and I ran in the air."[42] Twain's
Indians present as equally fearful. In sharp distinction to the figure of
Jim, these "primitives" are described by Twain as hostile savages, resem-
bling the ugly caricatures in dime novels. Less than human, they serve
as clear obstructions to the forces of civilization and present a threat
that requires a hostile response. In *Huck Finn and Tom Sawyer among the*

Indians, Twain abandons Turner's vision of ideal boyhood, read through
the primitive cast of nature, to flirt with a vision like Cody's, predicated
on the conquest of the bloodthirsty savage.

Ultimately, though, that vision does not hold. On the desolate and
foreboding plains, Tom's storybook logic is as useless as ever—in fact, it
is Tom who is chiefly responsible for the trio's venturing out west and for
Jim's capture. At the same time, Huck's connection to the land, felt so
powerfully at times in *Adventures of Huckleberry Finn*, has been severed as
well. The logical solution is for the boys to adapt to this hostile situation,
conforming to a vision of the pioneer more like Cody's battle-tested
scout than Turner's pioneer farmer. Twain does take some steps in this
direction. Before the Indians murder most of the Mills party, the boys
practice riding, shooting, and roping to the extent that, as Huck boasts,
"we got powerful good at them." Tom proves able "to cave in a squirrel's
or a wild turkey's or a prairie chicken's head any fair distance; and could
send both loads from his pistol through your hat on a full gallop, at
twenty yards."[43] Huck, ever more practical, kills a rattlesnake and then
"skinned and roasted him in the hot embers" on a fire they managed to
build (51).

Both boys seem capable of taking on the trappings of the archetypal
Western hero; in fact, Twain turns to a separate character, Brace Johnson, to fill this role. It is Brace, Peggy Mills's fiancé, whom the boys are
waiting for in the tall prairie grasses, and he seems to leap straight out of
the pages of a dime Western. As Twain describes Brace:

> He was more than six foot tall, I reckon, and had broad shoulders,
> and he was straight as a jackstaff, and built thin as a race-horse.
> He had the steadiest eye you ever see, and a handsome face, and
> his hair hung all down his back, and how he ever could keep his
> outfit so clean and nice, I never could tell, but he did. . . . And as for
> strength, I never see a man that was any more than half as strong
> as what he was, and a most lightning marksman with a gun or a
> bow or a pistol. (60)

Johnson is a natural white pioneer hero, set up to exterminate Indians and other miscreants alike. Huck gets to see these exploits first-
hand when Brace shoots down two horse thieves. Afterward, Huck notes,

"We had two dead men on our hands, and I felt pretty crawly, and didn't like to look at them." At the same time, as Brace points out, and the boy concedes, "it warn't a very unpleasant sight, considering they tried to kill me" (73). These seem like precisely the right exercises to help develop Huck from "vagabond" boy to masculine frontier hero. Twain intimates this kind of developmental arc earlier, after Tom and Huck first explain to Brace how they ended up out west. After hearing about Tom's idyllic delusions about Indians, "Brace said it was just like boys the world over, and just the same way it was with him when he was a boy" (54).

After traveling out west, though, the callow boy grows into the seasoned pioneer, and Brace's remarks suggest a similar trajectory for Huck. Despite his obvious fondness for dime novels, Twain did not complete that trajectory. Perhaps the author was stymied by the brutality of the frontier he had created or the grim possibilities of the plot he had sketched out. Perhaps he sensed the market would not respond well to the notion of a Huck Finn dime novel. Regardless, the unfinished project highlights the author's inability to reconcile his ideas of frontier violence and child development. Ultimately, the rough work of frontier heroism could not mesh with Twain's idealized boy-savagery. In this wild West, savage and civilized cannot work together productively, failing to provide either Tom or Huck with the tools to develop the raw materials of boyhood into successful American manhood.[44]

A third literary attempt at integrating narratives of the frontier and American boyhood comes from an author with little literary reputation to speak of. As Buffalo Bill, William Cody became the nineteenth century's most powerful symbol of the American frontier myth, a feat achieved in no small part through his ability to seamlessly fuse romance and realism. When he published his autobiography in 1879, Cody was already a multifaceted celebrity. He had gone from renowned Indian scout to dime novel hero ten years earlier with the publication of Ned Buntline's *Buffalo Bill, the King of the Border Men.* Shortly after that he became a stage star, acting out his dime novel exploits in freewheeling frontier dramas. Cody formed the traveling theatrical troupe the Buffalo Bill Combination in 1873 and ten years later starred in the hybrid performance genre of the Wild West show, profoundly shaping the production and transmission of American frontier narratives forever.

Cody's autobiography was published in the midst of his transition from stage star to Wild West impresario. Buffalo Bill dominated the pages of sensational literature in the 1870s and 80s and clearly had his sights set on different—and more profitable—modes of performance. Perhaps he saw the autobiography as a vital publicity tool for this transition. It is also possible Cody sought to issue a counter-narrative to portrayals of Buffalo Bill in "blood-and-thunder" stories. As Cody biographer Don Russell points out, "most dime novels about real persons were pseudo-biographical," but only "rarely did a Buffalo Bill dime novel bear any relation to anything ever done by the real Cody."[45] Whatever Cody's motives may have been, the book remains a fascinating mixture of genres and a powerful example of the vivid interaction between American boyhood and frontier myth in the second half of the nineteenth century.

By the time *The Life of Hon. William F. Cody, Known as Buffalo Bill* was published, Cody was a show business veteran who readily understood the value of appealing to as wide an audience as possible. Partly, this entailed pitching his exploits to the "right kind" of boys. Buffalo Bill's Wild West sought to broaden the appeal of its star—and surely did so. In the process, though, Cody and his partners needed to make Buffalo Bill palatable to audience members of all types. Cody launched the first version of his show in 1883. As Louis Warren describes, the traveling show's inaugural run came under criticism for its appeal to bootblacks, newsboys, and other "lower class elements."[46] In other words, it appealed to the same audience as the Buffalo Bill dime novels. Eventually, Cody would hook up with a new business partner, Nate Salsbury, and the two men made several changes to the show, creating a more wholesome image of Buffalo Bill and a product more likely to appeal to middle-class families.

The Life of Hon. William F. Cody, Known as Buffalo Bill suggests similar ambitions. The book was published by Frank Bliss's American Publishing, which published a number of Twain's works, including *The Adventures of Tom Sawyer.* While Cody's autobiography is not a Boy Book, it reprises the genre's central conceit of a successful man looking back on his adventurous boyhood. In contrast to most Buffalo Bill fiction, which rarely focused on the hero as a boy, much of the autobiography deals with Cody's childhood. Right from the start, the author adopts the tone and language of the Boy Book. Describing his "childhood days," Cody

confesses, "I often wonder that I did not get drowned while swimming
or sailing, or my neck broken while I was stealing apples in the neighborhood orchards."[47] As a child, Cody lived, like Garland's Lincoln Stewart,
in Iowa, where he "was sent to school more for the purpose of being kept
out of mischief than to learn anything" (21).

Cody's narrative moves quickly from the peacefulness of Iowa to his
family's 1852 migration to (still unsettled) Kansas. The risks of stealing
apples are immediately replaced by more daunting challenges; on the
trip, Cody recounts seeing "men carrying pistols and knives for the first
time" and notes that "they looked like a dangerous crowd." That danger
soon proved quite real. All in all, while Cody's boyhood recollections
indulge in (and embellish) his many colorful adventures on the plains,
they are also grounded in the Cody family's harrowing struggles. Cody's
father, Isaac, was an outspoken abolitionist, whose presence near the
Kansas-Missouri border wars of the 1850s quickly became incendiary.
In the chapter "Boy Days in Kansas," Cody recounts his father speaking
out against slavery, only to watch helplessly as a "hot-headed pro-slavery
man" pulls "out a huge bowie knife" and stabs the elder Cody twice (33).[48]

Lucky to escape with his life, Isaac Cody became something of a
fugitive and often remained in hiding when at home. William Cody
notes these developments stoically, admitting that his father's "indiscreet
speech . . . brought upon our family all of the misfortunes and difficulties
which from that time on befell us."[49] Sure enough, persecuted by their
pro-slavery neighbors, the Cody family struggled to make ends meet, and
four years after being stabbed, Isaac Cody died. William was only ten
years old, and from this point forward he became the family's primary
wage earner.

Cody's Kansas boyhood brought him into contact with an influential
new role model. After the Cody family settled into their new home in the
Salt Creek Valley, Cody describes encountering a "genuine western man."
This character, who later turns out to be Cody's long-lost cousin Horace
Billings, "was about six feet two inches tall, was well built, and had a light,
springy and wiry step. He wore a broad-brimmed California hat, and was
dressed in a complete suit of buckskin, beautifully trimmed and beaded"
(35). Cody soon becomes better acquainted with the stranger, who shows
him how to break ponies. As the Californian explains, he "was raised on

horseback," having run away from home as a boy, gone to sea, and eventually joined a circus, where he became "a celebrated bare-back rider"
(37). Later, drawn to California by the gold rush, he learned the trade of
"bocarro-catching and breaking wild horses." This romantic portrait se-
duces the seven-year-old Cody completely; he proclaims the Californian
"a magnificent looking man," admits he "envied his appearance," and
confesses his ambition "to become as skillful a horseman as he was" (41).

If the description seems reminiscent of Twain's Brace Johnson, that
is likely no accident; Armon and Blair list Cody's autobiography as one
of the sources Twain consulted for *Huck Finn and Tom Sawyer among the
Indians*. Additionally, Twain was a fervent admirer of Buffalo Bill's Wild
West, writing that "it brought vividly back the breezy life of the Great
Plains and the Rocky Mountains, and stirred me like a war-song."[50] At
the same time, it is Cody, not Twain, who successfully integrates the dime
novel hero with a literary model of successful American boyhood. Cody
also imbued his western upbringing with the glow of nostalgia, using the
stock heroics of boyhood adventures to fuel both his remembered past
and his (not so) distinctive creation myth.

Of course, Cody's autobiography is more amenable to such fictions,
as his boyhood wish to be like the bocarro-busting Californian is a fait
accompli by the time the author put pen to paper; the boy Cody has
grown into the man known as Buffalo Bill. Still, the author does strain
to balance the domestic ideals of middle-class American boyhood with
the violent realities of the frontier. At age ten, Cody stabs a boy in the leg
at school and kills his first Indian a year later. In each case, he embraces
the violence of the act while also taking pains to justify that violence—in
stark opposition to the blood-and-thunder stories bearing his name. Cody
stabs the (much bigger) boy, described as "the 'bully' of the school," to
defend "a sweetheart with whom I was 'dead in love'—in a juvenile way"
(64). He kills the Indian in clear self-defense and in the performance of
duty, confessing afterwards to being "overcome with astonishment," so
shaken up, in fact, that "I could hardly realized what I had done" (72).
Tempered by his conscience, the graphic nature of violence in the story
is unflinching. It also plays a significant role in shaping boy into man. As
Cody notes, from that time on, "I became a hero and an Indian killer. . . .
[M]y exploit created quite a sensation" (73).

Cody does all he can to bolster the effects of this type of "sensation." That much becomes plain in comparing how he and his older sister, Julia Cody Goodman, describe a scene when they were compelled to take up arms on their father's behalf. As Cody describes it in his autobiography, "I determined that the man should never go up stairs where my father was lying in bed, unable to rise." Acting quickly, he fetches "a double-barreled pistol" and stations himself at the top of the stairs. There, Cody "cocked the weapon and waited for the ruffian to come up, determined that the moment he set foot on the steps I would kill him" (59).

In Julia's memoir, she recalls being with her brother and father upstairs. Isaac tells them, "You will have to protect me because I am too sick. Willie you get your gun," which always stood beside the stair door. "And Julie, you get the ax." As the children move into action, Isaac provides further instruction: "If that man starts to come upstairs, Willie you shoot, and Julie, if Willie misses him you hit him with the ax."[51] The differences are notable. In Cody's version, he is the budding frontier hero, acting alone, "determined" to kill the hostile intruder. In doing so, he replaces his father as protector of the house. In his sister's version, young William's actions are essentially the same. It is the father, however, at the center of the action, directing the children. Furthermore, William does not act alone; rather, Julia is there, ax in hand, ready to join the fray.

This scene neatly encapsulates how William Cody infused real-life events with the tone and feel of sensational fiction in his autobiography to promote a more romantic vision of Buffalo Bill. These efforts to navigate realism and romance were at least partially successful in tempering the more familiar image of Buffalo Bill in blood-and-thunder fiction. As a reviewer for the *New York Herald* reassures, "We doubt whether the perusal of the book will lure a single boy to run away from school, steal a revolver and tramp to the border." Rather, the reviewer explains, Cody's story allows the boy reader to revel in dime novel exploits as kind of pedagogical tool, framing the boy-hero's adventures as an example of how life on the rough-and-tumble frontier develops boys into admirable men.[52]

These negotiations help Cody suggest a new model of American manhood, demonstrating how Anglo-Saxon boyhood can be best developed in the dynamic space of the frontier. An Indian killer at eleven and a Pony Express rider at fourteen, Cody does not offer the reader a boy dreaming of dime novel heroics but a fully realized boy-savage and frontier hero. Twain famously wrote of his ambitions to "take a boy of twelve & run him on through life (in the first person)." Tom Sawyer, he declares, "would not be a good character for it."[53] This moment is often invoked in tracing the genesis of *Adventures of Huckleberry Finn*. Of course, Twain proved unable to run Huck "on through life" as well. In his autobiography, Cody manages the task quite nicely, weaving the romance of his boyhood adventures together with hard realities of "civilizing" the frontier as he documents his growth from boy to man.

Cody, then, creates an idealized boy-hero without relegating American boyhood exclusively to the realm of nostalgia; rather, he holds out the tantalizing possibility that frontier heroics could be lived as well as remembered, acted out again and again. His story serves not merely to recapture the past but, rather, to channel it in actualizing the present and the future. In doing so, Cody uses boyhood nostalgia to tap into the same complex—and to some degree paradoxical—paradigm that undergirds Turner's frontier thesis. Looking backward and forward simultaneously, Cody's distinctive frontier narrative provided a successful formula for developing the crude materials of Anglo-Saxon boyhood into successful American manhood.

Buffalo Bill's fictionalized boyhood exploits ultimately appealed to a broad range of young readers. Cody's autobiography managed the neat trick of valorizing the West as space that was wild, unpredictable, and yet deeply imbued with the sensibilities of white middle-class boyhood. When the book was first published in 1879, Cody was beginning to shape the contours of a brand of frontier tale that balanced savage and civilized in ways that both instructed and titillated. In the 1880s, this tale would become a foundational piece of Buffalo Bill's Wild West, Cody's most enduring projection of the frontier as a symbol of America's potency and progress.

2

DANGEROUS ADOLESCENCE
AND THE DIME WESTERN

On September 28, 1890, two young men were found shot to death in a Wyoming boxcar. Their killer was Charley Miller, a fifteen-year-old orphan from New York City. The victims, Waldo Emerson, nineteen, and Ross Fishbaugh, twenty, left good jobs as clerks in Missouri to pursue their fortunes in Denver. They had money saved along with their parents' blessings for the journey. They were riding boxcars for a thrill, but Miller could afford no other way to travel. He was poor, alone, and an avid fan of dime novels, so much so that he had renamed himself "Kansas Charley."[1]

The murder made tantalizing headlines, playing on the fears of anxious middle-class parents and pedagogues. One report from the *Kansas City Times* warned that despite "his extreme youth," Miller was "a young villain of exceptional wickedness and depravity." The crime reinforced the conviction that sensational literature could turn poor urban boys into cold-blooded murderers. Emerson and Fishbaugh's decision to play at tramping illustrated how respectable boys could be seduced and ruined by the very same literature. Taken together, the fates of these three youths comment on the powerful relationship between emerging ideas of adolescence and popular culture in the second half of the nineteenth century. Specifically, public reaction to the crime gestures to broader cultural connections between boys, boyhood, and the frontier myth embedded in readings of the American dime novel Western. In these novels, ideas of young and old came into conflict, positioning the mythic frontier as a dynamic space for youth and an incubator of idealized American masculinity.

As we have seen, perceptions and constructions of youth and the frontier have long been mixed together in the American imagination. Frederick Jackson Turner's frontier thesis enshrined the frontier as the defining symbol of the American ethos and offered the symbolic frontier as a tool for actualizing the bright promise of the nature's future. In the final decades of the nineteenth century, white male elites imagined that future through the reconfiguration of American masculinity. Gail Bederman describes a time when "middle-class power and authority were being challenged in a variety of ways which middle-class men interpreted—plausibly—as a challenge to their manhood." The sources of this challenge ranged from economic—namely, the transformation of middle-class men to low-level clerical work—to cultural and political, with growing ranks of immigrant and working-class men threatening to undermine traditional claims to authority.[2]

Bederman describes a range of strategies employed by privileged white men to fight these challenges, and G. Stanley Hall and Theodore Roosevelt stand out as key figures in her analysis. Examining Hall's lectures, biography, and other writings, Bederman offers a potent examination of how the influential psychologist introduced a new model of child development, positioning boys as the raw material for idealized visions of manhood. Successful American men, Hall believed, could be made from the right kind of boys, and "educators could raise boys to be strong and virile, immune from civilization's effeminizing tendencies" (78).

Hall's theories valorized Anglo-Saxon manhood while addressing a central paradox in anti-modernist anxieties about the deteriorating effects of civilization. These anxieties pitted the weakness and effeminacy of civilization, coded as Anglo-Saxon, against the perceived strength and power of primitive races, leaving a thorny dilemma: How could white men access both the virtues of Anglo-Saxon civilization and the natural advantages of savagery? Hall's theory of recapitulation suggested an answer to that question that upheld contemporary racial hierarchies. As Bederman describes it, "a man might be civilized as an adult" because "*as a boy* he had been primitive." While enjoying the benefits of a civilized race, Hall suggested that "boys . . . had access to all the primitive strength lacking to civilized men," and, if raised properly, could achieve a paragon of new American manhood.[3]

Theodore Roosevelt's cult of the strenuous life dovetails neatly with Hall's theories. Roosevelt warned Americans urgently about the dangers of race suicide, and, as Jackson Lears points out, he became the early twentieth century's "poster boy for white-male renewal—especially among the Anglo-American elite, the effete 'better sort' whom Roosevelt scorned for their decadent and effeminate ways."[4] By taking up the strenuous life, these men could, as Bederman puts it, "prove their virility as a race and nation."[5] As in Turner's thesis, Roosevelt's ideal of frontier manhood required contact between the savage and the civilized; as in Hall's pedagogy, it worked explicitly through constructions of boyhood. Born and raised as one of those effete elites, Roosevelt was teased and bullied as a sickly child in New York City but reinvented himself as a vigorous western man, complete with buckskin suit and majestic Dakota ranch. Following this example, the frontier could turn Anglo-Saxon boys, with access to both the innate strength of the primitive and the boundless potential of white civilization, into superior American men.

Of course, as the case of Charley Miller demonstrated, the imagined frontier as a space for youth signified both promise and peril. In this way, Hall's theories posited two categories of boyhood: proper boyhood (the ideal) and improper boyhood (its pathological other). In the final decades of the nineteenth century, Americans became increasingly preoccupied with this type of pathology and the threat of juvenile delinquency. In the wake of the Civil War, many perceived a more lawless society and, as John Hallwas explains, "Rowdyism became a major problem," one increasingly connected to the nation's rapidly growing urban centers.[6] Boys such as Miller seemed headed for a life of destitution and criminality, corrupted by the deleterious effects of urbanity and their own presumed bad blood. Immigrants, especially young males, were a major source of anxiety in this regard.

Founded by Charles Loring Brace in 1853, the Children's Aid Society sought to rescue America's poor urban youth from a life of destitution and criminality. Brace notes that these youths, especially the boys, "are far more brutal than the peasantry from whom they descend." The city, Brace believed, hardened these boys, often the children of immigrants, whom he and others described as a future generation of frightening criminals. Already, he describes, "they are ready for any offense of crime, however degraded or bloody."[7] While clearly suspicious of their peasant stock, Brace was mostly concerned with the environment these children lived in, and his main goal was to remove them from the vice and squalor of the city.

To redeem these boys, Brace shipped them out to rural areas through the Children's Aid Society's placement program. In operation from 1854 to 1929, the program was driven by the same logic as Roosevelt's rhetoric of the strenuous life, positing that the nation's rugged open country was a transformative space. Still, while Brace and others conceived of the frontier as a redemptive space, some viewed his orphan trains, as they became known, much differently. To some critics, the trains were, as LeRoy Ashby puts it, simply "dumping criminally minded youths in western states," paving the way for a growing criminal class.[8] In this way, the frontier threatened to mold young boys in different ways than Brace imagined. Like former orphan-train rider Charley Miller, the displaced urban youth removed to the frontier would grow not into rugged and virtuous men but instead into the worst kind of criminals.

In the public imagination, dime novels only reinforced these fears. In addition to his adopted name, Miller modeled his speech after the outlaw heroes in dime Westerns, which as Joan Brumberg puts it, became "a guidebook for behavior worthy of imitation."[9] Labeled "the boy murderer," not on account of his victims but, as Brumberg argues, "because of his own youth" (5), Miller stood out as a startling example of how sensational literature and the American frontier could nurture the at-risk boy into dangerous adolescence.[10]

Nineteenth-century fears about dime novels might seem hysterical in retrospect, but these texts served, in ways that have largely gone unnoticed, as a provocative brand of adolescent literature. Numerous scholars, such as Joseph Kett and Kent Baxter, have examined how American ideas of adolescence took shape in the late nineteenth and early twentieth centuries. This chapter adds to that body of scholarship, assessing the adolescent characters and readers, both real and imagined, of the nineteenth-century dime novel Western. I argue that dime Westerns mediated cultural notions of proper and improper boyhood, contributing to emerging ideas of American adolescence in ways that have been overlooked. Mapping the frontier as a space for youth, these texts troubled nineteenth-century age categories, establishing the dime novel as an ideological battleground for notions of cultural identity and social order.[11]

DIME NOVEL SUBVERSIONS

As discussed in chapter 1, dime novelists were not the first authors to imagine boyhood through evocations of the American frontier. James Fenimore Cooper's Leatherstocking Tales established frontier adventure as preferred reading material for the American boy. Mark Twain, Hamlin Garland, and other chroniclers of genteel American boyhood also explored the relationship between boyhood and the frontier in their work. Twain and Garland were well acquainted with dime novels, alongside their predecessors the penny dreadful and the story paper. Garland confesses to maintaining a steady diet of dime novels during his prairie boyhood. Likewise, if Mark Twain had little patience for Cooper's frontier romance, he had no reservations about dime novel Westerns, which he read voraciously while working on *Huck Finn and Tom Sawyer among the Indians*. Twain would likely have balked at recommending this literature for children, though, and as noted in chapter 1, Tom Sawyer shows all the negative effects of too much "cheap reading."[12]

The dime novel label has been invoked to cover a range of popular literary forms, including those in different formats such as the story paper and the library. Some of these narratives predate 1860, while dime novel content surely seeped into the magazines and pulps that rose to prominence at the turn of the century. Still, most critics use the century mark as the end point for the dime novel, and this analysis focuses mostly on the years from 1870 to 1900, specifically the 1870s and 1880s. Taking advantage of technological advances in printing, low postage rates, and improved networks of distribution, dime novel publishing houses became known as "fiction factories;" novels were assembled quickly, with an emphasis on quantity rather than quality, and shipped all over the country. Produced in high volumes and fueling emergent distinctions between "high" and "low" culture, dime novels represent one of America's earliest and most prominent forms of popular culture.

Western themes dominated the early years of dime novel publishing, mixing fictional characters like Seth Jones and Deadwood Dick with the sensationalized exploits of real-life figures such as Jesse James and Buffalo Bill. Owing a clear debt to Cooper, these busy stories ratcheted up the violence (becoming known as "blood-and-thunder" tales), while willfully entertaining improbable scenarios, convoluted plotlines, and a cheerful disregard for traditional narrative conventions.

The content of the stories presented a challenge to mainstream literary culture. In his analysis of nineteenth-century sensational literature as working-class culture, Michael Denning reads dime Westerns as a collision of contested meanings and potential sites of resistance to the forces of Gilded Age capitalism. While Denning rightly points out that not all dime novels were Westerns, frontier mythology worked to engage the subversive potential of the genre and continued to be a prominent theme in sensational literature through the turn of the century and beyond.[13]

If dime novels posed a threat to existing class structures, they also contributed to the destabilization of dominant modes of masculinity. In fact, Christine Bold describes the Western genre's history as a story of competing visions of class-bound masculinity in the late nineteenth and early twentieth centuries. The modern day Western, she claims, growing out of Owen Wister's *The Virginian* (1902) and later finding full flourish in the macho swagger of John Wayne, was shaped by "a group of influential easterners who were prominent in politics and professional life—as well as being published authors—and who inhabited the most privileged class in Victorian America."[14] Bold describes these eastern power brokers, including Teddy Roosevelt, Frederic Remington, and Caspar Whitney, as the "Frontier Club," a group whose appropriation of both western land and western stories quickly became "accompanied by a running battle over who got to tell the story and in what terms" (6). As Bold describes it, Frontier Club fiction adopted the form and style of the dime novel Western while aggressively suppressing any notions of working-class resistance. Social class, she argues, "separates how the early dime novelists fictionalized cowboys and cattle barons and how frontier clubmen did" (92).

At the same time, as Daniel Worden perceptively argues, nineteenth-century dime novel Westerns did more than challenge masculinity across or through class lines; these novels also threated to sever the link between masculinity and the male body. Popular dime novel heroes such as Deadwood Dick demonstrate, as Worden claims, "the emergence of a performative masculinity that is unhinged from essential ties to bodies, politics, and social conventions."[15] In fact, throughout the second half of the nineteenth century, the dime novel became increasingly viable as a site where notions of American masculinity were conceived and con-tested, presenting myriad opportunities for characters to exist outside of conventional gender categories.[16]

The figure of Calamity Jane stands out in this regard. Based (in the loosest of possible ways) on the real-life Martha Jane Canary, this recurring character in Edward Wheeler's Deadwood Dick novels alter-nates between the role of friend, colleague, and even lover of the titular character. As Janet Dean points out, her complex performance of gender works to "effect a transformation of Western masculinity, as well as East-ern femininity in the imagined West."[17] Dean cautions against reading dime novels as a direct challenge to Victorian notions of gender, suggest-ing instead that the radical nature of the dime novel's form, "its hasty production, its reliance on literary formula and cliché, its adherence to the requirements of seriality," reflects "an unconscious struggle against restrictive identity categories" (46). Still, the radical form of the dime novel facilitated much of its subversive potential. On the whole, dime Westerns engaged with popular cultural narratives of the American frontier to create a dynamic space for slippery negotiations of class and gender roles. Just as the dime novel became established as a dominant form of popular culture in the 1870s, the frontier was being established as the dominant organizing principle for American ideas of character and identity.

There are clearly limits to the emancipatory potential of frontier dime novels. As Worden notes, these books were hardly "free of the prejudices of their time," especially racial prejudices.[18] Depictions of non-white characters, most notably Indians, are garish in the best cases, and the masculinity championed in these novels is always white mascu-linity. Interestingly, the haphazard narrativity intrinsic to the dime novel form provided opportunities for some nonwhite authors to utilize that form to their own ends. In one prominent example, black cowboy Nat Love claimed the name of Deadwood Dick for his fictionalized 1907 au-tobiography. In doing so, as Michael Johnson argues, Love employs the "western setting to demonstrate that a black man can achieve the dom-inant culture's masculine ideal." Leaning on dime Western tropes such as "Indian attacks, outlaws, gunslingers, six-gun justice, cattle roundups, and cowboy contest," Love achieves, as Johnson describes it, "his desired masculine identity" through an appropriation of the dime novel form and its stylized masculinity.[19]

While picking up on the subversive elements—and ugly racism—of dime novels, critics have underestimated the challenge dime Westerns presented to nineteenth-century age categories. Johnson's analysis is a reminder of how suppressed individuals can use dominant cultural forms and narratives for self-empowerment and can be instructive when considering the young readers of frontier dime novels. Nat Love's use of Deadwood Dick to establish his desired identity exemplifies the use of tactics Michel de Certeau discusses in *The Practice of Everyday Life*. "Culture," de Certeau argues, "articulates conflicts and alternately legitimizes, displaces, or controls the superior force." Efforts to disperse dominant cultural narratives create "an atmosphere of tensions," an atmosphere that enables individuals like Nat Love to use these narratives tactically. Making use of the existing form of the dime novel, Love manages to subvert the themes within that form to foster agency and identity regardless of the overt racism in the genre. This use of tactics demonstrates "the ingenious ways in which the weak make use of the strong."[20]

It is worth keeping de Certeau's ideas about culture and tactics firmly in mind when considering the relationship between frontier dime novels and adolescence. If Deadwood Dick provided a powerful vehicle for oppressed individuals like Nat Love to project strength and claim agency, that vehicle proved equally viable for a range of young readers. Deadwood Dick, as we shall see, was himself was a teen, as other dime novel heroes were, and frontier dime novels provided useful tools for young readers in pushing back against emergent—and restrictive—ideas of adolescence.

**A CHANGING MARKET AND
AN EMERGING THREAT**

An early force in dime novel publishing, Beadle & Adams built a successful publishing model that kept prices low and introduced aggressive marketing techniques to great effect. Their 1860 campaign for Edward Ellis's *Seth Jones* resulted in unprecedented sales, and the firm soon claimed the slogan, "Books for the Million!" At first, Beadle & Adams did not directly target a child audience, but their books undoubtedly found young readers, and as Paul Ringel argues, "many northern boys consumed them voraciously" in the wake of the Civil War.[21] Erastus Beadle's first publishing venture in the 1850s, *The Youth's Casket*, was a children's magazine, and years later, Beadle & Adams recognized the growing child audience for sensational fiction. In general, the market for books for young readers was developing during the second half of the nineteenth century. Steven Mintz labels the period from 1865 to 1910 "the golden age of American children's fiction," and Ringel notes that in the same period "children's magazines began marketing more directly to young readers."[22]

Considering the close proximity of these literatures of boyhood, it is odd that dime novels are rarely considered children's books. Denning argues that dime novels "could not be called 'children's literature,'"[23] citing an anecdote from the memoir of dime novelist William Wallace Cook. Cook relayed a directive, ostensibly from his editor at Beadle & Adams, explaining that the "stories in the Ten-Cent Library are not read by boys alone, but usually by young men, and in no case should the hero be a kid" (30). Of course, this anecdote evinces wariness on the part of dime novel publishers more than a lack of interest in cultivating a market of child readers.

In fact, dime novels found a sizable child audience in the 1870s, and publishers of sensational literature became increasingly open to courting young readers directly. In 1877, Beadle & Adams introduced the Half-Dime Library, a series Denning and others readily admit was meant to target boys. Through these efforts to target a youthful audience and through its sustained focus on adolescent heroes, the Half Dime Library could be considered an early form of adolescent literature, specifically a literature targeting young males. Blurring the line between boys and men, this constituted the haziest of demographic categories in the late nineteenth century, one prefiguring early-twentieth-century delineations of adolescence. In 1915, looking back on his career writing for Beadle & Adams, T. C. Harbaugh commented on the exacting style of his editor, Orville Victor. In shaping manuscripts, Harbaugh notes, Victor, "who made them great by his criticism, knew what the 'boys' wanted."[24]

Harbaugh's emphasis of the word *boys* is notable. In a series of letters written to dime novel collector Frank O'Brien between 1914 and 1921, Harbaugh looks back on the heyday of Beadle & Adams, reminiscing about his own youthful days writing dime novels. In considering the reissue of the Beadle & Adams titles, Harbaugh advises retaining the "old style that delighted the 'boys' of other days." While evincing a clear nostalgia for his "old dime novel days," Harbaugh uses *boys* to describe both his former audience and his fellow writers. As he describes it, the roster of (mostly) all male writers served as a family of boys with Orville Victor serving as their benevolent but exacting father.

The dynamic is captured neatly in a poem Harbaugh typed up and sent to O'Brien in 1921, entitled "A Christmas Sentiment." The poem laments how "the 'boys' who told the story / in the old 'Dimes' days of glory, / have nearly all passed away." He goes on to describe O'Brien as "the friend of Beadle's 'boys; / for they give you youthful pleasure, / often filled your boyhood's measure / With the happiest of joys."[25] Here, Harbaugh describes the former Beadle & Adams writers as avatars of eternal boyhood, noting that, even as adults, readers like O'Brien can draw "youthful pleasure" from the books they once read as actual boys. In the poem, and indeed in all of Harbaugh's letters to O'Brien, dime novels serve as a vital conduit linking author and reader alike to a timeless space of idealized boyhood.

Harbaugh stands out in this regard in his surviving correspondence with O'Brien, but many of the writers who worked under Orville Victor saw him as a father figure—ushering them, as writers, into full maturity. This comes across most clearly in a collection of letters sent to Victor upon his retirement from the firm, in which writer after writer heaps praise upon the venerable editor for molding their work and their lives. Harbaugh remembers coming to Beadle & Adams "almost a boy," before reaching "mature manhood in both years and literary work" under Victor's stewardship. Most strikingly, William Manning recalls sending his first manuscript to Victor "as a boy of nineteen," demonstrating that in at least one case, Beadle & Adams employed an adolescent writer to write sensational fiction.[26]

The 1870s were a time of rapid change in the dime novel industry, and the genre's growing boy readership helped motivate those changes. Beadle & Adams's founders, Erastus Beadle and William Adams, retreated from day-to-day operations, but the firm remained incredibly active. Beadle & Adams introduced five new series in 1877, changing the form of the books as well as the content, and the Half-Dime Library stands out on both fronts. As Albert Johannsen points out, the novels could be folded into fours and "were much handier to place inside a geography for intensive study, or to read beneath the projecting edge of a school desk."[27] If William Wallace Cook had written any half-dimes, he wouldn't have been reprimanded for including a "kid" as his hero. Many of the nickel novels featured young heroes, including Antelope Abe, the Boy Guide; Buffalo Bill, Prince of the Pistol (a youthful version of the real-life William Cody); Lasso Jack, the Young Mustanger; Wild Edna, the Girl Brigand; Corduroy Charlie, the Boy Bravo; Hurricane Nell, the Girl Dead-Shot; and of course Deadwood Dick, Prince of the Road. In Harbaugh's *Judge Lynch, Jr.; or the Boy Vigilante* (1880), the titular protagonist is not only a kid but a one-boy lynch mob. His business card boasts, "Court always in session! Villains executed with neatness and dispatch! Hangings cheerfully attended to at all hours!"[28]

These new developments in dime novel publishing raised the anxiety level for guardians of middle-class childhood. As Albert Stone explains, "blood-and-thunder" stories were "anathema to most proper parents in the Gilded Age" from the start, and "the forces of gentility drew together in an effort to stamp out this vulgar literary intruder."[29] Stone notes that between 1865 and 1879, four children's magazines—*Our Young Folks, The Riverside Magazine for Young People, The St. Nicholas,* and *Harper's Young People*—emerged to provide an alternative to the lurid fare proffered by the House of Beadle & Adams and their ilk (104).

In 1878, *Scribner's Monthly* published William Graham Sumner's powerful indictment of the dime novel, "What Our Boys Are Reading." Sumner laments that many young boys belonging "to families which enjoy good social advantages," are reading cheap periodicals about "Indian warfare, California desperado life, pirates, wild sea adventure, highwaymen, crimes and horrible accidents, horrors (tortures and snake stories), gamblers, practical jokes." These stories promote "the life of vagabond boys, and the wild behavior of dissipated boys in great cities."[30] Sumner goes on to bemoan the lack of "good" boy roles in these stories, along with, importantly, their degradation of domestic life as "stupid and unmanly." All in all, he concludes, the novels "poison boys' minds with views of life which are so base and false as to destroy all manliness and all chance of true success" (685).

Sumner's screed hits on several key elements that made dime novels
such a palpable threat to middle-class authority figures, betraying a rhetoric of boyhood embedded with powerful class infections. On the one
hand, as would be illustrated by the dead bodies of Waldo Emerson and
Ross Fishbaugh, this literature threatened to lead "good" boys into "bad"
behaviors, bucking adult authority and straying from the conventions of
middle-class respectability. In this way, dime novels were perceived as an
open attack on the middle-class family; they encouraged boys to cut ties
to the family, enticing them to believe they could thrive and prosper as
"men" without making any concessions to parental guidance or middle-
class domesticity. The "wild behavior" and moral dissipation threatened
by the dime novels could lead the "good" boy to destruction by bringing him down to the level of the "boys in great cities," clearly coded as
lower-class children from (largely) immigrant families—in other words,
boys like Charley Miller. As a product of degeneracy, through his absent
parents, the orphaned Miller was a potential criminal long before he
became Kansas Charley. For boys like Charley, dime novels seemed designed to maximize their inherent criminal potential.

While some critics, like Sumner, denounced dime novels publicly, others sought to mimic their themes in more wholesome literature. As Stone
suggests, children's magazines and authors of didactic children's fiction
recognized that their readers demanded a healthy dose of adventure and
not just moral instruction. For instance, in *Julius the Street Boy or Out West*
(1874) Horatio Alger Jr. sends his standard-issue protagonist, the plucky
but aimless street urchin, out to the prairies of Wisconsin on one of the
Children's Aid Society's orphan trains. Julius benefits from fresh air and
open land, while acquiring a proper father figure who instills in him the
discipline to become a responsible, respectable farmer. As Laura Apol
points out, from 1880 to 1910, seventeen *Youth's Companion* serials were
set in the West, and these stories all "exhibited a prescriptive quality" that
ensured the narratives fit comfortably "within widely cultural standards"
desired by the magazine's middle-class readership.[31] Operating in this
vein, Stone's "forces of gentility" had a fine line to walk, trying to woo
youthful readers with the trappings of the sensational literature they
decried.

Complicating matters, middle-class pedagogues did not agree on
exactly what kinds of literature middle-class boys should be exposed

to; for instance, many rated Alger as little better than a dime novelist. In *Eight Cousins* (1875) Louisa May Alcott devotes the bulk of a chapter to an extended condemnation of cheap literature, seemingly aimed at Alger and Oliver Optic. Upon catching her young sons reading "the adventures of the scapegraces and ragamuffins," Aunt Jessie gives them a thorough dressing down: "The writers of these popular stories intend to do good," she confesses, but in her estimation they fail completely, preaching a doctrine of "'Be smart, and you will be rich,' instead of 'Be honest, and you will be happy.'" Geordie, one of the boys, protests that the stories offer realistic portrayals of lower-class boys and how they live, but Aunt Jessie presses on: "my sons are neither boot-blacks nor newsboys." Ultimately, she concludes, the books cannot "help to refine the ragamuffins if they read them, and I'm sure they can do no good to the better class of boys, who through these books are introduced to police courts, counterfeiters' dens, gambling houses, drinking saloons, and all sorts of low life."[32] Aunt Jessie's diatribe reinforces the degree to which class considerations mediated the dangers of cheap reading. At the same time, Alcott herself wrote sensational romances under the alias A. M. Barnard, and her singling out of the "boys" here suggests these dangers were mediated by gender as well, with boy readers being all the more "at risk."[33]

Censorship represented a less subtle response to the dime novel threat. Anthony Comstock's rise to power as a moral crusader was partially fueled by the desire to keep sensational fiction away from American children, and he successfully framed dime novels as a moral panic. Comstock formed the New York Society for the Suppression of Vice, "a quasi-legal organization," as Denning describes it, whose campaign against immoral and obscene literature resulted in the 1873 Comstock Act, "prohibiting the mailing of obscene books and materials."[34] Comstock also operated as a special agent for the United States Post Office, employing those powers to harass publishers of cheap literature. He arrested the publisher of *The Fireside Companion* in 1872 and, in 1885, arrested Frank Tousey, who published story papers such as the *New York Boys Weekly* and *Young Men of America*. Efforts to censor dime novel publishers reached a fever pitch during the trial of Frank James in 1883, when, as Denning describes it, the postmaster general compelled "Frank Tousey to withdraw his outlaw tales" of the James gang (160). Ultimately, in 1910 the postal service revoked the permits of a number of dime novel publishers, leading the last of them to abandon the trade.[35]

It is important to recognize that these varied responses to dime novels do not amount to universal condemnation of sensational literature in the final decades of the nineteenth century. Rather, they reflect the growing awareness that a vibrant market existed for a different kind of children's book, one that was both less didactic and more engaging to child readers, and the recognition that this market, which was emergent but unstable—much like competing nineteenth-century conceptions of childhood—needed regulating.

The birth of this market, the desire of moral guardians to regulate it, and the later canonization of American "children's literature" coincide with the dime novel boom. At the same time, the dime novel backlash mirrored prevailing social trends, falling neatly in line with a raft of efforts aiming to both reform and regulate young Americans in the decades following the Civil War. According to Kathleen Chamberlain, in these years, "schools and libraries came to be regarded not merely as educational training grounds or repositories of knowledge, but as major agents of socialization and citizenship." The uproar about what children were reading, then, informed broader efforts to teach "both native-born and immigrant children . . . what it meant to be an American."[36] As a diverse array of writers, educators, and organizers came to see childhood as an increasingly crucial developmental period and the development of boys as especially relevant to the future of the nation, many of these efforts were focused on boys.

DANGEROUS ADOLESCENCE ON THE FRONTIER

Panicked responses to the dime novel also reflected a growing social awareness of adolescence as a life stage and growing concern about the regulation of adolescent boys. Kenneth Kidd borrows the term *boyology* to describe diverse cultural projects in the late nineteenth century, from didactic literature to organized boy work, encompassing various efforts, including organizational scouting and team sports, employed to usher white boys into successful American manhood. As David Macleod describes it, nineteenth-century boy workers saw great potential in the perceived purity of the boy; for Hall, "if purity was power, preadolescent boyhood seemed the ideal time to build masculinity,"[37] creating strong men and productive citizens—especially for those who suited Hall's model of Anglo-Saxon purity. For those who did not, like Charley Miller, boyhood was a critical time for managing and curtailing delinquency. From 1870 to the turn of the century, more than eleven million immigrants arrived on American shores, many settling in cities like New York and Chicago. As urban populations swelled, delinquent youth demanded increasing attention from social reformers such as Jane Addams and Jacob Riis who, as Jon Savage describes it, emphasized with "greater urgency than ever before the stark choices facing America's young."[38]

The popularity of dime novels in the 1870s and 1880s reflects a growing concern with adolescence—and adolescents who were tempted to make the wrong choices. Hall's *Adolescence* (1904) is a capstone moment in most histories of this life stage in America, though ideations of youth as a distinctive life stage clearly existed much earlier. Joseph Kett describes how, by the middle of the nineteenth century, American high schools had emerged as places where middle-class parents could provide supervision for their teenage children, shielding them from the "perils of adolescence"—weak judgment, lack of impulse control, and excessive and irrational passions.[39] Howard Chudacoff traces similar concerns as early as 1828, through pastor Joel Hawes's lecture on the "Dangers of Young Men," noting that Hawes "defined "'young manhood' as the stage bounded by ages fourteen and twenty-one."[40] In 2003, revisiting his foundational work on youth cultures, Kett distinguished between the category of "youth" dominant for most of the nineteenth century in America and Hall's ideas of adolescence. For moralists of that earlier era, he claims, it made "no difference whether a youth was 14 or 25," rather those were the years when boys typically left home and "hence had entered a critical and dangerous period."[41] For Hall and his followers, adolescence was distinguished by the need to maintain the period of dependency for young people.

Late-nineteenth-century ideas of adolescence were steeped in evolutionary theory, particularly the work of Herbert Spencer. Spencer proposed that girls and boys experienced distinct cycles of development; while girls seemed to develop faster, they also had a much lower developmental ceiling. As Crista DeLuzio explains, Spencer and his followers, including Hall and Edward Clarke, relied on this understanding of evolution to explain how female development prepared girls for reproduction and marked women as the inferior sex. The boy developed more gradually, these theorists believed, but his slower growth held greater potential. Prolonged development initially rendered the boy less refined than his female counterpart, but it also ensured that he would inevitably become the more advanced of the two.[42]

Spencer's theories provided the foundation for social Darwinism and created clear racial hierarchies as well. In Spencer's evolutionary model, which directly informed Hall's use of recapitulation theory, the individual's evolution replicated the evolution of the species. In this way, the boy had a higher developmental ceiling than the girl, and the civilized—that is, white—boy had the highest ceiling of all. Exposed to the frontier, it was this white boy, the Anglo-Saxon ideal touted by Teddy Roosevelt, who was best situated to develop into Turner's triumphant American pioneer—and, at the same time, most at risk to the lure of negative influences such as sensational literature.

Cultural historians have made some useful connections between the dime novel and early notions of adolescence. Often, this work focuses on the character of Frank Merriwell, who made his debut in Street & Smith's *Tip Top Weekly* series, launched in 1896. As Ryan Anderson describes him, Merriwell provided readers—middle-class boys in particular—with an adolescent hero who was young and powerful but "did not have to act bad to prove his manliness."[43] The Ivy League football star provided a counter to the equally manly, if far less principled, teen protagonists introduced nearly two decades earlier in frontier dime novels published by the rival house of Beadle & Adams. Many of these novels also highlighted a life stage separate from either childhood or adulthood, one that, unlike Merriwell's world, was defined by its independence from and open defiance to adult authority.

As cultural notions of adolescence started to crystalize in the 1870s, they interacted with sensational literature in diverse and interesting ways. Sarah Chinn writes about turn-of-the-century girls working in New York City, whose parents had immigrated to America in the 1870s; these girls absorbed "the lessons of dime novels and story papers" and demanded the right to spend their own hard-earned money as they saw fit.[44] Kett speculates about a different connection between sensational literature and emergent adolescence, wondering whether adolescents denied full agency "took refuge in the fantasy world of nineteenth-century adventure literature," finding escape "in the stories filled with sentiment, seduction, violence, pirates, Indians, desperadoes, and young stalwarts who brazenly cut loose from family ties."[45]

Beyond refuge and escape, frontier dime novels offered adolescent readers agency. A couple of decades earlier than Chinn's focus, these novels targeted adolescent readers and often portrayed white adolescent boys at their most powerful—and their most dangerous. If Hall came to describe adolescence as a time of greater dependency, these novels presented it as a time of unfettered autonomy. The Beadle & Adams half-dimes often featured a new brand of young hero, typically male, who has maximized his potential and taken full control of his life.

More competent and confident than previous generations of young characters, this adolescent hero presaged broader developments in children's literature. As Ringel points out, by the 1890s, even magazines such as St. Nicholas and The Youth's Companion were "portraying young Americans who were capable of succeeding in contemporary society."[46] Frank Merriwell's popularity can also be seen as part of this trend. As Anderson explains, for devoted readers of Frank Merriwell novels, "joining Merry's Flock was a way of working with and against people who would define them as children or adolescents and incapable of acting for themselves."[47]

Of course, the adolescent hero of the dime Western appeared some twenty years before Merry's Flock, exercising a degree of autonomy surpassing anything in the Tip Top Weekly's run. That autonomy likely brought together American youth with strikingly disparate daily lived experiences, be it the teenage boy in a small-town Connecticut high school or one of his age peers working in the Pennsylvania coal mines. Jacqueline Moore argues that boys growing up on the range were "just like boys everywhere in the country;" Texas boys, she notes, "idolized the cowboys they saw on the ranches or that they read about in dime novels and believed they embodied the very ideal of manhood. With their devil-may-care attitude toward society, cowboys mirrored the freedom that all young boys wanted from their parents."[48] In this way, the crisis of "what our boys are reading" becomes a cover for a much broader set of concerns than literary taste. Through dynamic heroes like Deadwood Dick, the dime Western created a space for different boy readers to imagine a host of alternate trajectories from childhood to adulthood, stimulating powerful visions of autonomous young people triumphing over the restrictions of age and the oppression of adults.

Critics have largely ignored the preponderance of adolescent heroes in the Beadle half-dimes. Henry Nash Smith argues that the "strongest link connecting the Beadle Westerns with the frontier narratives established by Cooper's Leatherstocking Tales is the presence of a benevolent hunter without a fixed place of abode, advanced in age, celibate, and of unequaled prowess in trailing, marksmanship, and Indian fighting."[49] It is hard to square that analysis with Deadwood Dick. He may not be a "kid," but he's not "advanced in age" (or celibate) either.

In fact, by positioning his hero as a liminal "youth," Edward Wheeler blurs the line between child and adult, while providing an alternative to the stereotypical frontier hero handed down from Cooper. Contemporary critics of the dime novel surely picked up on this trend. In an 1884 lecture on the evils of "vile literature," Comstock warns, "the hero of each story is a boy who has escaped the restraints of home and entered on a life of crime."[50] Ultimately, in showcasing this young hero as the star of a new format aimed specifically at an audience of boys, Beadle & Adams created a new kind of children's literature that featured liberal doses of adolescent autonomy and threatened conventional narratives of social order on myriad levels.

DEADWOOD DICK AND
EMPOWERED ADOLESCENCE

The success of the Beadle & Adams half-dime novel can be attributed, at least partially, to Deadwood Dick, the hero chosen to launch the series, which subsequently included 1,168 issues. Edward Wheeler's *Deadwood Dick, the Prince of the Road*, proved to be, as Johannsen describes it, "a very lucky choice for the new series,"[51] and Deadwood Dick went on to star in 130 Beadle & Adams novels, living on through innumerable reprints and pirated editions. He even outlived his creator, who authored a mere thirty-four of the titles (hundreds of additional titles appeared under Wheeler's name but were clearly written by others). The choice of Deadwood Dick as a protagonist for the first title in the series lends additional

weight to the notion of dime novel Westerns as adolescent-driven, refor-
mulating the chimeric frontier as a space of and for youth.

Critics have not failed to seize on the subversive potential of Deadwood Dick. Daryl Jones notes that Dick was the first Western hero who
"openly defied the law," reacting "to social restraint so violently as to waylay
stages and rob banks."[52] Smith laments Dick's abandonment of gentility
as the dime Western's last chance to "develop social significance,"[53] while
Denning offers a useful counter to Smith's analysis, reading Deadwood
Dick as a vigilante figure who not only seeks rightful revenge against
the villains who have robbed him of his family fortune but, more importantly, one who organizes local miners to fight the oppressive interests of
Gilded Age capitalism. Dick's main antagonist in the first novel is the Old
Mechanic, whose name, as Daniel Worden points out, "seems to mark
out the older artisan class, unionized and unwilling to join rank with
unskilled laborers."[54] Again, as Christine Bold points out, working-class
sympathies were commonplace in dime novel Westerns throughout the
nineteenth century. In the Deadwood Dick novels, these conflicts often
boil down to "old" versus "young."[55]

It is not surprising that the Deadwood Dick series gives free play to
varied readings, as Wheeler's main character is defined by his fluidity.
Wheeler first describes Dick as a lone rider passing through the Custer
gulch toward a notice offering a $500 reward for "the notorious young
desperado who hails to the name Deadwood Dick." This how Wheeler
introduces Dick: "He was a youth of an age somewhere between sixteen
and twenty, trim and compactly built, with a preponderance of muscular
development and animal spirits; broad and deep of chest, with square,
ironcast shoulders; limbs small yet like bars of steel, and a grace of position in the saddle rarely equaled; he made a fine picture for an artist's
brush or a poet's pen."[56]

That picture reveals a familiar ideal of frontier masculinity, from
the ease in the saddle indicating his close connection to the primitive
to the broad chest and square shoulders. "Only one thing," Wheeler
reveals, "marred the captivating beauty of the picture." Dick is dressed
head to toe in skin-tight black buckskin, with a black mask covering his
eyes, an appearance that "presented a striking contrast to anything one
sees in the wild far West" (280). The buckskin marks Dick's connection

to the frontier scout, an archetypal figure established by Kit Carson and
Daniel Boone, and later made into a global icon by William "Buffalo
Bill" Cody. The black clothing and mask suggest something less benign
and more mysterious, the effect so strong that Wheeler stops to remind
the reader how this apparel "marred" Deadwood Dick's natural beauty.

While unusual, Dick's appearance ultimately proves superficial.
Wheeler's hero is more than a master of disguise; he proves capable of
altering his appearance completely so that, essentially, there is nothing
to disguise. As Worden describes it, "Deadwood Dick is introduced as
entirely surface."[57] This surface can be perpetually inscribed and re-
inscribed with a changing set of names and features. Indeed, a few pages
later, Dick appears in the guise of Ned Harris, a well-appointed gentleman with "a pleasant, handsome, youthful face." Harris sits at the table
with a notorious cardsharp and his intended mark, and as those two play
cards "he commenced to pare his finger nails. The fingers were as white
and soft as any girl's."[58] Later, Dick reveals his given name to actually be
Edward Harris, a name he soon casts aside again to reclaim the name
and image of Deadwood Dick.

Manipulating his name and image, Dick turns blankness into a
powerful weapon, one that, in fact, he can't always control. In the next
book in the series, *The Double Daggers, or, Deadwood Dick's Defiance* (1877)
Dick finds himself hotly pursued by a questionable lot of vigilantes
known as the Deadwood Regulators. A young man appearing to be Dick
confronts Dashing Dave, the leader of the Regulators, in a saloon, with "a
cocked revolver in his right hand, which was as white as a woman's.[59] The
man accuses Dave of stealing his seat and demands it back. Instead the
Regulators arrest and hang him as Deadwood Dick, though he claims to
be Owen Hawk—as in fact he is. Justin McKenzie, Dick's brother-in-law,
is present at the hanging and even he believes Hawk to be Dick. After
the hanging, Deadwood Dick's "ghost" haunts the region, picking off the
Regulators. That ghost, of course, is Dick himself, whose physical appearance proves mutable and ephemeral throughout Wheeler's novels. In
many cases, as in *The Double Daggers*, this mutability drives the story's plot.

As noted earlier, Worden's chief interest is in how Deadwood Dick
destabilizes conventional notions of masculinity. He points out that
Dick's fluid masculine identity offers "vantage points for a critique of

class hierarchies" and, ultimately, effects "a way of belonging apart from hierarchical structures."[60] Equally notable, Deadwood Dick presents as neither clearly a "boy" nor a "man." In the first Deadwood Dick novel, Wheeler specifies Dick's age as "somewhere between sixteen and twenty," clearing marking him as a "youth," or, an adolescent. Other than his piercing black eyes, the one consistency in Wheeler's description of this character is a focus on his "youthful features." Dick may be purely surface, but in all guises he retains his youth. In this way, the category of youth operates as both fixed and fluid, its boundaries discernable while the territory within remains perpetually obscured, its contours and features open to be arranged and rearranged.

Alongside Dick, the novel's other prominent male characters are all identified by their youthfulness. Wheeler describes Fearless Frank, the first character to appear in the novel, as "an interesting specimen of young, healthy manhood, and, even though a youth in years, was one that could command respect, if not admiration, wheresoever he might choose to go."[61] Harry Redburn, whom Dick rescues from the cardsharp at the Metropolitan Saloon, is introduced as a "young and handsome 'pilgrim." Most intriguing of all, perhaps, is the mysterious outlaw who first appears to offer Harris and Redburn refuge from a gun-toting mob. As the duo flees the mob, "a trim boyish figure stepped before them, from out of the shadow of a new frame building" (291). After being led to a safe hiding place, Redburn pauses to consider his rescuer. Wheeler describes this figure as of "medium height and symmetrically built; dressed in a carefully tanned costume of buck-skin being fringed with the fur of mink; wearing a jaunty sombrero." The face was "slightly sun-burned, yet showing the traces of beauty even dissipation could not obliterate." After ensuring their safety, "the next moment the youth was gone." A "bewildered" Redburn asks who the youth was, and Harris replies, "That?—why that's Calamity Jane!" (292).

The eldest of Wheeler's young protagonists, Redburn is "somewhere in the neighborhood of twenty-three years of age" (285), placing him at the end of adolescence as Hall construed it. Unlike Dick and Frank, he has nothing of the outlaw in him, but rather is a straitlaced miner who has come to the Black Hills seeking fame and fortune. Notably, he is also the most naive and (initially) helpless of the bunch. Dick's intervention prevents Redburn from being swindled by the cardsharp, and it is Dick who spurs Redburn into action, commanding the tentative "pilgrim" to shoot the cardsharp down before the two fight their way out of the saloon.

Wheeler's emphasis on youth extends beyond the novel's main characters. He repeatedly describes the Black Hills region itself in terms of its age—the miner's Camp Crook is an "infant village" (282), and the city of Deadwood is an "infant metropolis" (283). Then there is "the Pocket," the hidden valley where Dick has settled with his sister, Anita, and where he and Redburn escape after the shoot-out at the Metropolitan Saloon. Accessed via a "large, narrow, subterranean passage, barely large enough to admit the horse and rider," this hidden valley spans fifty-odd acres, walled in on all sides by "rugged mountains as steep, and steeper, in some places, than a house-roof" (294). Fed by Brown's Creek, the valley "was one vast, indiscriminate bed of wild, fragrant flowers," alongside "a log-cabin, overgrown with clinging vines" (294). In short, it is the settler's paradise, an Edenic refuge hidden from the outside world. This is where Ned Harris and his sister have been living and hiding; it is where Dick brings Redburn, and it later becomes Fearless Frank's destination.

Of course, this "unspoiled nature" cannot be sustained. With Redburn's help, the Pocket is developed into a bustling and lucrative working mine, the full realization of any prospector's wildest dreams. This transformation is inevitable. As Wheeler describes it, "like a drama on the stage, a grand transformation had taken place; a beautiful dream had been changed into stern reality; quietude and slumber had fled at the bold approach of bustling industry and life" (326). Redburn, along with the eccentric General Nix, runs the mine, with a troop of Ute Indians working under them. At the same time, it is a youth space, where Fearless Frank, Calamity Jane, and Deadwood Dick are drawn to resolve the novel's (many) conflicts. This space survives an incursion from the Old Mechanic, who nearly kills Dick but winds up being hanged for his crimes, and witnesses a set of marriages: Fearless Frank to Dick's sister, Anita, and Redburn to General Nix's daughter, Alice.

At first glance, the story's conclusion suggests merely a strengthening of family bonds and the valorization of the transition from boy to man. Redburn becomes manager of the mine, marrying his business partner's long-lost daughter, both reuniting and expanding the family unit. Frank hangs up his guns, as it were, settling into married life, as he and Anita become heirs to the Harris family's considerable estate. Importantly, all these happy endings are achieved through the actions of the story's youthful protagonists. Redburn takes the initiative in establishing the mine and reunites Alice and her father. Frank rescues Alice from the maniacal Sitting Bull and brings her to the Pocket where she meets Redburn and is reunited with her father. Deadwood Dick, of course, kills the Old Mechanic, a clear instance of empowered youth triumphing over adult oppression, a pattern that continues throughout Wheeler's Deadwood Dick novels.

More important, Deadwood Dick's story does not end in marriage; in fact, he is twice rejected on this score by the novel's end, the second rejection coming from Calamity Jane, who curtly responds, "I have had all the *man* I care for! We can be friends, Dick; more we can never be!" Dick takes the news in stride, professing, "it is destined that I shall live single. At any rate, I'll never take a refusal from another woman" (356). In future installments, Deadwood Dick and Calamity Jane do marry—while in still future installments, he will be married to someone else or not married at all. The distinctions prove irrelevant, necessitated to be so by the dime novel's serial mode of production. In this way, as Worden suggests, the genre effects an important separation from traditional novel form. With the need for dime novel heroes like Dick to remain unattached for the next installment in the series, Worden argues, these texts "come to contest the desirability of traditional narrative closure—particularly the marriage plot—and produce a vision of masculinity that creates publics outside of the usual structures of social belonging."[62]

For the adolescent, "the usual structures of social belonging" mean the end of the adventure and autonomy. Marriage itself is not the problem; it is the settling down into the world of adult responsibilities. Settling down would entail the end of Dick's youthful adventuring and his ability to harness the powerful blankness of his identity. For instance, after Fearless Frank marries Dick's sister he assumes the name of Justin McKenzie and begins working the mines. When he appears in subsequent novels, there is no appearance of his alter ego, and his days of free-spirited banditry have been left behind. Dick cannot come to terms with this vision of the future. In *The Double Daggers,* he proposes to another girl, Leone, promising that he will one day give up his life as a road agent for a life of respectability. He declares to Leone:

> I shall not always cling to the road; already the day is dawning, when the Black Hills gold excitement shall sink into that semi-oblivion that you will find in the mining districts of Colorado and California.
>
> Then the world shall know Deadwood Dick no more, and Edward Harris will quit the West for his old Eastern home where he has yet a fair record and can start in life anew.[63]

Deadwood Dick's sister Anita takes a less optimistic view, telling Leone, "I fear Ned will never desert the Black Hills, while there is life and excitement here! Here he is in his element; elsewhere, he would be lost—literally out of place."[64] Ultimately, Anita is proved right; Dick and Leone get married, but the marriage does not survive the next installment of the series.

Critically, both Deadwood Dick and his sister align Dick's character with the space of the West, specifically the freewheeling frontier imagined through South Dakota's Black Hills. This frontier space is Dick's element, a space in constant flux, much like adolescence itself. As an adolescent outlaw, Dick is one with this space. He knows that his youth, like the frontier itself, must eventually end, but the broader world of Wheeler's novel rebuffs such eventualities, providing a space of perpetual freedom and adventure.

As Nat Love's autobiography demonstrates, this frontier space suggests a kind of fluidity, one that might be used by different actors for a range of identity projects. It is quite possible, likely even, that a variety of young readers—of different classes, races, and genders—drew inspiration from the empowered adolescent characters who dominated this space. Still, it is worth reiterating that the heroes of these novels are almost exclusively white males. Empowered female adolescent characters do populate these texts, especially Wheeler's novels, but despite the powerful example of Calamity Jane, these characters often meet grisly ends.

For instance, Wheeler's *The Black Hills Jezebel; or, Deadwood Dick's Ward* (1881) features Kentucky Kit, a powerful adolescent character who proves handy with a rifle and more than capable of holding her own against the frontier's rough-and-tumble characters. Kit is introduced as "a girl dressed in boy's clothes," though Wheeler makes sure to focus on her distinctive beauty, describing her as "graceful, and well developed, while her face was round, prettily chiseled and browned with exposure to the wind and sun."[65] Kit, like Calamity Jane (who also appears in this story), is a fallen woman. She has come west in vengeance, on the trail of her duplicitous mother—the titular Jezebel—and by the novel's end, both mother and daughter meet their doom, while Deadwood Dick emerges as the story's principal hero.

So it goes for most heroines in the Beadle & Adams half-dime Westerns. Adolescent heroines are featured often, but ultimately these characters are destined to die or reform—giving up their frontier adventuring. In Prentiss Ingraham's *Gold Plume, the Boy Bandit, or the Kid-Glove Sport*, the heroine is another powerful girl disguised as a man. The boy bandit, as Ingraham calls her, appears with "piercing black eyes, dark complexion, and long brown hair hanging upon his shoulders. All told, he looked like some handsome young man masquerading as a cavalier."[66] Tipping his hand a few pages later, Ingraham describes the boy bandit as "more like a beautiful girl" than a boy, with a form "as slender, and his movements as graceful as a woman's" (6). Indeed, the boy bandit is later revealed as Clotilde, a fallen woman "ruined" by the real leader of the gang, Kid Glove Gambler. A young Buffalo Bill, the true hero of the story, defeats Gambler, whom Clotilde notes had "wronged me deeply" and "made me the guilty thing I am." By the story's end, Clotilde has cast off her identity as the boy bandit, pledging that "in the future, I will pass my days in penitence and prayer" (15).

COMPETING IDEALS OF BOYHOOD

By fixing Deadwood Dick in an endless cycle of high-octane adventures, Wheeler's novels separated themselves from the fare offered by more pedagogical-minded authors of boyhood like Oliver Optic or Alger. Ken Parille's analysis of Francis Forrester's *Dick Duncan* demonstrates this point. According to Parille, Forrester, like Optic and Alger, frames his adventure stories with the acknowledgment that boyhood adventures must all come to an end. So, at the end of *Dick Duncan*, the titular protagonist loses an archery contest, "for middle-class respectability demands

that he never become anything like a Robin Hood-esque adventurer."
Ultimately, as Parille explains, "if a boy is to possess a healthy masculinity, he must distance himself from play, pleasure adventures, and, most importantly from his desires."[67]

Wheeler's Deadwood Dick novels provide no such distancing. In this way, the novels threaten to do more than poison the minds of impressionable boys; they set the wheels of adolescent conflict in motion in ways that promote a vision of powerful masculinity linked to youthful autonomy. For Stone, "Deadwood Dick and his fellows had a profound effect upon the American family, upon parents as well as boys and girls." Children, he notes, "were carried away by their hero's exploits," while adult readers perceived "these bad men and vagabond boys" as a direct threat to the social order. Ultimately, he concludes, these novels "played all the changes on the theme of adolescent rebellion against family, school, and society in general."[68] Through these themes, frontier dime novels valorized the empowered adolescent, freed from adult guidance, as a hero and role model.

In this way, Wheeler's Deadwood Dick novels represent more than a disruption of traditional narrative form; they refashion the most basic cultural assumptions of the bildungsroman. Dick does not come of age; he is *already* of age, having mastered the art of survival in the "wild" West. In fact, he takes on the responsibility of teaching "tenderfoots" like Redburn (who is actually older than Dick) how to thrive in the dangerous frontier that has shaped him from destitute orphan to fearsome road agent. At the end of *Deadwood Dick, The Prince of the Road*, Dick describes this process. He reveals that years earlier the Old Mechanic, revealed to be his and Anita's uncle, Alexander Fillmore, murdered their parents, leaving them as orphans. After becoming their guardian, the villainous Fillmore seized the Harris family's considerable financial assets and proceeded to torment the children. Dick relays how they "were whipped, kicked about, and kept in a half-starved condition." Eventually, Fillmore tries to murder them, but Dick escapes with his sister out west. The frontier then, creates Deadwood Dick, turning a powerless boy into a formidable outlaw.[69] Throughout the Deadwood Dick novels, the character remains fixed in a kind of suspended adolescence, one that recasts the sense of developmental delay implied by that term in favor of a sense of successful adaptation.

The West in Wheeler's novels truly is no country for old men. The Deadwood Dick novels offer a series of heroic characters that have been forged by the frontier into formidable adolescent heroes. On almost every occasion, these youths come west after being cast off by duplicitous adults. When brought together in the frontier, the villainous adult always suffers, and the adolescent always triumphs. The fundamental natures of these two types, the "youthful hero" and "the old villain," become immediately clear in any of Wheeler's character descriptions. In *The Double Daggers,* he introduces us to the seventeen-year-old Leone, informing the reader that she "was of medium height and possessed of a plump, symmetrical form, which in its delicately rounded outlines was little less than perfection." By contrast, the villain who hunts her is Jasper Leslie, a fifty-year-old man whose "face was a mirror of his black, evil nature; his eyes constantly emitted gleams of baleful light." Ruined by "dissipation and debauchery," Leslie was "a repulsive object to gaze upon with his furrowed, haggard, sallow face; his sinister eyes; his huge wolfish mouth, and the accompanying grotesque ivories, and all relieved by a matted shock of hair and beard of purest white."[70]

Wheeler was not alone, as this old vs. young dynamic dominates the novels in the Beadle & Adams Half Dime Library. For example, Frederick Whitaker highlights the disparity between the two types early on in *Dick Darling, the Pony Express Rider.* Whitaker begins the novel by introducing the reader to two men, "widely different in external appearance and seemed to be so in character, judging from many indications." The older man, described as a smoker, "was a short, broad, heavy-built man of about forty, whose shaggy hair and beard looked as if the comb and they were distant acquaintances that seldom met." The smoker is as poorly dressed as he is groomed, with his shirt dirty, jacket unbuttoned and "trowsers [*sic*] ragged in the seat and inside of the thigh to knee as if from riding." By contrast, Dick Darling, the story's adolescent hero, is "younger, taller, and slighter, as well as incomparably handsomer. He did not seem to be over twenty for his face was nearly smooth, a soft brown mustache barely shading his upper lip." All told, Whitaker notes, "the difference between his uniform and that of his comrade was amazing," giving Dick "the appearance of a different being."[71]

This imagined West is no place for domesticity either. Dashing Dave, the leader of the Regulators in Wheeler's *The Double Daggers*, represents a clear example of the dangers awaiting the frontier hero who goes in for family life. Dave "had won great name as an Indian-fighter during the troubles preceding the fatal Custer engagement, and was feared by a large class of the desperate characters who infested the Black Hills." As Wheeler describes it, though, Dashing Dave "had lost his family—a wife and a month-old babe—by the border ruffians, since coming into the Hills, and this had embittered his whole nature against mankind."[72] Blinded by hatred, Dashing Dave will do anything to destroy Deadwood Dick, leading, of course, to his own death at the novel's end, when Leslie also dies and Leone marries Dick—the young again triumphing over the old.

The distinctions between these frontier dime novels and other boyhood literature becomes evident in comparing Wheeler's Deadwood Dick novels and Horatio Alger's Ragged Dick novels as frontier narratives. In the eyes of nineteenth-century reformers, waves of immigration and simmering class tensions had made the American city resemble a kind of frontier. As in Turner's West, this urban frontier could turn boys into either the best or worst kinds of men. Aaron Shaheen describes how that urban frontier operates in Ragged Dick's New York City. For Alger, he argues, "the city and the frontier exist dialectically. In fact, the two sites are not only mutually dependent, but almost one and the same."[73]

In this analysis, Dick, the lower-class bootblack, straddles the line between savage and civilized much like the traditional frontier hero. In *Ragged Dick; or, Street Life in New York with the Boot Blacks*, Dick shows his young charge, Frank Whitney, around the town, confronting peril in the form of duplicitous con men and dangerous toughs rather than bloodthirsty Indians and ruthless road agents. Still, the New York streets offer many of the dangers a frontiersman might encounter in the West, and Dick, a "native" to this unpredictable environment, acts as scout, safely guiding the naive Frank through this hostile terrain. Dick's boy-savagery also proves key to his redemption. After being taken in by Frank and his rich uncle, Dick, much like Turner's frontiersman, uses his access to both the "savage" and "civilized" to navigate the road to respectable American manhood.

If Ragged Dick displays many attributes of the frontier hero, he fails to attain the autonomy Deadwood Dick enjoys in Wheeler's novels. In both novels, the uncertain frontier proves difficult for the uninitiated to read, and both protagonists work as guides. In *Ragged Dick* Frank Whitney cannot spot a swindler, just as in *Deadwood Dick* Harry Redburn fails to detect the cardsharp. In both cases, the titular Dicks step in to assist their helpless friends. In Wheeler's text, though, the protagonist answers to no higher authority. Ragged Dick's good deeds are part of an exchange that ultimately leads him off the streets and into a respectable position as a clerk. In the urban frontier, a poor bootblack needs middle-class adult guardians to open up the road to respectability. Deadwood Dick needs no such help—nor, for that matter, respectability at all. Alger's city may be a frontier, but ultimately, it is governed by typical hierarchies of class and age. Wheeler's Black Hills present a more tumultuous, less certain frontier, one that facilitates the passage from boyhood to adolescence by way of a powerful form of masculinity detached both from middle-class propriety and the adult male body.

The recurring character of Old Avalanche in the Deadwood Dick novels provides an interesting wrinkle to the dynamic of old vs. young in frontier dime novels. An old scout and inveterate Indian killer who serves as Dick's sidekick, Old Avalanche is a clear and direct descendant of Cooper's Natty Bumppo, a figure caught between the "savage" and "civilized" worlds. On the one hand, he is one with the space of the West, a dead shot who can track any outlaw and read the terrain like an open book. On the other hand, he is completely alienated by the rapid industrialization of the Black Hills and does not fit in with the new civilization taking root there; he has a foot in both worlds while belonging to neither. Old Avalanche bears more than a passing resemblance to R. W. B. Lewis's iconic description of the American Adam, who, as Lewis describes it, is "an individual emancipated from history, happily bereft of ancestry, untouched and undefiled by the usual inheritances of family and race," an individual both superior to other men and removed from the world they live in.[74]

Lewis's rhetoric echoes Turner's formula for how American identity is forged in the contact zone of the frontier. Turner notes that "the frontier is productive of individualism. Complex society is precipitated by the

wilderness into a kind of primitive organization based on the family."
At the same time, Turner cautions that this "tendency is anti-social. It
produces antipathy to control, and particularly to any direct control."[75]
If Old Avalanche fits Lewis's Adamic vision to a tee, Deadwood Dick
represents the most dangerous manifestation of Turner's frontiersman.
Emancipated from history and family, he threatens conventions of
domestic order. Not clearly embodying hegemonic notions of class or
gender, he threatens conventions of social order. Most importantly, as an
independent youth his "antipathy to control" represents a direct threat to
hierarchical structures of age. If Old Avalanche represents the old vision
of the frontier hero, the scout caught between two worlds, Deadwood
Dick represents a dangerous new vision, a vigorous adolescent shaped by
the frontier who, in turn, exerts a demonstrable influence on the social
world starting to flourish there.

Wheeler's Deadwood Dick novels were not anomalous in framing this
vision of powerful adolescence. Many of Beadle's half-dime Westerns
invoke a frontier where adolescent heroes flourish while the old and
corrupt are swept away. At the same time, the heroic adolescent was no
constant either—even in the Deadwood Dick novels. For instance, in
Wheeler's *Wild Ivan, the Boy Claude Duval, or the Brotherhood of Death*, the
titular character is an adolescent monster, or as he describes himself, "an
outcast, murderer, swindler, thief, rogue, and blackleg." Ivan boasts, "I
have all the peculiarities of a fiend—as the Boy Fiend I am widely known
in some parts of the West."[76]

Wild Ivan demonstrates his fiendish nature in various ways, notably
by tormenting his young cousin Edith, another victimized orphan, who
has "been prisoner in the power of a cruel uncle and aunt who sold my
mom and brought me away while my father was absent on a tour through
Europe" (5). Edith has rejected Ivan's offer of marriage, though she
quickly warms to Dick, "a gentleman, in appearance and manners, and
a man whom women are apt to admire, because fearless, courageous,
courteous, and tender" (5). Ultimately, Dick defeats Ivan, proving that
even among adolescent road agents and murderers, a sense of honor is
bound to prevail.

While Wheeler takes care to paint Dick as an "honorable" bandit,
other dime novelists were even more careful to frame their stories of

youthful adventuring with bold disclaimers. *Roving Joe: The History of a Young Border Ruffian*, an 1882 title from Beadle's Boy's Library of Sport, Story, and Adventure, is an autobiography of Joseph Badger, confusingly attributed to A. H. Post. The author prefaces the text with a letter, "To my Boy Reader." In the letter, Post offers the following advice:

All that follows I believe strictly true, but however interesting it may *read*, I would not advise you to follow the example set by "Roving Joe." A full score of years have passed since he ran away from home, but even now he has not forgotten the deep grief and anxiety his conduct caused his loving parents. His eyes glisten and his cheeks flush as he recalls the wild, free life he had in those boyish days—the "prairie fever' has never left him nor will it ever—but he often regrets that those youthful years were not more wisely spent. In these days, a school book is far more valuable than the hunter's rifle. Stick to your studies at least until your beard is grown.[77]

This disclaimer demonstrates that authors and editors recognized not only the power and possibility the frontier posed as an adolescent space but also the anxiety and fear that space generated in parents and other adult caretakers. In one way or another, the Beadle authors all demonstrate an awareness of these dynamics at play. Some react cautiously; others, like Wheeler, respond with a wink and a nod, as in a brief scene from *Wild Ivan, the Boy Claude Duval*. After joining forces with Old Avalanche, the aged scout tells Deadwood Dick a story about a bandit named Jack Shepard Jr.: "'Jack Shepard Junior, eh?' Dick jokes. 'I once read in a yellow-covered book of Jack Shepard the highwayman. Is this Junior a chip from the old block?'"[78] Sharing a joke with his readers, Dick demonstrates that he is well read in all the books that matter, acknowledging that his youthful heroics are steeped in the established tradition of blood-and-thunder tales.

In his later Deadwood Dick novels, Wheeler himself takes clearer steps to address the concerns of worried adult readers. This is strikingly evident in Dick's symbolic death and resurrection. In *Deadwood Dick's Dream, or The Rivals of the Road* (1881), Wheeler notes early on that his youthful hero has been transformed. Accused by a US marshal of being "the road agent, Deadwood Dick," Dick responds: "No, not the road-agent, Deadwood Dick, but the detective Deadwood Dick, sir." In his new role as detective, Wheeler assures the reader, "the man who, by hanging, forever paid his debt to justice then rose up to take up a different life-trail and hunt down law-breakers and villains, whether they be professional outlaws or citizens."[79] With this symbolic death and rebirth, Wheeler tries to reassure readers that empowered adolescents like Deadwood Dick are not destined to become dangerous criminals; rather, the frontier will develop them into ideal specimens of American manhood.

With this move, Wheeler follows the example set by William "Buffalo Bill" Cody, both the real-life man and, more directly, the dime novel hero. As seen in chapter 1, Cody was no stranger to the literatures of boyhood, and his 1879 autobiography straddled the line between the more genteel work of boy-book authors like Mark Twain and the bloody theatrics of the dime Westerns. Throughout his career, Buffalo Bill maintained a striking, and strikingly variable, presence in the cultural worlds of American children. In 1879, young fans could potentially encounter their hero in a range of forms and venues. They could read Cody's autobiography, see the man perform as Buffalo Bill on the stage, or read about his youthful adventures in dime novels. Notably, these adventures were published alongside those of Deadwood Dick in the Beadle & Adams Half Dime Library.

As noted earlier, a young Buffalo Bill emerges as the true hero of Prentiss Ingraham's *Gold Plume, the Boy Bandit, or the Kid-Glove Sport* (1881). Ingraham also penned a number of frontier Westerns focusing on the adolescent exploits of Buffalo Bill, all fully fabricated, while also authoring a more extravagant version of Cody's "official" autobiography. Other authors wrote Buffalo Bill stories for the Half Dime Library as well, featuring Cody as an adolescent hero like Deadwood Dick and others, defeating corrupt adult villains in the wild frontier. In Alfred Taylor's *A Strange Story of the Silver Trail* (1881), Cody is described as "a youth of fifteen, tall of his age, wiry and possessing a face that was frank, fearless, and handsome enough for an artist's study."[80] A powerful adolescent hero like Deadwood Dick, Cody is more clearly aligned with the forces of law and order and defeats a thief and murderer of local silver miners. In the course of the novel, he deals out death more judiciously than Deadwood

Dick, killing only the villain, Carl Moran, an unscrupulous murderer and thief himself.

Interestingly, Taylor, like Ingraham and others, willfully mixes fact and fantasy in telling Buffalo Bill's story. For instance, at the end of the novel, Cody learns of "Wild Bill's sad death by the hand of a professed friend, who turned assassin." This true story, Taylor confides, his "reader doubtless knows," and is woven in with fictionalized assertions of how "Buffalo Billy's roving nature quickly drove him to the plains again where he figured in a new character as a Pony Express Rider" (15). By mixing details from Cody's life with the highly fictionalized exploits of "Buffalo Billy," Taylor establishes the flesh-and-blood Buffalo Bill as an authentic frontier hero and an exemplar of empowered adolescence. While Deadwood Dick needs to die as unrepentant teen bandit to be reborn as a detective, Buffalo Bill can harmonize the wild and the civilized, presenting as both a developing adolescent and a fully realized man. In fact, as the next chapter demonstrates, Cody's ability to achieve this balance marks him as the ideal of western masculinity, a figure who fully taps the potential of the frontier as a vehicle for adolescent development.[81]

The dime Westerns in Beadle & Adams Half Dime Library did not originate the idea of the frontier as an ideal space for open-ended self-fashioning. However, these texts were among the first vehicles to appropriate this ideology to create a space of unfettered adolescence, marketed primarily for the consumption of American boys. In doing so, dime novel Westerns recast the existent frontier myth through a dangerous paradox: On the one hand, they imagined the frontier as a space where boys could flourish as adolescent heroes, offering, in the process, a bright vision of America's future. On the other hand, heroes like Deadwood Dick also suggested a less certain future, where the frontier acted as a breeding ground for dangerous adolescence and future criminals who, like Kansas Charley, threatened social order at the most basic levels.

In the final decades of the nineteenth century, as the frontier closed, these conflicting narratives reflected broader cultural negotiations over ideas of proper and improper boyhoods and the increasing anxiety of adult authority figures regarding how to define adolescence and regulate adolescent behavior. By the turn of the century, dime novels were catering more directly to boy readers and, as Ryan Anderson points out, were more explicitly concerned with "defining manly boyhood."[82]

At least partly then, this later wave of dime novels reads as a direct response to the frontier dime novels of the 1870s and their jarring challenge to conventional age hierarchies, while paragons of virtuous boyhood, such as Frank Merriwell, acted as a corrective to the unruly example set by Deadwood Dick. The youthful adventures of Buffalo Bill suggested another path forward. Teddy Roosevelt demonstrated that the frontier was a useful vehicle for the broader cultural reenvisioning of American masculinity at century's end, as the collision of young and old continued (and continues) to fuel a sense of national identity. The Beadle & Adams Half Dime Library made use of similar themes, showcasing the power of the frontier as a transformational youth space. Ultimately, if Deadwood Dick failed to demonstrate how that space could develop wild boys into ideal American men, Buffalo Bill emerged in the 1880s and 1890s as an increasingly viable alternative.

FIGURE 1. **GAAR WILLIAMS**, "The Last Exit," 1917.
Buffalo Bill Center of the West, Cody, Wyoming.

FIGURE 2.   **TRUE WILLIAMS**, "Buffalo Bill's Duel with Yellow Hand."
Buffalo Bill Center of the West, Cody, Wyoming.

On the 17th of July, 1876.

FIGURE 3. **THE SCALPING OF YELLOW HAND**, from Buffalo Bill's
Wild West 1891 program. Buffalo Bill Center of the West, Cody, Wyoming.

FIGURE 4.   **CODY AND CARVER'S** Wild West, 1883 program cover.
Buffalo Bill Center of the West, Cody, Wyoming.

FIGURE 5. **BUFFALO BILL'S** Wild West 1885 program cover. Buffalo Bill Center of the West, Cody, Wyoming.

FIGURE 6. "ATTACK ON THE BURNING CABIN," from Buffalo Bill's Wild West 1885 program. Buffalo Bill Museum and Grave, Golden, Colorado.

FIGURE 7. **JOHNNY BAKER**, Buffalo Bill's Wild West publicity photo.
Buffalo Bill Museum and Grave, Golden, Colorado.

FIGURE 8. **LILLIAN SMITH**, Buffalo Bill's Wild West publicity photo.
Buffalo Bill Museum and Grave, Golden, Colorado.

FIGURE 9. **JOHNNY BURKE NO NECK**, newspaper clipping.
Buffalo Bill Center of the West, Cody, Wyoming.

WA-KA-CHA-SHA (RED ROSE,) THE PET OF THE SIOUX.
Buffalo Bill's Wild West.
ELLIOTT & FRY   Copyright   55, BAKER S^{TR}, LONDON.W.

FIGURE 10.   **ROSE NELSON**, cabinet card.
Buffalo Bill Center of the West, Cody, Wyoming.

FIGURE 11. **CHILDREN BACKSTAGE** at Buffalo Bill's Wild West. Buffalo Bill Center of the West, Cody, Wyoming.

FIGURE 12.   **BENNIE IRVING**, "The World's Smallest Cowboy."
Buffalo Bill Center of the West, Cody, Wyoming.

FIGURE 13. **FUND-RAISING CERTIFICATE** for the Buffalo Bill
Memorial. Buffalo Bill Museum and Grave, Golden, Colorado.

FIGURE 14.   **BOY SCOUTS** with Buffalo Bill's casket. Buffalo Bill Museum and Grave, Golden, Colorado.

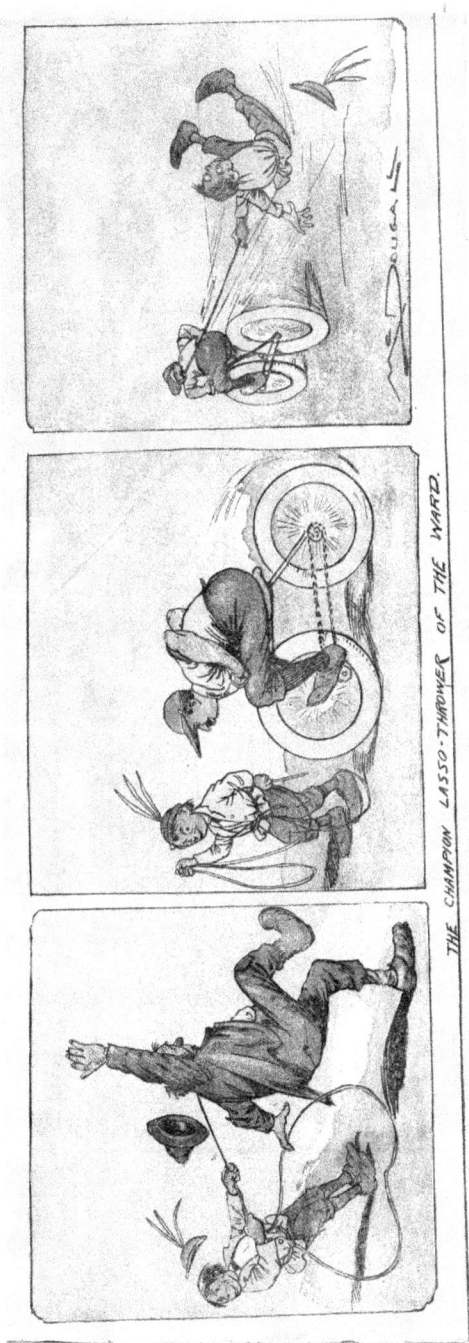

FIGURE 15.   "**THE CHAMPION LASSO THROWER OF THE WARD.**" Buffalo Bill Center of the West, Cody, Wyoming.

FIGURE 16. **SMITH & WESSON AD**, *Youth's Companion*, July 1, 1901. Author's collection.

WINCHESTER

Model 1900 Rifle.

HAMMERLESS, TAKE-DOWN.

THIS rifle is just the thing to take on your summer vacation for fun and diversion. It can be taken apart in an instant and packed in a trunk or suit-case. It is handy and reliable and an accurate shooter. It shoots .22 Short and .22 Long rimfire cartridges, and Bullet Breech caps. These cartridges cost so little that one can afford to shoot as many times as he likes and as often as he likes. The barrel of this rifle is round, 18 inches long, bored and rifled with the same care and exactness that have made Winchester rifles famous for their accurate shooting. It is fitted with open front and rear sights, the sights of every gun being adjusted by shooting. For boys it is safer than most guns, as it has no hammer to catch in the clothing or brush and cause a premature discharge. This rifle *lists* at $5.00, but dealers sell it for quite a little less. It costs only a few cents more than the cheapest small caliber rifles, but it's dollars better. Any dealer can furnish you with our guns and ammunition.

Winchester Repeating Arms Co.,
New Haven, Conn.

FIGURE 17. **WINCHESTER AD**, *Youth's Companion,* July 1, 1901. Author's collection.

3

THE WILD WEST
Making History and American Boyhood

On September 14, 1883, the *Philadelphia Inquirer* ran the following item under the headline "Missing Boys: Two Youngsters of Reading Infatuated with Buffalo Bill":

> William Dickinson, aged fourteen years, and William Stevenson, aged eleven, are missing since Monday, since which time nothing has been seen or heard of them. They both left home dressed with the intention of seeing Buffalo Bill. They had been in the habit of reading exciting stories such as Indian tales, etc., and it is supposed that they must have left with Buffalo Bill during Monday night. The mothers of the young lads are greatly worried, and if the boys do not return soon their minds might become deranged. Detectives have been notified and telegrams were sent to Harrisburg to Buffalo Bill, who is showing there today. No reply has yet been received.

In the 1880s, this type of story was not unusual. The disappearance of the two boys, their apparent decision to "go west," and the subsequent fear of inevitable derangement echoes panicked media responses to dime novels, as discussed in chapter 2. Major newspapers ran stories like these regularly, describing how blood-and-thunder fiction seduced children to leave good homes and go west, to play dangerous games—occasionally maiming or even killing a playmate unintentionally—and to form gangs that wreaked havoc on orderly neighborhoods and even venture into criminal behavior. Cody, as we have seen, was no stranger to the dime novel. In fact, Buffalo Bill was featured in more blood-and-thunder titles than any single figure outside of Jesse James, and he even penned a few of the novels himself.

These newspaper cautionary tales became ubiquitous companions to Buffalo Bill's Wild West, a prolific traveling spectacle logging, at one point, nine thousand miles to perform 131 shows in 190 days.[1] The show extended its reach to Canada and, by 1887, across the Atlantic, where its allure to rambunctious youth proved so powerful that British authorities established a "special staff of detectives" to stand guard at the Liverpool docks to "look out for runaway youth and restore them to their parents."[2] At the same time, Buffalo Bill's Wild West generated a disparate range of responses from adult audience members, as evidenced by the provocatively titled 1893 news item, "Cured of Indian Fever: A Father Presents his Son's Outfit to Buffalo Bill":

> Col. Wm. F. Cody (Buffalo Bill) had a strange visitor in his camp the other night. It was a middle-aged man with a fatherly look, who carried with him a strange assortment of rude wooden daggers, long pieces of rope and rusty pistols. He also had a valise full of old cartridges, one or two red feathers, and a leather belt.
>
> "You may have these," he said as he pushed them over to the Colonel. "My son has no further use for them. The Wild West has killed all his desire to eat the flesh of the red man and become another terror of the plains."[3]

The article goes on to explain how the boy had suffered for years from "cowboy fever," before finally being cured by attending repeated performances of the show, which demonstrated "the actual life of the far West," so that "the glamor has been rubbed off for him."

These two articles hint at the complex relationship between Buffalo Bill's Wild West and late-nineteenth-century notions of boyhood. In the *Philadelphia Inquirer* article, the show plays the part of the seducer, enticing good boys to leave comfortable homes and risk their lives in the unsettled West. In the second article, it alleviates a young boy of his romantic notions of the West and demonstrates the "actual life" of the place. These seeming contradictions are not coincidental. In the ten years between the two news stories, Buffalo Bill's Wild West underwent significant changes as Cody and his partners struggled to manage the conflicting impulses at the heart of the show.

American ideas of childhood remained fluid during these final decades of the nineteenth century. While middle-class ideals and notions
of Romantic Childhood were becoming more pervasive, the experiences
of children themselves continued to vary significantly, influenced by
myriad factors such as race, gender, and social class. A nine-year-old boy
homesteading in North Dakota and a nine-year-old boy working in a
factory in North Carolina lived vastly different lives. So, for that matter,
did a middle-class nine-year-old girl living with her family in New York
City and the orphan girl of the same age living on the streets of the same
city. Buffalo Bill's Wild West sought to appeal to as wide an audience as
possible and, thus, to appeal to as many children as possible. From his
inaugural season in 1883, Cody tinkered with his show's content considerably, and this tinkering gestures to the fluid relationship between
different constructions of the frontier and boyhood. Cody's show tapped
into this relationship's broader negotiations of race, gender, and power
in late-nineteenth-century America. In the end, Buffalo Bill's Wild West
pulled these disparate strands together to offer a cohesive narrative of
developing boyhood and national identity.[4]

As Louis Warren describes it, Buffalo Bill's Wild West was a "mass
entertainment" that catered to no overt political agenda. Cody and his
partners managed to draw "millions of Americans to its bleachers over so
long a career, and to achieve consistently glowing reviews from critics and
newspapers on different sides of so many political questions."[5] Assessing
the show's success more bluntly, Paul Reddin notes that "the desiderata
of the entertainment and the nation merged: both needed bloodshed,
galloping horsemen, and conflict."[6] Buffalo Bill's Wild West certainly
offered those things. Still, Warren suggests, the show's main appeal was
broad, drawing on a collective fervor for the imagined past, a shared
dream of American conquest and prosperity. Much as Frederick Jackson
Turner channeled in his 1893 essay "The Significance of the Frontier in
American History," Buffalo Bill's Wild West framed the settling of the
West as a powerful celebration of white masculine vitality.

In addition, Cody used the frontier narrative to imagine the West as a
space of and for boyhood. In Warren's estimation, Cody and his partners
succeeded by recognizing early on the need to temper the violent masculinity permeating his show. Ultimately, Warren claims, Buffalo Bill's

Wild West owed its success less to Cody's representation of bloodshed and conflict and more to "the way he framed his spectacle's violence to make it a show that middle-class women could attend."[7] Indeed, Cody and his partners domesticated Buffalo Bill's Wild West throughout the 1880s and 1890s—even if the show retained plenty of racial hostility and bloodlust. These efforts were not just about drawing women to the arena, though. In domesticating the show, Cody marked it as a safe space for children, and especially boys. Right up through his show's final run in 1916, Buffalo Bill's Wild West spoke directly to American boys, developing and disseminating an influential brand of frontier mythology deeply connected to varied and competing notions of American boyhood.

During this long and successful tenure, Buffalo Bill's Wild West fed off paradoxical impulses about both the imagined frontier and the American boy, promising the child spectator both entertainment and education. On the one hand, the show promised fantasy and escape, as staged reenactments of frontier life and history interacted neatly with children's play. After all, what else was Cody doing as Buffalo Bill but playing "cowboys and Indians," a script he did much to inform, if not create outright? On the other hand, the show marketed itself as much more than performance. Cody billed Buffalo Bill's Wild West as living history, an opportunity to see the frontier "as it was," precisely at the moment when, as Turner's essay suggests, western migration had reached its terminus and there was no frontier left to see. The authentic frontier life was unattainable, the show argued, so the best—and most exciting—way to experience the frontier was through reenacting it.[8]

In performing the frontier, Buffalo Bill's Wild West, like the larger-than-life figure of Buffalo Bill himself, traded on the idea that the space of the West developed American boys into the right kind of American men. In this way, Buffalo Bill's Wild West conflated human development and theatrical performance, imagining the frontier as a space of perpetual boyhood. Annette Kolodny argues that Turner's frontier thesis reveals "the experiential truth of the American continent: the West was a woman, and to it belonged the hope of rebirth and regeneration."[9] In Cody's West, the male pioneer settled the fertile West, producing a hearty new race of superior white American men. In the Wild West arena, this theme of rebirth is persistently vivid, preserved and continually inscribed through the performance of history. This history casts the West as a mythic space forever young, forever growing, a space where the virgin land births and nurtures robust specimens of American boyhood, a space that forms these specimens into robust visions of American masculinity, much like Cody himself.

With growing cultural awareness that the frontier was "closed," this kind of performance took on increasing importance. For the generations of boys who could not experience the frontier as Cody had, Buffalo Bill's Wild West served as a vital conduit. Reinforcing the bond between boyhood and the frontier, it played a crucial role in defining American identity in the late nineteenth and early twentieth centuries. Cody and his partners do not appear to have formulated any single strategy in cultivating child spectators or in establishing connections between the show and the development of American boyhood. Still, cultural notions and expectations of boyhood, along with a flesh-and-blood audience of boys, were critical to the creation and refinement of the show and, in fact, Cody's entire life and legacy as an entertainer. While appealing to a broad and diverse child audience, the show created an influential form of mass spectacle, presenting the mythic West as a vital space for imagining the development of Anglo-Saxon boyhood into triumphant American manhood.

MASS CULTURE'S NEW FRONTIER

Cody did not invent this brand of frontier; in fact, many aspects of his show seized on emergent trends in nineteenth-century popular culture. The size and scope of the traveling show shared much with the circuses popularized by P. T. Barnum, James Bailey, and others, while, as LeRoy Ashby points out, exhibitions of "roping, steer-riding, and bronco-busting" had been organized as early as the 1860s.[10] Barnum himself had taken a couple of stabs at frontier spectacle—most notably his failed 1843 buffalo hunt in Hoboken, New Jersey. Fascination with American Indians was also a long-standing American preoccupation. George Catlin toured the eastern seaboard and Europe in the 1840s, featuring Ojibwa performers, his own paintings, and reenactments of American Indian life. Cody partnered with sharpshooter (and former dentist) Doc Carver to launch his first Wild West show in 1883. The show struggled. It was expensive to mount and keep on the road, and a run of poor attendance could be devastating. Even Cody's successes came back to haunt him, as he soon faced competition from a legion of imitators. After splitting with Cody, Carver started his own traveling show, and circus owners like Bailey and Adam Forepaugh soon got in the game. In the final decades of the nineteenth century, Wild West shows proliferated so quickly that Thomas Altherr claims there "may have been as many as eighty companies touring in the decades at the turn of the century."[11]

Despite a crowded field and constant competition, Cody ultimately succeeded where others failed. In large part, his success stemmed from the strong impression Buffalo Bill made on his legions of young fans. In appealing to these fans, the show successfully balanced the lure of the sensational and the promise of the respectable to powerful effect, domesticating the West, as Warren puts it, while preserving a sense of freedom and adventure. As noted in chapter 1, Cody could strike this balance so successfully because his own life story represented a compelling model of the interaction between the dangerous and the domesticated. After all, in the wilds of the American West, Cody had grown from savage boyhood to gallant manhood.

This idea of Buffalo Bill was undeniably appealing, and Cody played the idea to perfection. He boasted a natural magnetism and striking appearance that, as numerous reviewers attested, left audience members of all types enthralled. Amy Leslie, writing about Buffalo Bill's Wild West at the 1893 Columbian Exposition in Chicago, describes how this appearance changed over the years. She notes that in "his earlier days a hint of the border desperado lurked in his blazing eyes and the poetic fierceness of his mien and coloring." By 1893, fierceness had been "subdued into pleasantness, and he is the kindliest, most benign man, as simple as a village priest and learned as a savant of Chartreuse."[12]

As Leslie discerns, Cody's appeal went beyond good looks; as Buffalo Bill, he could channel both the "desperado" and the "village priest," delivering the titillating thrills of blood-and-thunder Westerns with a safe veneer of gentility. Sandra Sagala points out that even in dime novels, Buffalo Bill was "often regarded as 'a knight of chivalry' or the 'prince of reins.'"[13] Above all, Cody presented a powerful image of distinct American masculinity. Edward Aveling marveled that Cody "is so manly a man," a representative of a "fine race," and most importantly "a type of a race vanishing as the Red Indian, its foe, vanishes."[14] Much like Cooper's Natty Bumppo, Cody is a symbol of ideal American masculinity and a member of a dying race. Unlike the fictional Bumppo, Cody could preserve this tension indefinitely, a charismatic showman summoning the vanished past through live performances on a nightly basis.

Of course, Cody did not fail to age. Performing from his late twenties into his seventies, he transformed from young scout to elder statesmen in the public view. His public aged as well, with the boys who saw Buffalo Bill on stage in the 1870s growing into men and perhaps taking their own sons to see Buffalo Bill in action. In this way, the character of Buffalo Bill and the space of Buffalo Bill's Wild West worked to subordinate age categories to the nostalgic gaze. In her analysis of age-bound identities and summer camps, Leslie Paris describes the American summer camp as a physical space and an imagined one, a site that was both fixed and fleeting. Every few years, Paris argues, "a completely new cohort of girls cycled through the camp," while "older adolescents aged out of the group and into young adulthood."[15] As a day-to-day space then, the camp was a place where age-bound identities were constantly in flux. As a cultural construct, the camp existed as a timeless space where campers of all ages viewed camping and childhood through the gauzy light of nostalgia. In the case of Buffalo Bill's Wild West, this nostalgia did important cultural work, fueling a master narrative that cemented the frontier as the foundation of American identity.

Successive generations of American boys filtered through the audience of Buffalo Bill's Wild West, but through the figure of Buffalo Bill the show became a place where generational differences were deemphasized, where boyhood and the West were always in the past, always there, and always directing aspirations for the future. Previewing Buffalo Bill's Wild West in 1897, one newspaper reporter muses that it "does not seem very long to middle-aged men when they were boys and reading Ned Buntline's thrilling romances about Buffalo Bill." Getting to see Cody in person, those men both learned "Buffalo Bill was a real identity" and a vital link to those boyhood romances. As the reporter explains, while the pioneers who advanced American civilization "over the boundless reaches of far Western plains have nearly all passed the boundary of existence," Buffalo Bill remains. Regardless of age, he connects boys (and men) of all ages to the "boundless" frontier. That connection will be severed, and the article suggests that "when he is gone the life he portrays so realistically will become only traditionary."[16]

Gaar Williams's cartoon "The Last Exit," commemorating Cody's death in 1917, crystalizes this dynamic perfectly. Buffalo Bill appears from behind a slightly parted translucent curtain. Behind the curtain, the viewer sees the sun setting over an unspoiled natural setting. Passing through the curtain, Buffalo Bill pulls the reins back on his horse, gesturing to an audience of four boys. The boys, also on the stage, ride toy horses made, with varying degrees of sophistication, from broomsticks. They stare up at Buffalo Bill as one salutes, one raises a wooden sword, and one raises a pennant that reads, "About four generations of us." All white, with minor variations in dress, the boys draw attention to Cody's long tenure as performer, while also suggesting that generational differences are immaterial; on this stage, age and time are subsumed by the powerful frontier narrative of Buffalo Bill's Wild West (fig. 1).

Buffalo Bill's popularity with audiences young and old also reflects broader changes in American entertainment during the second half of the nineteenth century. Lawrence Levine uses Shakespeare to demonstrate the growing division between "high" and "low" culture during these years. Levine asserts that Shakespeare was "presented and recognized almost everywhere in the country" in the first half of the century, just as likely to be performed in a barroom as in a theater.[17] Levine describes the gradual "sacralization of culture" after the Civil War, in which Shakespearean performance became privatized as elite, highbrow culture. While theater audiences in the first half of the century included people from all classes mingling together, the second half of the century was marked by "an increasing segregation" along class lines (57). As Cody transitioned his frontier spectacle from the stage to the outdoor arena, he and his partners were powerfully aware of that segregation. In fact, one of the triumphs of Buffalo Bill's Wild West was its ability to transcend the division Levine describes.

The typical history of Buffalo Bill's Wild West traces the show's genesis to July 4, 1882. Arriving home in North Platte, Nebraska, for the Fourth of July festivities, the story goes, Cody was dismayed to learn how little had been planned to commemorate the holiday, so he put together the "Old Glory Blowout," an outdoor celebration featuring a full parade, roping and racing contests, and other competitions and exhibitions that would later become staples of his Wild West. This concept grew naturally out of Cody's stage productions, which by this time, contained many of these elements, including sharpshooters, Indian performers, and live animals on the stage. In fact, by all indications, Cody had been imagining a large outdoor spectacle for some time, and as Sagala concludes, the "transitions from combination to Wild West show was inevitable."[18]

That transition was easier to imagine than effect, however. As noted, Cody struggled in his initial run at staging a Wild West show, and from 1883 to 1886 he kept his combination on the road, partly to generate needed revenue (180). In 1884, Cody teamed up with show business veteran Nate Salsbury, and they rechristened the show Buffalo Bill's Wild West. The naming is significant. Cody always emphasized that he wasn't presenting a show but rather the Wild West itself, while Salsbury also perceived the venture as more than "merely a Wild West show."[19] Both men sought to differentiate their product not only from their direct competitors but also from "lower" forms of entertainment like the circus; for instance, Cody and Salsbury staunchly refused to include a sideshow for many years. Though the two men had a tumultuous relationship and in later years quarreled about who was responsible for their success, Buffalo Bill's Wild West enjoyed its greatest success under the stewardship of Cody and Salsbury, and they continued working together up until Salsbury's death in 1902.[20]

CULTIVATING BUFFALO BILL AS A BOYHOOD HERO

From the start, Buffalo Bill's Wild West profited from its ability to draw a significant child audience. Explaining his early conception of the show, Salsbury makes it clear Cody's status as a dime novel hero would be the Wild West's best form of promotion: "Wherever the Dime Novel had gone Cody had gone along for Ned Buntline had so firmly written Cody into the contemporary history of the Great Plains."[21] Recognizing that Buffalo Bill was a fixture in the culture of childhood, Cody and company crafted a show that appealed to an imagined child audience, one that was built around the persona of Buffalo Bill and the perceived dime novel appeal of that persona to American boys.

As Salsbury implies, Buffalo Bill first found fame in the pages of sensational literature, specifically Ned Buntline's 1869 serial novel, *Buffalo Bill, the King of the Border Men*. Three years later, Buntline convinced Cody to play himself in frontier melodramas styled after his dime novel adventures. After some initial reluctance, Cody took the stage and never left it. In an 1878 review of Cody's *The Knights of the Plains*, one critic professed that Cody is "really the only man on the stage who gives representations of himself," marveling that this unusual actor "is the only true type of the frontiersman, as we have been taught to regard him by writers of travel and adventure."[22] Recognizing the authenticity of the frontiersman as simultaneously a work of fiction and a truth to be "taught," this critic offers insight into the distinctive mix that would later make Buffalo Bill's Wild West so successful.

Much like Buffalo Bill dime novels, Cody's stage shows catered to a largely male audience. Another review of *Knights of the Plains* notes that, regardless of the play's quality, it is "highly relished by the self-reliant membership of the masculine sex." Furthermore, this type of theater "does much towards inculcating freedom and independence in boys who seem to have a natural 'hankering' after this style of thing."[23] Before Cody's later attempts to domesticate his Wild West show, boys attended Cody's stage shows in great numbers. Thronging in the gallery, they were christened the "gallery gods" by reporters. One 1878 review of the play *May Cody* notes that "there was a great rush of boys on opening night" in Baltimore, "fond of reading dime novels and Indian stories in boys' periodicals, and worshipped Buffalo Bill as a great hero."[24]

As he became more comfortable as a performer, Cody carefully cultivated his image as a boyhood hero both on the stage and off. While Buffalo Bill dime novels indulged in fantastic adventures, Cody's 1879 autobiography, as discussed in chapter 1, managed a skillful balance of dime novel adventuring and authorial restraint, presenting his life story, as Don Russell describes, in "a straightforward, unpretentious recital."[25] Of course, that recital still boasted many improbable exploits, such as Cody's heroic, and most likely fictionalized, service as a Pony Express rider and no shortage of Indian-killing, including the controversial scalping of Yellow Hand, immortalized by Cody as the "first scalp for Custer." Rife with controversy and developed to its full potential as pure spectacle, no single incident highlights Cody's careful performance of himself as Buffalo Bill better than his run-in with Yellow Hand.[26]

By 1876, Cody had made a habit of dividing his time between scouting and the stage, a combination with more than financial advantages. By spending his summers out on the plains, Cody bolstered his authenticity as a genuine Indian scout. In fact, on more than one occasion, Indian "hostilities" prompted rumors that Cody was planning to head out to the front immediately, rumors quickly followed up on by reporters who worked them into news items that served as publicity for Cody's stage show. Of course, the Indian Wars were quite real, and Cody did scout for the army, which made his enthusiastic blending of fact and fiction even more potent. Well aware of this formula, Cody sought to exploit it at every turn, as he did in his confrontation with Yellow Hand.

The 1874 discovery of gold in the Black Hills and the subsequent violation of the treaty ceding that land to the Sioux provoked an escalation in armed hostilities in the summer of 1876, leading to the shocking defeat of General Custer and his men at Little Bighorn. Cody happened to be on the plains at the time. Having been sought out by General Carr and appointed as an army scout, he rode with the Fifth Cavalry when word reached them of Custer's defeat. Some 150 miles to the south of Little Bighorn, the Fifth Cavalry encountered a small group of Cheyenne at Warbonnet Creek. As a military exercise, the encounter between Carr's regiment and the Cheyenne was largely insignificant. It did, however, result in at least one Cheyenne casualty, a warrior killed by Cody. In the showman's account, the death of that warrior became an iconic symbol for America's "winning of the West" and a prime example of how Buffalo Bill "made" history.

The details of what actually happened at Warbonnet Creek remain murky, and the truth of the encounter has long since yielded to fiction. Cody was prepared that day not just to fight but to perform, decked out, as Warren describes it, "in a stage costume of black velvet slashed with scarlet and trimmed with silver buttons."[27] In a brief skirmish, Cody allegedly shot and scalped a Cheyenne warrior. The remaining Cheyenne soon fled, and the Fifth Cavalry went on to Fort Laramie, where Cody promptly set about publicizing the encounter. Enlisting the services of the future frontier novelist Lieutenant Charles King and a correspondent from the *New York Herald*, Cody shaped the killing of Yellow Hand into a powerful narrative of American frontier heroism: Buffalo Bill had taken the "first scalp for Custer." Even the name of the slain warrior was a distortion, mistranslated as Yellow *Hand* instead of Yellow *Hair*, suggesting the dead warrior to be in possession of a "cowardly hand." Cody discerned that accuracy was beside the point. As Joy Kasson argues, "the significance of the killing of Yellow Hair lies not in what 'actually' happened but in the uses that Cody made of it."[28]

Those uses were extensive. By the fall of that year, Cody's combination was performing the *Red Right Hand, or First Scalp for Custer* on stage. Night after night, Cody reenacted the killing of Yellow Hand, lifting the scalp above his head and shouting, "The first scalp for Custer!" The scalp itself traveled with Cody, often displayed in the lobby. Drawn by True Williams, the image of Cody raising the scalp and ornamented headdress soon became iconic. It appeared in Cody's 1879 autobiography, where Cody is shown dressed in the same buckskin he wore for publicity photos, with a knife in one hand and Yellow Hand's scalp raised high in the other, as the Cheyenne appear, a distant blur, riding across the prairie toward the scene of their fallen warrior (fig. 2). Years later, a similar image would appear in Wild West programs, with Cody wearing not fringed buckskin but a dark shirt, much like the black velvet costume Warren describes, standing on a high ridge overlooking the scene, further isolating him and Yellow Hand in the center of the frame. The composition emphasizes Cody and his vanquished foe, while the soldiers look up, awestruck, from below. If the context of the image changed, the message remained the same: Cody had claimed the first scalp for Custer, solidifying his reputation as Indian killer and national hero (fig. 3).

In targeting young fans, Cody presented such exploits carefully. By mimicking dime novel theatrics too closely, he left himself open to attacks that he was corrupting the minds of impressionable young boys. Indeed, reviewers of the Buffalo Bill Combination occasionally found Cody's show stage show too grisly, likely to attract the "wrong" crowd and drive away the right one. An 1882 review in the *Springfield Republican* argued that Cody is "more attractive off from the stage than on it." While allowing that Buffalo Bill is a "genuine scout, whose achievements are well spoken of in Nebraska," and noting that the performers "present a good enough play of its kind," the reviewer worries about the impact of the show on its young audience: "It is to be feared that an increased demand for dime novels follows the annual appearance of Buffalo Bill," the critic bemoans, "and that's the pity of it."[29] Cody actively sought—and planted—publicity that countered such perceptions. For instance, a critic previewing the 1875 show put on by the Buffalo Bill Combination stresses that it "is said to be free from blood and thunder dime novel scenes," and instead "is of the romantic and emotional order, and is said to possess considerable merit."[30]

These concerns about the "wrong crowd" of boys took on a heightened importance beginning in the 1870s. As noted in chapter 2, the second half of the nineteenth century saw increased anxiety about the threat of juvenile delinquency. Not reflected in any reliable data, these fears were likely linked to new waves of immigrants coming to America in the 1870s, notably an influx from Eastern Europe and Asia. Just as these foreigners became viewed as a threat to Anglo-Saxon visions of manhood, their children were viewed as a potential generation of degenerates and criminals. It became all the more important, then, for Buffalo Bill's Wild West to offer a vision of young masculinity that propped up Anglo-Saxon ideals, while failing to incite the baser instincts of the show's rowdier young fans.

Building on Cody's reputation as both deadly Indian killer and chivalrous "knight of the plains," Buffalo Bill's Wild West thus emphasized American progress and white supremacy while trying to distinguish this narrative from the rehearsal of similar themes in sensational literature. Achieving this balance was particularly important when it came to the show's young fans, and early reactions to the show demonstrated a familiar mixture of wariness and awe in this regard. On the show's 1883 debut in Chicago, a reviewer notes that Buffalo Bill's Wild West, depicting "realistic events of the plains, with the aid of buffalo, elk, cowboys, and redskins was seen for the first time in this city." Despite poor weather, the reviewer concludes that "at least 5,000 people assembled to witness the exhibition, which is really worth going a good ways to see." The gallery gods from Cody's stage shows were reportedly on hand, and "the newsboys and bootblacks formed a large and important element of it." Much like critics of Cody's stage show, the reviewer attributed Buffalo Bill's appeal to these boys to "the yellow-covered novels and five-cent libraries through which they had waged in company with daring scouts," joking that the boys' "energy in selling papers and giving shines was redoubled."[31]

Though the enthusiasm of newsboys and bootblacks for Buffalo Bill performances was nothing new, the format of Buffalo Bill's Wild West provided these boys with new ways to experience the show. No longer isolated in the gallery, boys were free to wander the grounds, and, according to the reviewer of the 1883 Chicago debut, a few "of them scraped an acquaintance with the Indian kidlets by carrying water for them," facilitating admission to the "sacred circle of the Indian village." Cowboys and Indians alike camped out on the grounds while Buffalo Bill's Wild West was in town, offering unprecedented access to the performers in the show. In this way, and through the parade preceding the show, Buffalo Bill's Wild West offered myriad opportunities for working-class audience members to get close to Cody and his performers. Priced at fifty cents for adults and twenty-five cents for children, tickets were not cheap, and these opportunities to experience Buffalo Bill's world up close must have been invaluable to the newsboys and bootblacks the *Chicago Tribune* reviewer was so struck by.

Of course, this increased access only heightened the show's potential danger to attract the wrong crowd. An 1885 *Chicago Tribune* review describes how Buffalo Bill's Wild West seemed to take over the entire city for an afternoon: "From noon till nearly 4 o'clock," the reviewer notes, "there was matter for moralizing at every corner of the West Side. The ungodly were out in masse." Swarming to the show, this "ungodly" mass "resolutely turned their backs on churches and every other mark of civilization to take up, and echo along the line the cry of westward ho!"[32]

Even the show's defenders acknowledged this perceived threat to social order: "One thing the management ought to make more prominent in their advertising," an *Illinois State Journal* writer suggests in 1883, is that the Wild West "is in all respects a moral show. There is nothing that ladies and children may not see; indeed, it is an exhibition particularly interesting to them." Admitting Buffalo Bill's Wild West was once perceived as "a rough show," it "is as decorous as a Sunday School, and far more interesting" (13). Cody and his partners were not remiss in addressing such criticism. Their 1884 program emphasizes the question of safety with the following guarantee: "I desire to remind the Heads of Families that ladies and children can attend my exhibition with Perfect Safety and Comfort, as arrangements will be made with that object in view."[33]

While Cody and his company presented their show as safe and wholesome, they struggled to shake the sense of danger associated with Buffalo Bill himself. In July 1887, a boy was shot and "probably fatally injured" while at play. The brief story reports that the boys "were playing Buffalo Bill and discharging what they believed to be blank cartridges from a parlor rifle."[34] Similar incidents reported boys injured or killed, while other stories struck a more lighthearted note. Regardless of tone, the message was consistent: Buffalo Bill's powerful magnetism had a profound effect on boys, impacting the games they played alongside their perceptions of the imagined West and the world they lived in.[35]

NEGOTIATING PROMISE AND PERIL IN THE WILD WEST

Buffalo Bill's potential to seduce wayward boys to leave home and go west constituted a grave threat to guardians of American domesticity. This fear touched on a key tension underlying the appeal of Cody and other scouts-turned-showmen. Rough-and-tumble frontier childhoods were key components of their creation myths; at the same time, to appease adult caretakers, these showmen needed to dissuade young fans from following in their footsteps. Through most of the show's life, cautionary articles like the one introducing this chapter proliferated in newspapers, and in some cases boys did run away from home to seek out Buffalo Bill and the romantic life of the West. Take Gordon Lillie. Born in Indiana in 1860, Lillie read frontier dime novel stories voraciously as a youth. As a boy, he saw the Buffalo Bill Combination and, in Michael Wallis's words, "knew he would never be happy until he moved west."[36] Shortly after his family moved to Kansas, the fifteen-year-old Lillie went to work for a trapper and later left town to live among the Pawnee. Adopting the name Pawnee Bill, he worked for Cody as an interpreter in 1883 and then launched his own successful career as a Wild West showman. In 1908, he partnered with Cody for Buffalo Bill's Wild West and Pawnee Bill's Great Far East Combined.

Cody's appeal to boys drew on his status as a "child of the plains," a heroic figure shaped by his frontier upbringing. In Beadle & Adams's 1881 *Adventures of Buffalo Bill from Boyhood to Manhood*, Prentiss Ingraham describes how when a young William was "but nine years of age his first thrilling adventure occurred, and it gave the boy a name for pluck and nerve that went with him to Kansas." Ingraham stresses that the West was, in fact, a dangerous place, so much so that Cody's father "allowed his son to go armed," and in fact, Billy always hung up his pistol with his hat, a pistol he "prized . . . above his books and pony and [he] always kept it in perfect order." In fact, Billy's gun proves far more useful than his schoolbooks in Ingraham's telling. When outlaws attempt to steal his father's horses, Cody shoots one dead, holding the three others at bay until help arrives. Afterwards, he was "voted the lion of the log cabin school, for had he not," Ingraham asks, "killed his man?"[37]

Much of Ingraham's book mimics Cody's own autobiography, which emphasizes similar themes—if in a more restrained tone. As Cody notes, the dangers of the frontier shaped him into a man, and he attests that his "love of hunting and scouting, and life on the plains, generally, was the result of my early surroundings."[38] In fact, Cody recounts running away from home himself. He is offered a job herding cattle at the age of ten, but his mother withholds her consent. Cody reasons his "ideas and knowledge of the world" to be "in advance of my age," and decides to take the job anyway, claiming the offer of "twenty-five dollars a month was a temptation which I could not resist" (55–56).

Cody was not the only frontier showman negotiating this thorny paradox. Cody's former partners Doc Carver and Jack Crawford later teamed up to stage Life on the Plains and Wild West Combination. Their 1883 program introduces Carver as having been shaped into a manly frontier hero after running away from home. At the age of seven, "Dr. Carver bade good-bye to his log cabin home, and, without saying farewell, he stole quietly away into the wilderness of Wisconsin, bent on living entirely by hunting and trapping." The program boasts that Carver spent his youth "on the wild frontier, and this great outdoor freedom did very much towards developing his wonderful constitution and gigantic figure."[39]

Carver's partner Captain Jack Crawford later performed as "the cowboy poet," and he persistently warned his audience that blood-and-thunder novels could lead boys to run away from home and into a life of ruin and debauchery. Crawford, who had the rare distinction among the showman-scout community of abstaining from drink, often conflated dime novels and alcohol as a powerful formula for eroding the virtues of youth. In one colorful lecture, "How I Met Billy the Kid," Crawford describes an improbable run-in with the famed boy-outlaw. Billy confesses, "I'm awful, awful bad, but if I'd a know'd you five years ago I'd never been an outlaw . . . I want you to do me a favor. When I'm gone tell the boys . . . cigarettes was my starter, then hard cider, then a little wine given to me by a girl and then bad books [dime novels] and then whiskey. Tell the boys and tell 'em I asked you to afore they killed me."[40]

In this inventory of boyhood temptations, bad books come after wine (and girls) and just before whiskey, suggesting that fears of frontier dime novels conveyed hysteria and not just hyperbole. Crawford also uses his own wayward youth as cautionary tale. While performing one of his plays, *Colonel Bob*, Crawford addressed the boys in the audience: "When I was a little boy like some of you, I read a lot about Deadwood Dick. . . . So one day I ran away from the Newsboy's home and worked my way out to the plains, where I came near goin' to the dogs. I wanted to be a bad man" (102). Of course, this desire to be a bad man was essential to Crawford's appeal, and the cowboy poet surely knew as much; despite his frequent condemnation of dime novels, Crawford starred in a number of them, including *The Adventurous Life of Captain Jack*, published by Beadle & Adams, which also published the Deadwood Dick novels. Like Carver, Crawford, and others, Cody used sensational fiction to provide his credentials as a true Western hero.

After all, Buffalo Bill's boyhood exploits were a central part of his allure to the boys in his audience. For Cody and others, the trick was to extoll his youthful adventures while managing to simultaneously satisfy parents and other adult caretakers. The battle with Yellow Hand may have been gory, but Cody didn't hesitate to pitch this piece of his personalized history directly to younger fans. In doing so, he framed the encounter as both dime-store bloodletting and a crucial step in America's conquest of the West. The "first scalp" was included prominently in Cody's autobiography and in Ingraham's *Adventures of Buffalo Bill from Boyhood to Manhood*. In 1899, Cody wrote up another version, entitled "My Duel with Yellow Hand," for *Harper's Round Table*, targeting young readers, especially boys. Draping this murderous act with patriotic urgency, Cody effectively tempered its sensationalized violence for diverse audiences. In its early years, from 1883 to 1886, Buffalo Bill's Wild West took a similar tack, framing themes of frontier conquest with overt nationalism, evidenced by the show's brightly colored program covers, while trying to balance those themes with Cody's value as an educator.

The 1883 show featured a full-color program, awash in red, white, and blue, with Cody and Carver on the cover, an American flag behind them, and "U.S. Scouts" emblazoned on a star-spangled badge beneath a buffalo head in the center of the frame (fig. 4). The back cover makes the theme of Indian warfare more explicit with a vivid representation of Indians and settlers in combat. An advertisement for the show promises "A True Picture of Life on the Frontier," including "Indian Dances and Races, Fancy Shooting, Indian Sham Battles, The Attack of the Stage Coach, Riding Bucking Horses, Indian Camp Scenes" and other western attractions, including "cowboy fun." The work of civilization is the focus, emphasizing the pioneers who settled the frontier and the Indians who stood in their way. Buffalo Bill is presented as a by-product of this work and the frontier, which "created an atmosphere of adventure well calculated to educate one of his natural temperament to a familiarity with danger and self-reliance." Gleefully promising both "real" western life and "sham" Indian warfare, the advertisement testifies to American progress, promising the show will be "novel, instructing, and entertaining."[41]

The 1884 program presented similar themes with a more effective structure. Salsbury and Cody crafted a sequence beginning with the Grand Parade and ending with the attack on the settler's cabin by Indians and the rescue by Buffalo Bill with his scouts, cowboys, and Mexicans. This basic setup remained intact until 1892; while various acts shuffled in and out of the lineup, emphasis on the progress of white civilization remained. That emphasis is reflected in the visual iconography of the programs and the massive posters Cody and Salsbury's advance team plastered, as Jack Rennert describes it, "within a 200 mile radius of the city to which the Wild West was coming"[42]

These formidable images visualize Buffalo Bill as authentic frontier hero and agent of white conquest—read as civilizing progress. On the 1884 cover, Cody is presented in full buckskin, rifle in hand, as he pulls back on the reins of his horse. Buffalo Bill and his mount dominate the frame on a grassy hill. On the plains beneath him, a long line of covered wagons ride into the distant horizon. Buffalo Bill appears as scout and protector, watching over the settlers as they make their way west. The cover of the 1885 program shows no settlers, presenting Cody as a showman in red and yellow chaps, racing his horse from right to left as he twirls a lasso overhead, revealing an image within an image (fig. 5). The picture of Cody appears to have been set down in the middle of the forest, with grass peeking out beneath and the branches of a tree hanging out in front of the image. Crouched by this tree, a much smaller trio of Indians, one armed with a rifle, peek warily out at the imposing figure of Cody as it threatens to squeeze them out of the frame altogether. The complex visual arrangement brings the two sides of Cody together. A dominant visual icon of frontier performance, he still strikes fear and awe into the war-minded Indian.

These images participate in critical discourses about race and nationality in 1880s America. In the early days of Buffalo Bill's Wild West, the frontier was still being contested, both as physical space and theoretical construct. General Custer's defeat in the Battle of Little Bighorn was only a few years old, and American victory in the Indian Wars seemed inevitable but not yet assured. The 1890 census would declare the western frontier closed, a report Turner used as the foundation for his frontier thesis. In the 1880s, these ideas were present but less certain, and the evolutionary logic undergirding Turner's summary of the essential American character was still being teased out. As Jonathan Martin explains, throughout the 1880s, Buffalo Bill's Wild West "romanticized a frontier past that had pitted civilization and savagery under their respective racial standards of white and red," while presenting "that racialized past as the keys to surviving a tumultuous, though still progressive present."[43]

In the 1885 program cover, all these themes are at work. Equal parts frontier hero and showman, Buffalo Bill dominates the space of the frontier, a space that exists as a projection of idealized America. In that projection, the romantic vision of the white masculine scout literally replaces the primitive Indian other who, relegated to the past, still lurks to threaten the full realization of an idealized white civilization. A comparison of the two programs suggests that Cody and Salsbury highlighted these themes deliberately, updating the show from "prairie exhibition" to Wild West reality. The same themes dominated programs for Buffalo Bill's Wild West throughout the 1880s. Those programs grew fatter over these years as well, with increasingly detailed descriptions and endorsements of the show's narrative of frontier conquest.

BUFFALO BILL AS EDUCATOR

From the very beginning of Buffalo Bill's Wild West, this narrative of conquest was inflected by the rhetoric of education. Starting in 1884, the programs contained a "Salutatory," attributed to John Burke, Cody's close friend and publicist, stressing the educational value of Buffalo Bill's Wild West. Claiming the true story of the West "has never been half told; and romance itself fall short of the reality when it attempts to depict the career of the little vanguard of pioneers, trappers, and scouts, who always in the front have always paved the way." Celebrating the role of these scouts as civilizers, Burke stresses that "east of the Mississippi, the methods of these people are comparatively unknown, and it is for the purpose of educating them that this little pamphlet has been prepared."[44] By 1885, the program extolled Buffalo Bill's Wild West for its educational value more directly. A new description of Cody appeared under the subheading "As an Educator," with journalist Brick Pomeroy writing, "I wish there were more progressive educators like Wm. Cody in this world."[45]

In the next few years, the programs increasingly touted Cody as an educator. By 1887, the "As an Educator" section had grown to a half page in length. Pomeroy describes Cody as "a sturdy, generous, positive character," a "gentleman" who "as a lover of his country, wishes to present as many facts as possible to the public, so that those who will, can see actual pictures of life in the West, brought to the East for the inspection and education of the public." Cody sought not merely to profit from his distinctive brand of entertainment but "to give people in the East a correct representation of life on the plains, and the incidental life of the hardy, brave, intelligent pioneers," men who secured the open West as a space where white American civilization could prosper. Descriptions of "sham battles" are no more, as Pomeroy suggests the show should be called "the Wild West Reality."[46]

This focus on Cody as an educator simultaneously softened and promoted Cody's reputation as an Indian scout. In this way, popular features of the show, such as the typical finale known as the attack on the settlers' cabin, offered multiple messages to its audience. Leading a troop of cowboys, Cody plays the dime novel hero to the hilt in this staged mini-drama, gunning down "marauding Indians" as they attack a helpless family of white settlers. As the stalwart scout paving the way for civilization, Buffalo Bill presents his audience with a glimpse at the "facts" of western expansion—both the fragility of frontier domesticity and the sure victory of that domesticity over savage incursion. Simultaneously, he presents himself as a teacher, bringing the ignorant easterner realistic depictions of the West as a kind of public service. In the early 1880s, Cody and his partners mostly staged Buffalo Bill's Wild West for eastern audiences, implying that the show posited all easterners, regardless of age, as children in need of instruction.[47]

Continued emphasis on education helped Cody and his partners redefine Buffalo Bill's relationship to his child audience, casting him as a protector not only of the vulnerable child on the frontier but also the ignorant child who has grown up without experiencing it. Newspapers eagerly picked up on these themes. A typical 1886 review of Buffalo Bill's Wild West notes that nearly "1,000 school children on Staten Island visited the Wild West Exhibition of Buffalo Bill one afternoon last week." The happy children "cheered, clapped their hands till the sound of their voices overpowered the band and the firing by the cowboys and Indians." The reporter concludes that the entertainment provided by the show was matched by its educational value, concluding, "Every school in the country ought to witness the exhibition, and learn what is meant by Out West."[48]

At the end of the 1885–86 touring season, Cody and his partners broke from their established pattern of putting the show in storage for the winter. Renting out Madison Square Garden, Cody and Salsbury prepared to move their show indoors and stage, as Martin calls it, a "more coherent narrative" of white American progress, one that separated the history of frontier settlement into distinct epochs, each of which "constituted an act in the performance and supposedly exemplified a distinct period of American history."[49] Subtitled the Drama of Civilization, the show was an explicit and extended meditation on westward settlement, operating on the principle that such settlement was now complete.

Dramatist Steele MacKaye was hired to shape the narrative for the Drama of Civilization, and he set out to "illustrate all the obstacles to the white man's advance that exist in the wilderness." The show's four "epochs" were the Primeval Forest, the Prairie, the Cattle Ranch, and the Mining Camp; a reenactment of Custer's Last Stand appeared as a later addition. The show's creators surrounded the live performers with impressive stagecraft, including massive painted backdrops—with each painting approximately 40 feet high and 150 feet long—wind machines, meticulous lighting, and a vast array of props. The show presented westward expansion as an unfettered celebration of white American progress, offering Buffalo Bill as the preeminent symbol of the nation's triumphant ascendance.[50]

Warren argues that this show's "appeal lay in its projected amnesia about the nation's most recent wounds."[51] For Warren, in 1886, a period of rapid change and increasing political polarization, America was less concerned with the Indian Wars than the dangers posed by waves of immigration and escalating labor unrest. He reads the Drama of Civilization as both a mythmaking exercise and an escapist fantasy, "a soothing and reassuring spectacle for audiences mostly united in their fear of anarchy and seditious foreigners" (267). If the Drama of Civilization made the Wild West's narrative of white American supremacy more pervasive than previous productions had, it did little to sap the show's appeal to the nation's youth, with William Deahl noting that large "groups of school children attended the matinees in order to witness the reconstructions of America's past."[52]

On the heels of the Drama of Civilization, Buffalo Bill's Wild West headed off to England, a move that, in hindsight, seems inevitable. The frontier had been won, so foreign conquest was all that remained. After a triumphant return and, later, a second and more expansive tour of continental Europe, Cody arrived at the 1893 Columbian Exposition. It would turn out to be a crowning moment for "America's national entertainment," as the show was billing itself. Interviewed that summer, John Burke reflected on the Wild West's appeal to foreign audiences: "They looked upon Colonel Cody apparently as a messenger of peace," claiming that Buffalo Bill "brought American frontier history to their own doors and showed that the march of Western Empire meant the triumph of the plow over savagery and bullets." If it sounds as if Burke is describing Turner here and not Cody, the publicist goes on to alleviate any such confusion, noting that Buffalo Bill's "triumph" also demonstrates the rise of America, wherein "the lasso of the cowboy had conquered not only broncos, but their fierce Indian riders, who gladly exchanged the tomahawk for the arena of the Wild West."[53] Burke's rhetoric exposes a central tenet of the history taught by Buffalo Bill's Wild West, namely that the mythology of the frontier need not be confined to the space of the West. Rather, the frontier was an experience to be packaged and exported, reenacted by Buffalo Bill and his company in a nightly affirmation of American triumph.

Shifting constructions of American boyhood were closely entwined with the show's central theme of patriotic progress. As Buffalo Bill became enshrined as a boyhood hero, the show's dominant frontier narrative became increasingly pervasive in children's culture. In 1887, McLoughlin Brothers published *A Peep at Buffalo Bill's Wild West*, a children's picture book with the story in rhyming verse. The book faithfully parroted the frontier themes emphasized by Cody and his partners. Buffalo Bill is presented as a child of nature who dreamed of living "in the wild-wood free." The bucolic paradise of the plains is threatened by "red men," and the book celebrates Buffalo Bill and the white men, "brave and bold," who subdued this threat, advancing the progress of white civilization. In describing "the game of hide-and-seek / The white and red men play / On the prairies wide, where on every side / They fight for the right of way," the book sounds the familiar refrain of Cody's frontier heroics while providing the template for children to reenact those heroics through play.[54] *A Peep at Buffalo Bill's Wild West* depicts Buffalo Bill not only as a frontier hero but, importantly, as a role model for children, helping to counteract stories of runaway boys and children injured by enacting scenes from

Cody's show. This trend carried over into the 1890s as Buffalo Bill became a fixture in the culture of children's play, with his name gracing toy guns, puzzles, action figure cutouts, and more.[55]

A NEW ERA: COWBOYS AND ROUGH RIDERS

From 1886 to the end of the century, Buffalo Bill's Wild West underwent changes that corresponded both to new nationalistic ambitions and to changing notions of American masculinity and boyhood. Two major changes to the show in these years were the expanded role and prominence of the cowboy and the addition and expansion of the Rough Riders of the World. While the influence of the latter is more immediately clear (one need look no further than Teddy Roosevelt's pinching of the name), the former reveals an equally powerful reframing of American frontier narrative.

The changes Buffalo Bill's Wild West underwent in the closing decades of the nineteenth century reflected broader changes in American society. As noted earlier, new ideas and attitudes about education and leisure were critical to the success of Cody's show. These new ideas were heavily inflected with important cultural reformulations of social class, a process that was itself directly tied to shifting notions of American childhood. In nineteenth-century America, Karen Sánchez-Eppler argues, childhood becomes a site where class identity is constructed, while "childhood itself is increasingly recognized as a sign of class status." Specifically, for Sánchez-Eppler the working child becomes a marker of a lower social class, while the (idealized) middle-class child becomes increasingly "protected from the difficulties and responsibilities of daily life—ultimately including the need to work."[56]

This changing valuation of what Viviana Zelizer has termed "the useless child"—the child valued not for its utility as a worker but its representation of a domestic ideal—neatly mirrors the changing content of Buffalo Bill's Wild West and is highlighted by the cultural transformation of the cowboy in the second half of the nineteenth century. Initially, cowboys were considered wild and degenerate, a criminal class of men living on the fringes of society. During an 1881 address to Congress, President Chester Arthur himself described the troublesome presence of "armed desperadoes known as cowboys" in Arizona.[57] As frontier mythology spread through different forms of American popular culture, the cowboy's reputation got a boost. Already a consistent presence in dime novels, the cowboy attained hero status in Frederick Whitaker's *Parson Jim, King of the Cowboys* (1882). Buck Taylor soon followed, with *Buck Taylor, King of the Cowboys* (1887). Unlike Parson Jim, Taylor was a real person and, not coincidentally, a longtime employee of Buffalo Bill, having worked his way up from ranch hand to Wild West attraction.

From his earliest days on the stage, Cody and his partners worked hard to rehabilitate the cowboy's image. Cody's frequent costar in the Buffalo Bill Combination, Texas Jack Omohundro, was particularly active in this regard, writing a glowing defense of the cowboy that found its way into the newspapers and later into programs for Buffalo Bill's Wild West:

> The Cow-Boy.—The cowboy! How often spoken of, how falsely imagined, how greatly despised (where not known,), how little understood! I've been there considerable. How sneeringly referred to, and how little appreciated although his title has been gained by possession of many of the noblest qualities that form the romantic hero of the poet, novelist, and historian: a plains-man and the scout.[58]

A forceful correction to "false imaginings," Omohundro's rhetoric makes it clear that the cowboy has all the qualities of the frontier hero, standing as a direct descendant of the scout and a symbol of future American prosperity: "As tall oaks from little acorns grow, the cow-boy serves a purpose, and often develops into the most celebrated ranchman, guide, cattle-king, Indian-fighter, and dashing ranger" (25).

Of course, few cowboys would ever lay claim to the title of ranchman or cattle king. Highlighting a clear, if often unrecognized, social hierarchy in the language of the frontier, Jacqueline Moore argues that no one "would call a cow*boy* a cattle*man* unless he owned the ranch,"[59] a status few of them ever enjoyed. Moore claims that cowboys were "essentially working-class men . . . subject to the same restraints nineteenth-century workers faced across the country" (3). Indeed, socialist advocate Edward Aveling, who traveled with Buffalo Bill's Wild West in 1886–87 and wrote with surprising admiration about the show, was quick to lump the cowboy in with other exploited American laborers, claiming "the 'free' cowboy is as much that of a slave as that of his Eastern brother, the Massachusetts mill-hand."[60]

Their status as frontier laborers helps explain the cowboys' bad reputation, especially in the eyes of wealthy western landowners and eastern elites. Coming five years after the Haymarket Riots in Chicago, for which "anarchists" were charged with killing several policemen, Wyoming's Johnson County War revealed similar class tensions, as Johnson County's wealthiest ranchers worked hard to present their opposition to lawless rustlers. As noted in chapter 2, Owen Wister's *The Virginian* (1902) cemented the cowboy's status as an American icon of white middle-class masculinity, in clear opposition to the villainous half-breed Trampas who, as Jacqueline Moore describes him, "is more in tune with working class ideals."[61]

Read in this light, Wister's novel marks the culmination of long-standing efforts to frame frontier masculinity as distinctly American, white, and upper class. As Gail Bederman argues, Roosevelt's four-volume *The Winning of the West* had one central thesis: "superior manhood had allowed the American race to prevail against the Indians, win a continent, and build a mighty nation," such that "America's nationhood itself was the product of both racial superiority and virile manhood."[62] And as Christine Bold points out, coding that virile manhood as upper class was a central concern of Wister's fiction. In *Parson Jim*, the hero is Harvard-educated Jim Arthur, who stands up for "homesteaders, townspeople, and independent cowboys" against big, wealthy ranchers. By contrast, Bold argues, Wister's Harvard years taught the frontier novelist "to celebrate the 'natural aristocracy' of big ranchers and their loyal cow-punchers and to demonize small, independent settlers."[63] Whether or not Cody shared Wister's interest in championing big ranchers, Buffalo Bill's Wild West played a key role in transforming the cowboy from an unsavory working-class laborer into a chivalrous hero, a powerful aristocrat of the plains—a figure much like Cody's idealized Indian scout.

This transformation can be traced through the increasing attention paid to cowboys in show programs. In the 1884 program, Buck Taylor was described as "a typical Westerner by ancestry, birth and heritage of associations as this noted herd." His "eminence is based on the sterling

122   CHAPTER 3

qualities that rank him as 'King of the Cowboys,'" a title he inherited
from his grandfather and uncle, who both died in the war with Mexico,
and father, who died as a member of the Texas cavalry. Unlike the Virginian—and Roosevelt, of course—Taylor was not a transplanted easterner. Nonetheless, he possessed the same qualities later attributed to
Wister's hero, and the cowboy himself, as an emblem of frontier heroism.
If Aveling saw fit to compare cowboys to "slaves," Cody and company were
keen to promote the cowboy as the paragon of American supremacy
and Anglo-Saxon superiority. A key part of this process involved distinguishing the cowboy from other articulations of frontier masculinity.
Programs from 1884 described the attack on the settler's cabin, with the
subsequent rescue by Buffalo Bill with his scouts, cowboys, and Mexicans. By 1887, any mention of Mexicans has disappeared, with the attack
repulsed by "Cowboys, under the leadership of Buffalo Bill."[64]

In the years that followed, Wild West programs didn't dismiss Mexican riders so much as make sure to distinguish them from cowboys.
In the 1893 program, "The Vaquero of the Southwest" is described in
a separate section: "Between the 'cow-boy' and 'vaquero' there is only a
slight line of demarcation." The program then clarifies the importance
of that distinction: "The one is usually an American, inured from boyhood to excitement and hardships of his life, and the other represents
in his blood, the stock of the Mexican, or it may be of the half-breed."
Beyond the question of bad blood, it's clear that clothes make the man,
with the vaquero described as "more of a dandy in the style and get-up
of his attired than his careless and impetuous compeer." More frivolous
than his Anglo-Saxon counterpart, the vaquero is noted to be "fond of
gaudy clothes, and when you see him riding into a frontier town, the
first thought of an Eastern man is, that a circus has broken loose in the
neighborhood."[65]

In these years, Buffalo Bill's Wild West increasingly worked out its
narrative of frontier conquest through a complex relationship between
the Indian scout and the cowboy. Both figures, after all, were symbols
of white American masculinity and both were "made" by the frontier,
"inured from boyhood" to all the promise and peril of the West. In the
final decade of the nineteenth century, the cowboy's ascendance was
clear, while the star of Buffalo Bill's Wild West remained Buffalo Bill,

a buckskin-clad Indian scout. Programs increasingly described the relationship between cowboy and scout as a passing of the torch. The 1902 biography for Johnny Baker, who had long performed with the show as "the Cowboy Kid" or "the Young Marksman" even though he was thirty-three years old at that point, cloaks this transition in the language of growth and development: "Cradled amid such pioneer surroundings and dandled on the knees of the most celebrated frontiersman, the genuine old buckskin trappers—the first frontier invaders—his childhood witnessed the declining glories of the buffalo hunter's paradise (it being the heart of their domain), and the advent of his superior, the 'long horn of Texas,' and his necessary companion, 'the Cow-Boy.'"[66]

Baker is described as a child of the Indian scout, a product of the frontier "paradise" once patrolled by "old buckskin trappers." By 1902, though, his future—like the nation's future—is aligned with the cowboys, those "brave, generous, self-sacrificing rough riders of the plains, literally living in the saddle, enduring exposure, hunger, risk of health and life." Importantly, while the Indian scout risked life and limb to cleanse the land of hostile Indians and pave the way for civilization, the cowboy serves "as a duty to the employer." It is this noble laborer who gave Baker his "first communion with society beyond the sod cabin threshold and impressed his mind as well as directed his aspirations, to an emulation of the manly qualities necessary to be ranked a true American Cow-boy" (20). The frontier myth of Buffalo Bill's Wild West has shifted, deemphasizing the Indian scout who lived on the fringes of society in favor of the disciplined and loyal cowboy. In both cases, the frontier generates these ideals of white masculinity, forging—as in Baker's case—formidable young manhood from the crude material of boyhood.

A second major shift in the show was more plainly evident; starting in 1893, Cody and Salsbury started billing the production as Buffalo Bill's Wild West and the Congress of the Rough Riders of the World. On some level, the change was practical. Unsure if indigenous performers would be granted permission to tour with the show after the Wounded Knee Massacre, Salsbury began securing other attractions. Russian Cossacks were billed in the 1892 programs, and Syrian and Arabian horsemen soon followed. Warren suggests this move reflects a shrewd marketing response to the increasing number of immigrants in the audience.[67] On some level, the new name also reflects an acknowledgment of a new chapter in American frontier history. If cowboys and Indians became the most enduring feature of the show, Buffalo Bill's Wild West made sure to address America's ambitions to carry on frontier conquest in the global arena.

The inclusion—and expansion—of the Congress of Rough Riders surely added diversity to Buffalo Bill's Wild West, though it also reflected the expansion of frontier narratives through American imperialist ambitions. In addition to featuring Syrian and Arabian horsemen, the 1893 program featured "Military Evolutions by a Company of the Sixth Cavalry of the United States" alongside regiments from the German, French, and British armies, while the 1894 show added a "Military Music Drill."[68] The emphasis on military themes—Cody had, by then, awarded himself the fully ceremonial title of colonel—picked up in anticipation of the Spanish-American War and, by 1902, included scenes from the war. Alongside a "U.S. Artillery Drill," "Life Saving Service Drill," and a "Musical Ride, featuring "Veterans from the Sixth U.S. Cavalry," the show featured the Battle of San Juan Hill, "introducing detachments from Roosevelt's Rough Riders." In addition to "civilizing" the frontier, the program reveled in showing the "Resplendent Realism of Glorious War."[69]

While the parameters of their frontier narrative may have shifted, Cody and his partners continued to emphasize the educational value of their show. By the 1890s, these efforts had successfully changed perceptions of Buffalo Bill's Wild West. An 1893 reviewer from the *Daily Inter-Ocean* attests to the show's evolution. Acknowledging it as a "crude exhibition given back in the seventies," the writer describes a transformation from "a 'catch-penny fake' into one of the most interesting, innovative and instructive exhibitions of the world." Buffalo Bill's Wild West serves to "disabuse the public minds of any wrong impression that may have gone abroad through misrepresentation by historians or unreliable reporters."[70]

Two reviews from the *New York Times* also trumpet the transformation of Buffalo Bill's Wild West. An 1886 review describes a trip to the "pleasure grounds" of Cody's Wild West, where the "more there was of banging pistols and scurrying Indians the better."[71] By 1894, though, the paper lauds Buffalo Bill's Wild West's long stand in Brooklyn for "the presence of so many children," who had a "universal desire among them to see this unique, original, and instructive exhibition." Likewise, an 1894 review in the *New York American and Mercury*, written during the show's six-month stay in Brooklyn, claims it offers "a summer school of instruction to youth of our country who may be called upon at any time to come into contest with other countries."[72]

Cody and his partners also addressed child spectators directly. An 1898 *Bison Courier*, cut in the shape of a large bison's head (serving as the book's cover), bears the heading "For the Children's Eyes," informing the reader:

> Your parents will combine duty with pleasure by taking you to see it and when they do, they will say to Col. Cody, as did General Sherman, the hero of the March to the Sea: *"Billy, for my children and grandchildren, who can never see these things as we saw them, I thank you."* And long and happily may you all live to profit by and pleas-antly remember a day with that true, brave friend of every child, Buffalo Bill.[73]

The message to children is clear, noting that viewing Buffalo Bill's Wild West will surely dispel any myths about "the miseries, sacrifices and horrors of war." Educated by this experience, "sensible boys will not be misled by demoralizing blood-and-thunder stories," though they'll remain "ever ready to defend 'Old Glory'—as did their ancestors in the Revolution, and their sires and grandsire in the sacred cause of the Union—whenever their beloved country calls upon them to defend her" (2). Young readers are encouraged to conflate westward expansion and the conquest of American Indian peoples with the recent Spanish-American War, and by 1898, Cody and company had successfully woven the Indian Wars into a narrative of America's "sacred cause," beginning with the American Revolution and continuing with the expansion of American global imperialism. In the *Bison Courier*, violence is part of progress, and the story of the West is the story of America, a narrative aimed both at children and their parents: "What the children see at Buffalo Bill's Wild West they will enjoy, appreciate, understand, and re-member. What parents see there they will wish their children taught" (2).

By 1893, Buffalo Bill's relationship with American boyhood had been significantly reoriented in the popular press. Reviewing Buffalo Bill's Wild West at the World's Fair in Chicago, one reporter speculates that should Buffalo Bill become the governor of Nebraska, "it will take forty cars to pull the boys of Chicago who will want to go to Nebraska to see him inaugurated." The reviewer declares, "A man who makes friends of all the children as Buffalo Bill does have something good in him. His name sounds a little wild, but Buffalo Bill is a patriotic American."[74]

Over the years, Cody's reputation as patriot and friend of all American children would only gain in strength, while the notion that he had "something good in him" became a consensus among adults. Cody came to be seen as a surrogate father for the nation's boys. When the organizers of the World's Fair rejected an idea to grant ten thousand poor children free entry for a day, Cody stepped in, admitting six thousand children to a free performance of the Wild West. The press celebrated his goodwill: "Waifs and Newsboys Have a Whole Day's Sport," declares one headline,[75] while the boys themselves presented Buffalo Bill with a solid gold plate in the shape of a messenger card, acknowledging Cody's great service to the "Chicago Waifs Mission Messenger," and signed by the "Waifs of Chicago." As popular inspirational author Orison Swett Marden aptly put it, in 1895, Cody was "the friend of everybody and especially of poor boys who have no chance in life."[76]

By the turn of the century, then, Buffalo Bill's Wild West made room for all boys, rich or poor, in the show's imagined frontier. Much as children of all types and from all backgrounds were encouraged to live up to the ideals of middle-class childhood, all children were encouraged to participate in the show's forceful narratives of development and identity formation—both of boy and nation alike. Through performance and, as we will see in chapter 5, play, Buffalo Bill's Wild West provided opportunities to interact with the triumphant narrative of white American masculinity, wherein myth became history and the frontier became a powerful tool for rehearsing the past and imagining the future.

4

CHILDREN, SPECTACLE, AND AGENCY IN WILD WEST PERFORMANCE

In the second half of the nineteenth century, Buffalo Bill's Wild West offered a spectacle like no other. Building on the success of impresarios like P. T. Barnum, William "Buffalo Bill" Cody and his partners staged a mass entertainment that drew millions of fans to its bleachers, touring relentlessly across North America and much of Europe. Like Barnum's American Museum or the traveling circuses of Richard Bailey and Adam Forepaugh, Cody's show was a novel form of early popular culture. Unlike most popular entertainments of the time, Buffalo Bill's Wild West featured an explicit narrative of national progress. Launched in 1883 and running into the first decade of the twentieth century, Buffalo Bill's Wild West told no single story. Still, the show's prevailing central theme was the settling—and "civilizing"—of the West. As noted in chapter 3, Cody and company tapped into a collective fervor for the past and a shared dream of white American conquest and prosperity, much as Frederick Jackson Turner channeled in his 1893 essay, "The Significance of the Frontier in American History."[1]

Much has been written about Buffalo Bill's Wild West and its contributions both to American popular culture and to enduring narratives of national character and identity. Less attention has been paid to the relationship between Buffalo Bill's Wild West and children and childhood in the late nineteenth and early twentieth centuries. In staging the show, Cody and his partners drew on Buffalo Bill's appeal as a dime novel hero. They anticipated an audience of children and made use of distinct ideas of American childhood in catering to that audience. They presented Buffalo Bill as a frontier icon and, at the same time, as a boy worker and even a father figure. In this way, Buffalo Bill's Wild West spoke directly to children, specifically to boys, and leery adults concerned with their welfare. Imagined through ideals of boyhood wherein young white boys were developed into paragons of rugged masculinity, the frontier created in the Wild West arena delighted generations of American children who would grow up without any "actual" frontier to experience.

Child performers played key roles in Buffalo Bill's Wild West, though their contributions to the show and its dominant narratives remain underexplored. These contributions informed and accentuated the relationship between boyhood and the frontier, both in the Wild West arena and the nation itself, during the second half of the nineteenth century and beyond. While hardly unique to Buffalo Bill's Wild West, the presence of child performers in the show stands out on two fronts. First, Cody and his partners reinforced specific constructions of childhood and youth through their singular narrative of American conquest and character. Second, Buffalo Bill's Wild West blurred the line between performer and spectator, creating a type of performance unlike anything else on the nineteenth-century stage.

Notions of American childhood remained fluid through much of the nineteenth century. As previously noted, the ideal of the Romantic Child, imbued with purity, innocence, and natural goodness, became a bright symbol of American middle-class childhood. While notions of Romantic Childhood grew increasingly influential in the second half of the century, their appeal was far from universal, and definitions of childhood fluctuated and clashed across lines of class, race, and gender. In the theater, competing ideas of childhood played out in the most public of forums. Examining representations of childhood on the nineteenth-century stage, Marah Gubar argues that the popular theater provided a dynamic public vehicle for this process, serving "as the site of a lengthy struggle over the question of how to define and delimit childhood."[2]

Buffalo Bill's Wild West contributed to this struggle in multiple ways. For one, it promoted ideals of Romantic Childhood, emphasizing the vulnerability of the show's child performers and their closeness to nature. At the same time, Cody and his partners tapped into nascent ideas of youth and adolescence, forging links between the developing child and the developing nation. G. Stanley Hall's landmark study of adolescence was not published until 1904, but the parameters of a distinctive phase between childhood and adulthood had started taking shape much earlier. As we have seen, some forms of popular culture, such as the frontier dime novel, played on late-nineteenth-century fears of adolescent juvenile delinquency, but Cody and his partners took a different tack, building on the vision presented in his 1879 autobiography to present the frontier as a place where the right kinds of American boys were nurtured into shining models of American superiority.

On its imagined frontier, Buffalo Bill's Wild West linked past and future through a nostalgic vision of white boyhood developed into triumphant masculinity. Nevertheless, some young performers found unintended flexibility in the show's central narrative. Eric Lott argues that the significance of any popular cultural form lies in its resonance, its ability to tap into collective fantasy, and the young performers in Buffalo Bill's Wild West demonstrated that ability at work on several levels. Through performance, they simultaneously reproduced visions of hegemonic masculinity and American imperialism and left space for the kind of counter-narratives that, as Lott puts it, manage to "retain subversive dimensions, or for a time be invested with them."[3] In some cases, young performers disrupted the show's constricting discourses of race and gender, exerting a kind of agency they have been given little credit for.

A close look at the child performers in Buffalo Bill's Wild West demonstrates how important ideas of childhood and youth were to the frontier narratives crafted by Cody and his partners. We can trace this relationship through analysis of the show's featured child performers; the many indigenous performers, or "show Indians," who traveled with the show; and the young audience members who interacted with performers, both inside the arena and out.

BOYS, GIRLS, AND GUNS

Johnny Baker served as the longest-tenured "child performer" in Buffalo Bill's Wild West. Often described as the Cowboy Kid, Baker was a fresh-faced, brown-haired boy who was with Cody from the show's run in 1883. He grew up in poverty in North Platte, Nebraska, and met Cody when he was seven years old. After seeing Buffalo Bill on stage in 1876, Baker recalls that Cody quickly "became my idol and I soon was on friendly terms with him."[4] In fact, Cody was mourning the loss of his young son, Kit, at the time. He warmed instantly to Baker and the bond between the two grew strong enough that Cody all but adopted the boy. Baker traveled with Buffalo Bill's Wild West up to its final performance, in later years serving as one of the show's business managers. After Cody died, Baker looked after his grave site, running the small museum dedicated to Buffalo Bill on the top of Lookout Mountain in Colorado. When Baker died, he was buried next to Cody's biological children.

Baker was more than a member of Cody's extended family; he was a steady and consistent presence in Buffalo Bill's Wild West. While Baker would play a number of roles in the show over the years—from offstage manager to actor, donning a blond wig to assume the role of General Custer—he had originally been trained by Cody to do rifle tricks and was often celebrated as "the cowboy kid" or "the young marksman" (fig. 7). Baker began performing publicly as a marksman at fourteen; was first advertised in the Wild West's 1885 program; and became a fixture in the show's prime years of the late 1880s and 1890s, performing various rifle tricks, including his signature move of firing at targets while standing on his head. Throughout those years and into Baker's adulthood, Wild West promotional literature stressed Baker's youthful vigor. In an 1895 pamphlet promoting the show, John Burke describes Baker, twenty-six at the time, as "a typical boy of the type only produced in America." Baker, Burke notes, is in full possession of "that elasticity and conscious strength and self-reliance which marks the young frontiersman.[5]

At fourteen, Baker was neither child nor adult. Rather, he fell into the nebulous category of youth, a period between childhood and adulthood with dimensions that differed radically across lines of class, race, and gender for much of the nineteenth century. By 1876, when Baker first met Cody, there was considerable cultural anxiety about unsupervised American youth as a perceived threat to social order. As a powerful youth figure, Baker could be perceived in starkly different ways, from juvenile delinquent to paragon of developing manhood. Buffalo Bill's Wild West successfully framed him as the latter. Raised on the frontier, Baker embodied traits of American boyhood. Possessing the "self-reliance" to succeed in the harshest of environments and the "conscious strength" to master the task at hand, he performed difficult feats of marksmanship beyond the ability of most grown men. At the same time, the "elasticity"

Burke mentions reminded audiences that Baker, like America, remained
unbound, still growing and developing. As discussed previously, for Child
Study experts like Hall, this kind of adolescent flexibility was critical to
developing Anglo-Saxon boys into the right kind of American men. In
the laboratory of the frontier, boys such as Baker became men like Cody,
growing up with the country and with the nation itself.

The 1885 program for Buffalo Bill's Wild West features an illustra-
tion labeled "Attack on the Burning Cabin" that celebrates this vision of
frontier boyhood. In it, Cody and his mates rescue a white family from
"savage" incursion (fig. 6). As the Indians emerge from the forest and
swarm the settler's small cabin, Buffalo Bill and company swoop in, guns
blazing. The settler family is armed as well, with a woman firing a rifle
out an open window and a man standing guard at the front door. Prominently featured, a boy stands in front of the cabin. Meeting Cody and his
advancing force, he fires his rifle at an unseen attacker. An inset image
shows Cody isolated with this boy in the aftermath of the successfully
repelled attack. Holding the rifle confidently over his shoulder with one
hand, the boy greets Buffalo Bill with his other. The image highlights the
two as conquering heroes, suggesting a passing of the torch, as Buffalo
Bill helps frontier boyhood transition into the next generation of indom-
itable American manhood.[6]

Show promoters made use of Baker, both explicitly and implicitly,
to reinforce this narrative. In one newspaper account, Major Frank
Powell, "best remembered as an intimate friend of Colonel W. P. Cody,"
tells the story of Cody arriving at the site of an Indian attack too late,
discovering a boy whose father and mother had both been killed. Cody
"took the boy with him, cared for him and has had him with him ever
since . . . His name is Johnny Baker."[7] The story, which is completely
fabricated, lays out the main components of Baker's creation myth: he
was born out of frontier violence, reared by Buffalo Bill, and nourished
by the inhospitable conditions of the frontier itself. In performance, of
course, that trajectory is promoted but never achieved. As Cody's long
hair grayed, he grew comfortably into his celebrated role as the heroic
father of all American boys. Baker, though, was posited as an ageless
youth by the show's promotional materials. Even as Baker entered his
thirties, the promoters of Buffalo Bill's Wild West promoted him as an

exemplar of vigorous American boyhood, an eternal youth fixed on the vanishing frontier.

Like Baker, the show's most prominent young performers all performed with guns, uniting the child, rifle, and nature in the story of American frontier conquest, a construction that grew out of long-standing links between the Romantic Child and the natural world. Interestingly, most of Buffalo Bill's Wild West's notable crack shots were girls. Annie Oakley, the most famous of the show's attractions, was not alone in this regard. Lillian Smith was fourteen when she began touring with Cody in 1886, billed as the California Huntress. Girl sharpshooters populated other Wild West shows as well, and their youth and connection to nature were routinely emphasized (fig. 8). When she joined Pawnee Bill's Wild West show in 1904, Smith was rechristened Winsome Wenona, the Wonder Woman Shot of the World. The 1904 program describes her as a "charming child of nature, reared among the birds, wooed to sleep by the lullabies of a sparkling stream," a girl who "grew to be a great shot before she was a grown child. When she was very young her father presented to her—to her great joy—a small rifle." Soon, "no bird or beast could escape her unerring aim."[8]

Publicity photos posed girl sharpshooters in nature—much like staged photos of Johnny Baker—further emphasizing this connection. Smith was in her thirties by the time she took on the identity of Wenona, but promotional materials still described her as a "child of nature." This connection fostered her development into, as the 1904 program from Pawnee Bill's show boasts, a "great shot before she was a grown child." Carefully manipulating her ethnic identity over the years, she assumed the identity of a full-blooded Sioux as Wenona—her alleged indigenous identity marking her as a kind of primitive "eternal child"—but always presented herself as a Romantic Child: frisky, free, and at one with nature.

In addition to race, age was clearly a factor in this construction. Middle-class social norms encouraged hoydenish behavior in girls, with the expectation that those girls should take on the trappings of genteel womanhood by their teen years. Oakley clearly felt pressure to compete with Smith on account of Smith's youth—Smith was eleven years younger than Oakley. As Shirl Kasper explains, Oakley managed her image carefully, endearing herself to the public "as a kind of schoolgirl-next-door, full of life and vigor." Threatened by Smith, Oakley "simply lopped six years off her age."[9] For these female sharpshooters, the younger they appeared to be the better.[10]

While the presence of these girl sharpshooters challenged conventional gender roles, Buffalo Bill's Wild West imposed clear checks on this challenge. In addition to stressing their youth, female sharpshooters balanced shooting skills with the trappings of proper and respectable femininity. As both a young girl and a respectable feminine figure, Oakley tempered the transgressive potential of her performance. An emphasis on youth kept sharpshooters like Oakley and Smith from challenging conventional gender norms. Teresa Jordan argues that unlike the cowboy, who functions as "the quintessential man—most of us see the *cowgirl* as a child who will grow up someday and be something else."[11] The same logic held for the female sharpshooter. Her mastery of the gun was admirable but temporary, not a stepping-stone to the future but the embodiment of an alluring and carefree present.

On another level, the prominent role of these girl sharpshooters might have actually reinforced the rhetoric of the frontier as a male-dominated space. Writing about mid-century frontier drama, Kim Marra describes the stage as a symbolic frontier space. "Beyond the pale of respectable civilization," the stage provided a place where representations of the wild could be projected, processed, and consumed. In this space, Marra contends, the male theater manager could engage in the symbolic "escape from domestic tyranny and opportunity, through his conquest of savagery embodied in actresses, to shed the skin of his European heritage and become an American man."[12] By civilizing the "wild" or "savage" actress on the stage, the male manager-actor reenacted the civilizing process of the scout on the frontier. Marra describes popular theater manager Augustin Daly's tactics for dealing with overly emotional actresses: "Rather than quell actresses' exciting displays of fervid emotionalism, he endeavored initially to manipulate and deploy such displays as his own creations in order to impress more respectable audiences with his mastery of nature in all its savage beauty" (60).

Buffalo Bill's Wild West demonstrates the progression of frontier theater into a multi-dimensional performance spectacle, and Cody's use of female sharpshooters can be seen as a variation on the process Marra describes regarding Daly. In the show, the poise and control of Oakley and her peers demonstrated the control scouts like Cody exerted over the space of the West itself. In this regard, Oakley stands in sharp contrast to a very different female icon of the time, Calamity Jane. It was all well and good for a woman like Oakley to practice marksmanship, but the question of a female scout or frontierswoman of a kind with Buffalo Bill was a different matter. Jane, the most prominent such figure, was typically described as a fallen woman and social outcast—a boon to her dime novel persona, perhaps, but a notable stigma otherwise. Speaking to the press after her death, Cody noted, "Calamity was a character—an odd one," describing her as "unique among women so far as I know. Perhaps this is just as well . . . but Calamity Jane had nearly all the rough virtues of the old west as well as many of the vices."[13]

Oakley steered clear of such associations. In her dress and demeanor, she projected child innocence, a connection to untrammeled nature manifested through her aptitude with guns. In her public persona, she balanced free-spirited and vivacious girlhood with respectable womanhood. Advertised as Miss Annie Oakley, she kept her marriage to manager Frank Butler quiet, indirectly paving the way for some spontaneous marriage proposals from her fans. At the same time, Oakley made sure to avoid untoward associations with members of the opposite sex. Oakley contrasted sharply with Smith in this regard, helping in part to explain the latter's much shorter tenure with Buffalo Bill's Wild West; after marrying one of the show's cowboys, Smith had a dalliance with another in 1889 and left the show.[14]

Positioned between childhood and adulthood, between frisky and innocent, these female sharpshooters occupied a highly restrictive and liminal space. These girls were not future pioneers—and certainly not soldiers—but proof of how the show used the frontier to conjure different visions of young America. For boys, this process facilitated their development from rugged boyhood to superior masculinity. For girls, the process was transitory; ultimately, it strengthened their affiliation with the land through the civilizing of the savage, the cultivating and controlling of the wild.

ASSIMILATION AND PERFORMANCE

The presentation of young performers as prototypical Romantic Children is most pronounced in descriptions of indigenous children in Buffalo Bill's Wild West. Describing these children, Burke even turns to Wordsworth: "That the boy is father of the man, is not more truly exemplified than in the case of the Indian boy. Lithe and active and fearless as young panthers," these boys display "a vim and go, which no artificial system could inculcate." Part boy, part panther, Burke's young Indian presents, like Johnny Baker, a vision of emerging masculinity that only the "real" struggles and hardships of life on the frontier can produce. Unlike Baker, of course, the Indian boy lacks restraint, his inner savagery leaving him ever "active and fearless," reacting from a place of pure animal impulse rather than Victorian self-mastery.[15] Like the frontier actresses Marra describes, these savage youth stand in for the frontier itself, and Buffalo Bill's Wild West manages to contain their savagery and, in fact, manipulate it for performance, which is meant to represent the success of white masculinity in taming those open spaces.

Buffalo Bill's Wild West drew on ideas of Indian child-savagery in myriad ways. In the arena, young show Indians were not only fearless; they could be hostile and aggressive, taking part in simulated attacks on the Deadwood stage and the settler's cabin. Outside the arena, these young performers were key players in the show's reproduction of frontier domesticity. In this way, performance in Buffalo Bill's Wild West was not confined to the arena; rather, it commenced as soon as the traveling members of the show disembarked from the train. Everywhere Buffalo Bill's Wild West played, a "real-life" frontier village was erected where cowboys, Indians, and Cossacks alike all pitched their tents and settled in. The indigenous performers in Cody's show were almost all Sioux, though they impersonated various tribes in the arena. In the camp, they presented without any tribal affiliation in a generic "Indian" setting, and their tepees proved a source of great fascination, with the public flocking to see Indian men, women, and children living in their "natural" environment.

Especially during the show's long runs, when these camps were set up for weeks at a time, the everyday performance of Indian domesticity proved a defining feature of the Wild West experience for the thousands of visitors who flocked to the show. In fact, these camps, where visitors could visit free of charge, exposed the show's performers to a broad cross section of society. For Philip Deloria, the encampments served as a counterpoint to the violence Indian warriors performed in the arena: "If the arena seemed a place of masculine conflict and domination . . . the camp was, like the newly pacified reservations, domesticated, with women and children visible and tipis well tended." These two facets of the show interacted with one another, establishing, as Deloria puts it, "a constant dialogue" between arena and camp, "with the real of the backstage being fed into the performance's imaginative universe."[16]

Each of these modes presented Cody's show Indians through assimilation narratives, which took on added weight for the show's child performers. Both in Buffalo Bill's Wild West and the broader American culture, narratives of Indian pacification were tempered by concepts of age. Charley O'Kieffe describes going to Rushville, Nebraska, in 1890 to witness Sioux performers head out with the show for the season. Eleven at the time, O'Kieffe watched awestruck as the Sioux danced, noting they "were not paid to perform—they wanted to do it, and there was spirit and fire in every movement they made."[17] O'Kieffe stayed up until five in the morning to see the troupe when they returned, though he bristles at the spectacle: "Here were the Indians whom we had last seen in war paint and feathers now clad in Prince Albert coats, Stetson hats, patent leather shoes, and all the accouterments of the well-dressed man of the period." Having left "filled with good advice," he reports, "now they were full of bad whiskey." Departing with "all they owned on their backs or in their hands, now they were returning with more useless junk than they could carry" (115).

O'Kieffe's disgust at the returning show Indians reflects popular criticism of Wild West shows. Many reformers thought these shows anathema to the prospect of successful Indian assimilation. In their eyes, the life of show Indians was degrading and deceitful; it prevented them from breaking with the past and delayed their acceptance of civilized America as a desirable future. Thomas Jefferson Morgan, who became the commissioner of the Bureau of Indian Affairs in 1889, argued that "When the lowest type of Indian, with his war dances, paint and blankets is exhibited the public mind accepts him as typical of the Indians of today."[18] For Morgan, the "lowest" type of Indian exhibited himself for profit, and he denied these performers any sense of agency. Reformers like Morgan posited younger performers as the most at risk. Forced to take part in regressive exhibitions, these children stood to learn the wrong lessons about the past and harbor distorted visions of the future.

O'Kieffe's memoir aptly reflects the generational split described by Morgan. While disgusted by the adult Indians in Cody's show who were corrupted by the fineries of modern living, he reacts much differently to a quartet of young Sioux returning to the Pine Ridge Reservation from the Carlisle School. O'Kieffe describes the girls in the group as "far too well dressed and refined in appearance to be called squaws by any decent white man." After some conversation, he concludes that the Sioux "were now well-educated young people, and impressed me as amply equipped to take their place in any community as useful and responsible citizens."[19] For the adults returning from a season with Cody's Wild West, nice clothing and modern airs suggest degradation. For these youth, however, similar trappings signify education and respectability. Unlike the older generations of the tribe, O'Kieffe sees these younger Sioux as primed for assimilation into the white man's world, ready to take their places as "useful" citizens.

In this way, Buffalo Bill's Wild West presented a model of assimilation in staunch contrast to Morgan and other like-minded reformers. Importantly, the show also provided an alternative educational model in which child performers learned to become American citizens without completely suppressing their tribal identities. This marked a radical break from the rhetoric of educators like General Richard Henry Pratt, who established the Carlisle Indian Industrial School in 1879. According to Pratt's famous and, at the time, influential doctrine, one had to "kill the Indian" in order to "save the man." At Carlisle, students were given new names and clothing and were prompted to cast off their indigenous identities. Unsurprisingly, Pratt was openly critical of Buffalo Bill's Wild West, and the popular press often presented boarding schools and Wild West shows as opposing visions of Indian futurity.[20]

The Indian village in Buffalo Bill's Wild West was a place where scenes of pacification and assimilation played out daily. Visitors who witnessed life in the camps came away with the sense that "real" Indians were peaceful, cooperative, and fully capable of assimilating into American society. The child performers in Buffalo Bill's Wild West played a significant role in this process. They had minor roles in the arena; older boys took place in the Indian races, on horseback and foot, while younger children served as extras in scenes dramatizing authentic "Indian life." Offstage, these children played more visible roles, through their display in the camps or marching in the show's public parades.

Certainly, reporters made much of this "authentic Indian life," and their investigations of the encampments inevitably focused on domesticity and the Indian child. In one 1894 account, a reporter describes his anthropological interest in going "down to Ambrose Park in the morning when the little Indians feel they are unnoticed to watch them play their games just as if they were in their native villages." The reporter describes how "Lizzy Spotted Tail, five, and her sister Many Eagle, who is three, build a miniature wigwam, like the tent they live in, and play with dolls." While a "New-York girl wouldn't think much of these dolls, with their bodies of buckskin and beads for eyes and nose and mouth marked with black paint," the reporter insists the toys are "without a flaw" for the "little Indian girl." In fact, the comparison with the "New York girl" reassures readers that these young indigenous girls play much as their own girls do; unaware their dolls "aren't much," they are essentially harmless. These "simple" and peaceful girls confirm both the indigenous girl's inferiority to the idealized white girl and the child's universal instinct for play. In fact, that instinct suggests the potential of these children for assimilation.

The assimilation scripts projected onto indigenous performers in Buffalo Bill's Wild West were inflected by gender as well as age. For instance, the reporter who visited Ambrose Park in 1894 offers a strongly gendered reading of indigenous children's behavior. He points out that Johnny Burke No Neck, ten years old and "quite a brave," judges the girls' "childish amusement as rather beneath him" (fig. 9). Burke, the reporter describes, teams up with two boys, Seven Up and Little Money, "to throw the bola, the weapon of the South American Gaucho," and then, using some chairs, to "perform some wonderful feats of horsemanship after the Cossack style." Unlike the indigenous girls, the play of these boys contains a hint of danger. The "thing dearest to them is playing war," the reporter claims, wryly noting "there are not enough of them at Ambrose Park for a good game, but they have played it often at home." In an extended description of this game, the reporter reveals an interesting mix of anxiety and amusement:

> First these small warriors put paint on their bodies and arm themselves with little bows, arrows, and shields, which they have made for the occasion. Then they select two chiefs, who are supposed to be leaders of hostile tribes. The war dance comes next. One of them plays on the tom-tom, while the others sing in a strange tone and gives [sic] vent now and then to savage yells. Scouts are sent out, and at last the fight begins. There are fierce charges. The air becomes thick with flying arrows and braves are falling on every side.[21]

In this description, the Indians' warlike behavior is portrayed as a central part of their essential nature. The reporter notes that "early in the lives of Indian children, games are put aside and life begins in earnest." For the boys, it is suggested, that life involves war; reassuringly, this playful reenactment features two tribes facing off against each other rather than a confrontation between whites and indigenous people. The still-real threat of that conflict becomes more notable when considering that Johnny Burke No Neck had allegedly survived just such a battle three years earlier.

As Burke's story attests, some child performers were asked to balance narratives of assimilation and aggression in complex—and disturbing—ways. Publicity materials from Buffalo Bill's Wild West proudly (and falsely) touted seven-year-old Johnny Burke No Neck as the sole survivor of the Wounded Knee Massacre on December 29, 1890. The boy accompanied Buffalo Bill to England in 1891–92, and, as Alan Gallop explains, Burke played "an active part in the show that year and his cheerful manner and winning smile make him a firm favourite with audiences all over England."[22] For the audience, Johnny's billed status as a survivor suggested the still-real threat of conflict, while his "cheerful manner" suggested the possibility of successful Indian assimilation. Publicly adopted by Burke, a prominent white man, and No Neck, a respectable

Standing Rock leader, he became a potent symbol of assimilation; as
Deloria describes it, he symbolized "an Indian future made possible by
Indian partnership with a great white father figure."[23]

These readings of young indigenous performers in Buffalo Bill's
Wild West also fit neatly into nineteenth-century rhetoric on child development. The Child Study movement gained credence in the second half
of the nineteenth century as a growing number of European and American pedagogues sought to apply the emerging principles of evolutionary
science to the study of child development. As James Sully argues, this
"modern science is before all things historical and genetic, going back
to the beginnings of things . . . so as to understand the later and more
complex phases of things as the outcome of these beginnings."[24]

In his 1877 article "A Biographical Sketch of an Infant," Charles
Darwin offers a representative sample of this modern science in action.
Through close observation of his son Doddy, Darwin traces the development of the child to the adult and of the human species itself. After
visiting the zoo with Doddy, who was then two years old, Darwin notes
that the boy "enjoyed looking at all the animals which were like those
he knew," while he "was much alarmed at the various larger animals in
houses." Darwin suggests such fears "quite independent of experience,
are the inherited effects of real dangers and abject superstitions during
ancient savage times."[25] Somewhat confusingly, this seems to contradict
the Darwinian theory of evolution as it later came to be understood.
However, as Claudia Castañeda explains, that theory, which distinguishes
carefully between evolution and development, held less sway in the
second half of the nineteenth century. At that time, Herbert Spencer's
ideas of evolution were more persuasive—even, it appears, to Darwin
himself—and those ideas "used individual development as the basis for
human evolution, and narrated both as a progressive story."[26]

Spencer's theories clearly influenced Hall in the formulation of
his own developmental paradigm. Updating Ernst Haeckel's theory of
recapitulation, famously distilled in the phrase "ontogeny recapitulates
phylogeny," Hall suggested that the child's inner savagery held the key
to understanding humanity's past and imagining its future. British psy-
chiatrist James Crichton-Browne had warned parents to "remember that
children are not little nineteenth-century men and women, but diamond

editions of very remote ancestors, full of savage whims and impulses, and savage rudiments of virtue."[27] Hall took things further, believing the child's essential link to the savage provided a golden opportunity to maximize development of both the individual and the species. "In play," Hall claimed, "every mood and movement is instinct with heredity." Through these moods and movements, boys "rehearse the activities of our ancestors, back we know not how far."[28] Through such rehearsal, Hall believed, the play of the individual could advance the progress of the species.

Particularly interested in the development of boys, Hall argued for allowing them to fully indulge savage whims. By doing so, he maintained, the boy increased his potential to develop into an ideal specimen of manhood. That specimen was, of course, white, as the inherently racist dimensions of Hall's recapitulation theory dictated he must be. As savages, all boys may have been equal; as potential men, each boy could only develop to the limits imposed by his race. Hall's theory created a hierarchy of race, and the young indigenous performers in Buffalo Bill's Wild West were at the bottom of that hierarchy and destined to stay there. Read against this hierarchy, and coded both as savage reenactment and assimilationist progress, the performances of Johnny and other young show Indians raise intriguing questions about performance and agency: Were the children simply reproducing Wild West scripts they saw enacted all around them? Were they performing hybridity in some way, mixing these frontier narratives with their own play scripts?

Certainly, these performances served as powerful vehicles for archiving culture. Rosemarie Bank describes this process at work in Charles Wilson Peale's museum during the early decades of the nineteenth century. Peale, she argues, was at the forefront of the emerging trend of collecting and displaying the rare and exotic—be it a person or thing. His museum eventually incorporated performative aspects, including public lectures and technological demonstrations, and it became an early vehicle for "the transference of cultural 'archiving' from museums and galleries to performance."[29] Through this process, indigenous cultural objects became increasingly popular, and the live bodies of indigenous people themselves were increasingly called upon as historical objects. This notion of performance as archive later flourished in Barnum's museum and in George Catlin's live exhibitions of "authentic" Indian culture. Before the Civil War, Bank argues, these exhibitions imposed order on "the natural world according to the 'scientific' principles that informed it," fixing indigenous people in a state of primitivism and promoting their status as historical artifacts" (49). After the Civil War, this process intensified in Buffalo Bill's Wild West, and Cody staged scenes, such as the attack on the settler's cabin, as "living history."

For all that, prominent critics have defended Buffalo Bill's Wild West as a place where indigenous performers preserved some degree of autonomy and cultural identity. Vine Deloria Jr. claims that American Indians in Cody's show "were able to observe American Society and draw their own conclusions." In this way, he adds, Buffalo Bill's Wild West "was worth more than every school built by the government on any of the reservations."[30] Louis Warren also argues for the educational value of Cody's show, claiming that "the knowledge Indians gained from their tenure with the show offered them at least some hope of protecting themselves from the government."[31]

Regardless of the intentions of Cody and Salsbury, Buffalo Bill's Wild West provided a loose structure that indigenous performers made use of in interesting ways. To some degree, the conflicting cultural impulses embedded in Buffalo Bill's Wild West provided indigenous performers with opportunities to exercise agency. Lucy Maddox points out that many white Americans first encountered indigenous people "through the medium of performance, and for many indigenous people, the only way of representing themselves to white Americans was through performance."[32] As such, show Indians had a certain freedom in choosing how to represent themselves. In the arena, the (mostly) white audience learned about "authentic" Indian dress and behavior from the indigenous performers themselves. These performers could then, as Joy Kasson puts it, "enjoy a joke when Sioux performed Omaha dances, or understand a subversive monologue when Kicking Bear recited his deeds in Lakota."[33] The degree of this subversion may have been limited, but the potential for these performers to author some aspects of their performance should not be underestimated. Linda McNenly argues against reading these performances as simply "a coproduction or a blending of two representations to produce a hybrid expression." Indigenous performers, she argues, were afforded the space to produce "two parallel representations."

A show Indian performing as a warrior could generate "the production of the savage warrior, and personal meanings of warrior identity."[34]

For child performers, negotiating these questions of agency and identity could be especially tricky. Having grown up on Indian reservations or with the show itself, many of these children may have had little to no exposure to their tribe's traditional culture. If his show biography is truthful, Johnny Burke No Neck offers an extreme example. Within a few short months, he would have gone from seeing his family wiped out by the United States Army to touring with a new family of show Indians, recreating scenes of Indian defeat and American conquest. Watching those around him, both the indigenous men dressed up as warriors for sham battles and the women peddling Sioux crafts to curious visitors, Burke learned to entertain the show's visitors, providing the cultural authenticity they clearly hankered for by mimicking the massacre he had miraculously survived.

For Johnny and his peers, performing the frontier involved imitating performances they saw around them, both on the stage and in the camp. Georg Simmel defines imitation "as the child of thought and thoughtlessness," claiming the act of imitation denies individuality, transferring "not only the demand for creative activity, but also the responsibility for the action from ourselves to another."[35] For Simmel, this makes social life a "battleground" between the individual's desire to create or conform. Prompted to imitate authentic "Indianness," the young indigenous performers in Buffalo Bill's Wild West grew up on this battleground. With varying degrees of purposefulness, these performers helped the audience imagine a generation of indigenous people read neither as threats to civilization nor as victims of the white man's brutality. Instead, they were understood as happy recipients of civilizing generosity. Their playful exploits worked alongside the phony battles in the arena to bolster narratives of white American conquest and Indian assimilation.

Anthropological inquiries into the Wild West's "authentic" Indian village prompted, promoted, and shaped these acts of mimicry. In turn, these performances did more than entertain curiosity seekers with visions of day-to-day life on the plains. They offered nuanced constructions and explorations of the assimilated (and conquered). Johnny Burke No Neck may have been a young warrior in training, but this training

was presented as mere play, signifying that warlike braves could be reha-
bilitated and the next generation of Indians would be absorbed by white
American civilization. In 1894, when a *New York Recorder* reporter visited
Buffalo Bill's Wild West at Ambrose Park, such reassurances were critical. While the Indian Wars were coming to a close, Wounded Knee was
still a recent memory, and the notion that white America had successfully
conquered the hostile "red man" was a new one. The playful exploits of
Johnny Burke No Neck and Lizzy Spotted Tail played as important a role
as the battles staged nightly in the Wild West arena in positing narratives
of white American conquest and Indian rehabilitation.

In fact, reporters visiting Buffalo Bill's Wild West paid special attention to indigenous children who bucked this assimilationist trend and
whose misbehavior suggested some degree of real threat. In 1900, a reporter visited the show, and his *Times Democrat* account is dominated by
an account of Little Willie, described as the "only real bad, bloodthirsty
Indian" the reporter came across: "Little Willie has a precocious appetite
for the gore of the palefaces, and, if he wasn't watched pretty closely,
would undoubtedly try his hand at scalping when he got the chance." At
eight years old, Willie "can swear like a pirate and doesn't hesitate to do
so when he is on the warpath," and he "is usually on the warpath." The
reporter singles out an incident when Willie, after being teased by a cowboy from the show, "calmly proceeded to sharpen a small penknife on a
stone and then went for that cowboy with the evident intention of cutting
his heart out." On another occasion, Willie watched as two other Indian
children gave a "little white boy a ride." Noting the generous nature of
the show Indians who gave this young boy a ride, the reporter describes
Little Willie's reaction: a "fierce hatred for the paleface kid filled his
heart. He took up the trail . . . with the evident purpose of watching
his opportunity to lift a golden-haired scalp when he got close enough."
Fortunately, the reader is reassured, a "friendly chief" intervened before
said scalp could be taken, explaining to the reporter that "Little Willie
heap bad boy."[36]

Surely, there is a playful side to Little Willie's misdeeds. As the reporter describes it, he partakes of the kind of antics that Mark Twain's
Tom Sawyer and other characters from "bad boy" literature indulge
in, antics that are hallmarks of that genre. Of course, "playing Indian"

meant something different for Tom Sawyer than it did for Little Willie. Threatening to break from the script of the assimilated next-generation Indian, Little Willie's "fierce hatred for the paleface" threatens the (newly) established social order, and his proclivity for scalping presents as anything but harmless. In Little Willie, the *Times Democrat* reporter describes a different kind of Indian, one who promises hostile resistance rather than peaceful assimilation. In this account, the intervention of the chief and the generous cooperation of the other indigenous children reassure the reader that this "bad" Indian is an exception rather than the norm. Still, this exception was a dangerous one, a potential threat to the social order and narratives of successful Indian assimilation.

ISSUES OF AGENCY

As these interactions and examples suggest, public fascination with the young show Indians in Buffalo Bill's Wild West reveals more than a desire for entertainment. We know little about how the show's young performers understood the frontier narratives surrounding Buffalo Bill's Wild West. Rehearsing sham battles in the arena or day-to-day life "on the plains" in the Indian village, young indigenous performers reproduced cultural scenes with which they likely had little direct experience. As such, these performers accessed history as much through revival as recollection. In her work on cultural revivals such as renaissance fairs, Wendy Griswold argues that "archive and activity, or what is saved and what is done, are two aspects of the same cultural system."[37] In reviving culture, the performer has access to both archive and activity, so that unlike the older generations of show Indians, these child performers were able to perform history as personal while reflecting on the personal as a form of conscious imitation. This potentially enabled younger performers to use performance to frame and assess their cultural identity, both in the past and the present, with heightened levels of awareness.

Many questions remain about the young performers in Buffalo Bill's Wild West, specifically the young show Indians. How did they perceive the complex rigors of these performances? How much protection and agency did the show really facilitate? Unfortunately, child performers in Cody's show left behind few records of their experiences, and the accounts we have cast little light on the rigors of negotiating identity through performance. Still, the evidence suggests that, at the very least, these performers were aware at a very young age how "Indian culture" was processed and presented through mass culture.

Rose Nelson was one of the show's prominent young show Indians. She was the daughter of Jenny Lone Wolf Nelson and John Nelson, the infamous "squaw man" who enjoyed a long tenure with Buffalo Bill's Wild West. *Squaw man* was a nasty term invoked to disparage a white man who had married an indigenous woman. In Buffalo Bill's Wild West, however, squaw men enjoyed an elevated status that was carefully cultivated by the show's publicists. Linked to upper-class nobility, Louis Warren argues, these squaw men avoided being perceived as mixed bloods or half-breeds. At the same time, they stood in contrast to Buffalo Bill and other "pure-bloods," helping to emphasize the superiority of the white male hero.[38]

For most of the show's tenure, the squaw men in Buffalo Bill's Wild West remained a popular attraction, none more so than John Nelson. Little Rose also became a fan favorite. In 1887, when she was seven, she and her family traveled with the show to England, where her brash behavior—including failing to curtsy for Queen Victoria and slapping the Prince of Wales—made her a darling with the British press. Buffalo Bill christened her Princess Blue Waters, in honor of her Atlantic crossing, and photographers prized her image. In cabinet cards sold at the show, Rose was billed as the "Girl-pet of the Sioux." Carefully groomed and dressed in native costume, she is presented as every bit the Indian princess, signifying her distinctive status as a union of the "savage" and civilized (fig. 10).[39]

This image stands in stark contrast to candid shots of indigenous children from Buffalo Bill's Wild West. In one undated photo, the children are still dressed to reflect the highly gendered nature of Indian performance, with the girls clad in simple dresses and the boys appearing as young warriors in feathered headdresses (fig. 11). Intriguingly, one child at the bottom right of this group disrupts the unity of the image. Dressed in a beaded vest, she stares at the viewer, brandishing a drum in one hand and a tiny (toy?) revolver in the other. Did she choose this pose herself? Was she, like the others, dressed this way for effect?[40]

These questions remain unanswerable. Warren points out that in off-stage photographs indigenous performers "frequently put on cowboy gear," gear that many of them had donned when working for livestock ranchers on the Great Plains.[41] The children in this group photo may have chosen to dress this way. More likely, parents or other adults dressed them; Luther Standing Bear describes the great pleasure others took in dressing his young son for the arena.[42] Perhaps the young girl brandished the gun in imitation of performers she saw, but there is no way to be sure.

In at least one instance, Cody and his partners consciously blended the tropes of cowboy and Indian for performance. Bennie Irving was the son of translator "Bronco" Bill Irving and his Sioux wife, Ella Bissonett. Like Rose Nelson, he was part of one of the show's celebrated squaw families, and like Rose, he was singled out for exhibition on his own. Photographed in full cowboy regalia, pistol tucked into his waist band and lasso in hand, Bennie performed in the arena during the show's 1890 tour of Europe and was billed as "the smallest cowboy in the world" (fig. 12).[43]

The blurring of racial lines was not unusual in Buffalo Bill's Wild West, certainly not for Cody's show Indians. They routinely stood in for other groups, such as the (similarly degraded) Chinese in the show's 1901 depictions of scenes from the Boxer Rebellion. In some cases, indigenous performers appeared in the ring as cowboys. More interestingly, Warren suggests Rose Nelson and her siblings may have, at times, played white children in Buffalo Bill's Wild West's climactic scene, the attack on the settler's cabin.[44] This kind of flexibility, helping Rose Nelson move through a handful of identities—including a typical child in the Indian village, the Indian princess, "girl-pet of the Sioux," and a white pioneer child—likely influenced Nelson's understanding of how performance shaped identity and, more importantly, how such performance could be employed to facilitate agency.

For indigenous child performers, that agency was clearly limited. At the same time, younger performers proved more adept than previous generations at navigating the commercialization of their identities. Rose, for her part, went on to study art and music at the Franklin Institute and appeared in several Hollywood movies. She, like other Indian performers, had little control over her image and did not prosper from the sale of cabinet cards at or around Buffalo Bill's Wild West. As an adult, though,

Nelson clearly became capable of managing—and profiting from—her performed self.[45]

Luther Standing Bear, who toured with the show as a translator in 1903, developed a nuanced perspective on the opportunities—and lack thereof—offered by the life of a show Indian. Standing Bear recorded his insights in five books, starting with *My People the Sioux* (1928). At eleven, then named Plenty Kill, he entered the Carlisle School, quickly proving to be a bright student. Still, if Standing Bear excelled at his studies and even followed the assimilationist logic undergirding Carlisle's educational philosophy, his recollections of those days suggest little ignorance about the school's attempts to transform his identity. After getting his hair cut, Standing Bear describes feeling "that I was no more an Indian, but would be an imitation of a white man." He goes on to note, "We are still imitations of white men, and the white men are imitations of the Americans."[46] The perception that late-nineteenth-century notions of racial and national identity were questions of performance is a keen one, and certainly Standing Bear and his peers at the Carlisle School had plenty of opportunities to form such perceptions.

Standing Bear had more opportunities than most. In 1883, at seventeen, he was sent to work at the Wanamaker Department Store in Philadelphia; like other model students, he was meant to exemplify how Indians could be properly assimilated by fully embracing the influence of white civilization. While in the city, Standing Bear saw Sitting Bull on a lecture tour. He recalls that Sitting Bull gave a thoughtful speech of reconciliation, declaring that "there is no use fighting any more." In translation, the speech became a retelling of the battle at Little Bighorn, with Sitting Bull falsely described as the man who killed Custer. "He told so many lies that I had to smile," Standing Bear remembers of the translator. A few weeks later, he saw another troupe of Sioux Indians in the city. The show consisted of a group of men with their wives and children. They had no interpreter and "were shown in a little side-show, on a small stage." As he watches, Standing Bear notes the "children had a little box down in front of the stage into which people would drop coins. Then the Indians would shake hands with them." (185–88).

Unlike the men of his father's generation, Standing Bear had been exposed at an early age to various kinds of indigenous performance, from his time at Carlisle to his brief stint with Buffalo Bill's Wild West. His insight that racial and national identities are, in their essence, sites of contested meanings, and that these meanings are mediated largely through both formal and informal performance, likely influenced his decision to exhibit his children for profit and, later, become an author and an actor in several Hollywood films.

Though Standing Bear did not join Buffalo Bill's Wild West until he was an adult, his early experiences likely shaped his approach to indigenous performance. When his wife gave birth to a daughter during Buffalo Bill's Wild West's stay in England, Standing Bear agreed to exhibit the infant in the sideshow. "It was a great drawing card for the show," Standing Bear reports, noting that "before she was twenty-four hours old she was making more money than my wife and I together." Standing Bear's son also traveled with Buffalo Bill's Wild West as a child. As his father describes it, the boy enjoyed standing outside the tepee, where "the English-speaking people would crowd around to shake his hand and give him money" (266).

In later years, the show's roster of young performers became increasingly diverse. As noted in chapter 3, the 1893 rebranding of the show as Buffalo Bill's Wild West and the Congress of the Rough Riders of the World reflected a more internationally themed program, and a more international cast of performers accompanied the name change. How the young performers from different backgrounds interacted with one another largely remains a tantalizing mystery. Surviving accounts offer glimpses of these interactions—such as the newspaper account cited earlier in which young show Indians were described attempting to ride in the "Cossack style." A pair of children's books written by George Hamid Jr. provides another glimpse into the distinctive youth cultures developed in Cody's show.

George Hamid Sr. enjoyed a prosperous career as an entertainer and circus owner, cofounding the Hamid-Morton Circus and later operating Atlantic City's famous Steel Pier for nearly three decades. Before that, though, he was a child performer in Buffalo Bill's Wild West. Born in Lebanon, Hamid joined the show in France when he was nine years old in 1906, and he came to America as a member of the cast a year later. Hamid stayed with Cody until Buffalo Bill's Wild West and the Congress

of the Rough Riders of the World folded abruptly in 1913. Later, his son
wrote two children's books about his father's life as a performer, *Circus*
and *Boy Acrobat*. Both published in 1950, the books are variations of the
same story with some notable differences. Both books focus extensively
on Hamid's time with Cody, helping to flesh out the experiences of the
young performers featured in the show.[47]

From his initial encounter with Cody's show in Marseilles, Hamid's
alienation as a cultural outsider stands out. Wandering in search of
the show, Hamid and his two cousins are struck by the spectacle of the
parade, which featured "prancing horses such as they had never seen"
and "strange creatures in costumes—Indians and cowboys!" Riding "the
most beautiful horse in the world," Buffalo Bill himself appears, looking
"as if he were a prophet straight from the Bible."[48] Excited to join up with
the show, Hamid and his cousins find it difficult to fend for themselves
at first. They do not speak any English and have no one to interpret for
them. Desperately hungry, they miss the bell for dinner on their first
night in camp and the next morning are trampled by the bigger performers trying to get food, managing "go get hold of a few pieces of
bread before everything was gone" (74).

Hamid credits Annie Oakley for coming to his rescue. In Oakley, the
boys find "the first real smile of friendliness since leaving home" (75).
Hamid labels Oakley their fairy godmother, describing how "that first
night and a hundred times after," she fed the boys "bits saved from their
own meal" (76). Later on, she teaches him to read and write in English.
Oakley's kindness stands in stark contrast to the isolation and intimida-
tion Hamid describes in navigating the world of Cody's show as a young
person from a different culture. Indeed, other than Oakley's assistance,
Hamid paints the camp as a place where one fends for oneself. This is
not a tight-knit community in which individuals from different cultures
learn to live together; rather, it is a place where even a nine-year-old child
prospers, or fails to prosper, as an individual.

Beyond this initial sense of alienation, the book's description of the
violence that defined life in the show is eye-opening. *Boy Acrobat* includes
several pages describing weekly boxing matches held for members of
the cast. Every Sunday a makeshift boxing ring was set up after church.
This was a space for performers and workers to "satisfy all grudges and

entertain everyone in the process," and the spectators included Oakley and Buffalo Bill (78). On their first Sunday, Hamid enjoys watching the fights until he is horrified to discover he will fight George Simon, one of his cousins. Against their will, the two boys are goaded into battle, and Hamid eventually wrestles his cousin to submission, reporting that he "didn't feel any too happy about winning" (81). After this, Hamid and his cousin become regular combatants at the Sunday dustups, though they never again had to fight one another. The casual violence seems surprising in a book written for children, but it reinforces the idea that savage play was good for boys, while providing a more contentious vision of life in Buffalo Bill's camp than the playful newspaper accounts of domestic life in the Indian village.

In *Circus*, these weekly fights are depicted in even more graphic detail. After performing as an acrobat for three years, Hamid earned Buffalo Bill's trust and was chosen to ride a horse in the Far East line. Hamid describes how each performance began with riders navigating the maze, which he describes as "a spectacular stunt of riders racing in opposite directions in concentric circles," a feat so dangerous, he reports, the performers called it the "Ride of Death." On his first day of practice as a rider, Hamid reports being given "a cowboy suit and a horse."[49] Taunted by a young Japanese performer who was also dressed up in cowboy gear, George fumes until he can get his revenge, an opportunity that comes in the boxing ring the following Sunday.

The encounter Hamid describes is bloody and brutal. "The Jap," as Hamid describes the other boy, attacks first, gouging and biting until Hamid wriggles away. After getting on top of his opponent, Hamid describes how "I smashed my fist into his face" and kept "pounding my fists into the face that had laughed at me, into the mouth that had bitten me." Afterwards, the Japanese boy is "bloody, sobbing only half conscious," and Hamid reports being warmed by a "great thrill" after Buffalo Bill calls him a "good boy." At dinner that night, Hamid remembers getting "a fairly large portion of food without my fighting for it. "This," he reflects, "was really being a hero!" (42). In Hamid's telling, the bloody pummeling of the boy stands out as an act of heroism, one singled out for commendation by the ultimate frontier hero himself, Buffalo Bill. Regardless of the two books' veracity, it's notable how much time Hamid devotes to describing these violent confrontations in the ring. His brutal beating of the Japanese boy might deviate from the show's master narrative of white conquest, but it suggests that boy culture at the show valorized the most savage types of "play," condoning the violent subjugation of the other and lionizing the hero who could pummel his opponent into submission.

BLURRING THE LINE BETWEEN
PERFORMER AND AUDIENCE

Beyond these rare glimpses, it is impossible to know for certain how the show's varied child performers viewed their lives in the camp or perceived their roles as performers. The few records left behind certainly disrupt the notion of cultural archiving as purely a top-down process. If Buffalo Bill's Wild West presented a cohesive and persistent narrative of white civilization triumphing over savagery, the interactions of child performers in and around the show suggest a more fractured and less monolithic set of interpretations. In practice, they more closely resemble Robin Bernstein's conception of the repertoire. As Bernstein defines it, "a repertoire is by definition in constant flux, always being re-made. These re-formations occur with the exercise of agency as well as accidentally, on a small scale, through authored and unauthored elements."[50]

By its very nature, Buffalo Bill's Wild West's dominant narrative of white American progress was unauthored, filtered through the broad dimensions of Cody's life story. That story lived not only in performances of Buffalo Bill's Wild West, the range and scope of which underwent significant changes over the years, or even solely through Cody's telling. Manifest in countless other literary productions, Wild West shows, toys, promotional materials, and newspaper accounts, this frontier narrative functioned, as Bernstein describes the repertoire, as "a formation of influence and cross-influence that is internally contentious and surprisingly tightly woven without ever becoming unified" (14). Imagined through an array of diffuse cultural genres, Buffalo Bill's Wild West allowed various social actors to refract and reform this frontier narrative. In fact, the show relied on this flexibility, allowing actors and audience to tap into the collective fantasy Eric Lott describes as the root appeal of all influential popular culture.

CHILDREN, SPECTACLE, AND AGENCY

The young performers in Buffalo Bill's Wild West grew up keenly aware of their role in this process. As the reporting of Little Willie's antics suggest, their ability to openly challenge the show's scripted realities was limited. Nonetheless, indigenous children were a source of fascination for white spectators, and, as we see from Rose Nelson and Luther Standing Bear, some young performers found opportunities to manipulate their performances to suit their own needs. According to Rose Nelson's granddaughter, Marirose Nelson, Rose fully understood that "the show's narrative was bogus" but used it as a vehicle for self-empowerment; "she enjoyed having people treat her as a peer and letting them know she felt she was a peer if not more."[51] Rose used that vehicle to her advantage and later appeared in several Hollywood movies. Most of the young performers in Buffalo Bill's Wild West did not enjoy the same fame, but many did find openings to exercise agency within the show's master narrative.

These opportunities often came outside the arena, where curiosity seekers joined in the performance. Again, it was in the camp and the streets around it that the greatest opportunities for mingling existed; it was here where children of all classes could seek out their heroes without paying the price of admission for the show. Certainly, many young boys came to Cody's Wild West show to visit their hero. As the *New York Sun* declared in 1894, Buffalo Bill's Wild West had a hypnotic effect on the "small boy" who "wakes up the family by uttering weird coyote yells in his sleep. He lassoes the bedpost and the family cat, and fires a toy pistol at imaginary objects while riding the back fence at full speed." Much like the "gallery gods" who thronged to theatrical performances put on by Buffalo Bill's Combination, the boys waited patiently for Cody's arrival in the arena, and when he arrived, "how they did yell!"[52]

The rapturous enthusiasm of the boys spilled out of the arena into city streets, at times becoming a public nuisance. One reporter concluded that Indian wariness of the white man "is readily understood, after witnessing how his life was made miserable all day yesterday by the juveniles of Boston." These young acolytes of Cody "invaded the tents of the show almost as thickly as ants in a cracker barrel," disturbing the performers at all hours, while "keeping up a discordant chorus of wild war whoops, that were probably all the more exasperating for their fidelity to nature."[53]

Notably, this fidelity to nature marks the boys as even more savage than the indigenous occupants of the village. Accessing their inner savage, as Hall described it, the boys "play Indian" better than the Indians themselves. In both cases—the Indians performing peaceful domesticity and the white boys performing the primitive—social expectations are simultaneously inverted and confirmed.

These intrusions represent more than the rambunctious misdeeds of boys being boys, even if that is exactly how the reporters describing these scenes attempted to frame them. All told, the stories of these children playing, acting, and performing in the myriad ways facilitated by Buffalo Bill's Wild West suggest a more nuanced estimation of American identity formation in the late nineteenth and early twentieth centuries than the show is typically given credit for. Analyzing one performance with an audience of four thousand New York–area orphans, Kathryn White describes how the child spectators delighted at the unscripted performance of "an Indian child who snatched a cartridge off of the ground and proceeded to hurl it at his elders." In this moment, she argues, the child spectators identified "with someone with whom they shared a common culture, that of childhood and its values," and through that identification, "the children experienced the liminal space between non-shared culture."[54]

It is uncertain to what degree the boy and his audience drew on a "common culture" of childhood, but White's analysis of this moment is instructive. Intentionally or not, the young performer disrupted the show's script, rejecting, to some degree, the adult authority sanctioning it. Reviewing a different performance, a *New York Times* reporter takes note of a little girl "so restless and active that she is never still." In the area, "she darts daringly between the feet of the moving horses, races with flying feet where she ought not to go, and laughs derisively at the cries and scoldings of her mother."[55] Such instances, White suggests, reveal child performers challenging adult authority. Performer and spectator alike can be seen working through Buffalo Bill's Wild West's scripted realities to offer competing visions of the late-nineteenth-century American frontier myth. Returning to Simmel's metaphor of social life as a "battleground" between creativity and conformity, these moments facilitated autonomy and self-making, as young performers channeled individual performance in ways that transcended imitation and created opportunities for self-expression.

At the same time, Cody and his partners set up Buffalo Bill's Wild West in a way that actually—if incidentally—supported such moments. The literature produced to promote the show, both the official programs and the editorials placed in newspapers, emphasize the importance of educating young audience members through exposure to the vanishing frontier. What sets Buffalo Bill's Wild West apart, an 1899 program boasts, is that it is "actually a part of the romantic past it perpetuates, and vitalized by the presence of some of the most noted makers of the frontier history they illustrate." Ultimately, "what the children see at Buffalo Bill's Wild West they will enjoy, appreciate, understand, and remember. What parents see there they will wish their children taught."[56] The power of witnessing or experiencing is critical for this process. For the child spectators of Buffalo Bill's Wild West, learning took place through witnessing, and the educational value of the show was transmitted through the visceral experience of living history.

These experiences played out both in the formal setting of the arena and the informal world of the Indian village. The show's child spectators fawned over heroes like Cody, Baker, or Oakley; mixed with performers in the Indian village around the show; and participated in a real-life embodiment of the romantic frontier they had read about in newspapers and storybooks. Winston Roche was born in 1898 and saw the Wild West show as a small boy. "We were part of the fight," he recalled with hushed reverence in a TV interview many years later. "We were living our fantasies, our imagination. Living it out was part of the show. It was wonderful."[57]

Parker (Paddy) McGoff expresses similar feelings in a 1945 reminiscence of visiting the show as boy. He recalls "what a thrill it was for us youngsters to strut along the sidewalks in the wake of such famous people as that great hunter and army scout, Buffalo Bill Cody, the crack rifle shots Annie Oakley and Johnny Baker," remembering also his efforts to "strive manfully to imitate the walk of fun-seeking cowboys as they head for McCormick's Wild West Hotel up on 3rd Avenue." McGoff also remembers the kind of unscripted play facilitated by the show's presence in Brooklyn, with the performers camped out along the city streets. "Later on, as the older folks were doing a bit of trading with show folks," McGoff and his friends "mingled with and made friends with the younger occupants of the show grounds and in no time at all we had two of the Arab boys joining us in our games of pah (leapfrog)."[58]

Unfortunately, much of the play McGoff describes fails to appear in records of Buffalo Bill's Wild West. The accounts that remain suggest child spectators of Buffalo Bill's Wild West had ample opportunity to structure their own meaning from the show's frontier narratives. As Bernstein points out, children are not passive recipients of these kinds of cultural narratives: "Rather, children expertly field the co-scripts of narratives and material culture and then collectively forge a third prompt: play itself." Through this kind of play, cultural narratives are constantly reworked and "children collectively exercise agency."[59]

At the same time, these boyhood recollections stress the critical role of memory in the type of history "made" by Cody and Buffalo Bill's Wild West. They emphasize that, despite the potential of Wild West performance to facilitate agency, the act of memory often reinforced familiar tropes of masculinity, casting the show's frontier repertoire as a space where impressionable boys aspired to the ideal manhood exemplified by cowboys and Indian scouts. Much as Cody and his fellow performers kindled their own memories of frontier living through performance, Buffalo Bill's Wild West manufactured myriad opportunities for men to engage in a similar type of nostalgia.

Mark Twain saw the show twice in 1884 and, as noted earlier, confessed that he enjoyed it immensely. Twain commended the show for its authenticity, and in an 1885 letter to Cody he connects that authenticity to memories of boyhood, noting that the feelings the show stirred in him "were identical with those wrought upon [him] . . . a long time ago by the same spectacles of the frontier."[60] As it did for Twain, the space of boyhood became vital for much of Cody's audience in nurturing a distinctive vision of frontier history. Through memories of childhood, white men like Roche and McGoff not only sustained the frontier as a place where history becomes myth but also where mythmaking is bound inextricably to memory, nostalgia, and willful self-fashioning.

Like the show's young indigenous performers, spectators like Roche and McGoff effectively *became* part of the history they were witnessing.

Through their visceral connection with Buffalo Bill's Wild West and through the opportunities to interact with the histories suggested by Cody and the other performers, these children revived stories of the past and gave shape to visions of the future. "America is making history faster than any country in the world," boasts an 1891 program for the show.[61] The idea of childhood and, in particular, the figure of the boy, was a crucial vehicle for processing and packaging that history. Writing about the early days of the Child Study movement, Sally Shuttleworth argues that nineteenth-century child "experts" perceived children in exactly this way. "With its potentiality waiting to be unfurled, the child becomes in this view an embodiment both of all past history and an expression of future possibility."[62]

In Frederick Jackson Turner's reading of the frontier, America was formed through a similar dialectic, with the European settler encountering the frontier in order to engender the distinctive character of the American. As the child was for Hall and others, Turner's frontier served as an embodiment both of the past and the future. For Hall and Turner alike, American progress worked through narratives of growth and development, and as we have seen, this theme dominated frontier literature in the nineteenth century, from the genteel Boy Book to blood-and-thunder stories of the West. In its central narrative, Buffalo Bill's Wild West reformulated Turner's frontier thesis as a timeless space of and for boyhood, where dominant notions of white American masculinity are produced and reproduced through frontier conquest. Certainly, the show appealed to audience members through its triumphant framing of westward expansion as a symbol of national character. At the same time, the frontier narratives embodied in Buffalo Bill's Wild West drew their strength from flexibility as well as familiarity.

The varied actions of the child performers in and around the show reveal that flexibility at work, proving its dominant narratives to be simultaneously promoted and contested. Featured performers like Baker and Oakley framed the space of the frontier as a youth space. Girl sharpshooters like Oakley demonstrated a subversive strain, even as the precisely managed nature of her performances worked to control that strain. The cultural repertoire of Buffalo Bill's Wild West was also defined by a diverse international cast, most notably a roster of young show

Indians, including Rose Nelson and Johnny Burke No Neck, both in the arena and in the more anarchic performances in the Indian village. In all these guises, young performers highlighted Buffalo Bill's Wild West as a space where the self could be fashioned through repeated rehearsal of a heavily fictionalized history. "The Greatest thing Buffalo Bill ever did," Chauncey Thomas extolled on the occasion of Cody's 1917 passing, "was to give a new game to the children of the world."[63] Buffalo Bill's Wild West established the framework for that game, a vital space where generations of child performers and spectators imagined the frontier in ways both expected and unexpected, shaping the scope and range of the frontier narratives constructed by Cody and his peers well through the early decades of the twentieth century and beyond.

5

WORK AND PLAY
Building Character on the Imagined Frontier

William Cody died January 10, 1917, twenty-four years after Frederick Jackson Turner published his frontier theory. In those years, that theory had completed its dramatic transformation from history into myth. Subsumed in Theodore Roosevelt's narrative of how the West was won, the story of the frontier became the creation myth of an American nation with broadening global ambitions. When Cody passed, the Indian Wars were over, and Americans watched uneasily as World War I unfolded across the Atlantic. By the time Cody was laid to rest in June on Lookout Mountain in Colorado, the nation had officially entered the war.

While America's dominant frontier narrative became more influential in the early decades of the twentieth century, the performance of that narrative became increasingly multifaceted, adapting to new modes and forms. By 1917, Wild West shows were dwindling in popularity. Financial necessity dictated that Buffalo Bill perform up until his dying days, but the distinctive brand of frontier performance Cody and his partners had invented felt antiquated rather than cutting edge in those final years. By midcentury, the dusty arena of Buffalo Bill's Wild West would be replaced by the bright lights of the silver screen, and by the time of Cody's death this process was well underway.

The early twentieth century gave birth to a slightly different type of frontier hero as well, as evidenced by Owen Wister's novel *The Virginian*, published in 1902. Richard Etulain argues that the novel's appeal lay largely in its ability to tap into a broad cultural anxiety that the open range had all been fenced in and the "wild" West thoroughly domesticated. *The Virginian*, Etulain observes, more than any other novel, "represented a break from nineteenth century stories of an open, endless frontier." For Wister, and for many other novelists and filmmakers that

159

followed him, "the magic frontier had disappeared over the horizon."[1] An immediate blockbuster, *The Virginian* sold over one hundred thousand copies in three months and became a bestseller for years to come, setting the stage for decades of frontier films and TV shows, all centered on the type of solitary white masculine hero so neatly embodied by John Wayne.

This figure, from Teddy Roosevelt to Ronald Reagan, or the Virginian to John Wayne, dominates twentieth-century frontier narratives. As radio and film started to replace literature, and the buckskin-clad Indian scout of the nineteenth century was obscured by the solitary cowboy of the twentieth century, the Western became synonymous with an amped-up form of hypermasculinity. In the twentieth-century Western, Jane Tompkins argues, everything else recedes to the background as the Western male hero dominates the frame. In the introduction to *West of Everything*, Tompkins marvels that the twentieth-century Western features hardly any significant Indian characters. No longer about "the encounter between civilization and the frontier," Tompkins concludes, this new Western is "about men's fear of losing their mastery, and hence identity, both of which the Western tirelessly reinvents."[2]

Of course, these fears had always been integral to the Western, from Natty Bumppo to Buffalo Bill, hypermasculine figures in their own right who paved the way for the work of Wister and Wayne. Noting that the Virginian is a direct descendent of Natty Bumppo, Christine Bold argues that Wister's hero proves more adaptable than Cooper's, ultimately managing to create "harmony out of his opposing inclinations to savagery and civilization."[3] In the late nineteenth century, Buffalo Bill's Wild West managed a similar effect, taming the wild frontier through performance. In the twentieth century, despite changes to the Western's medium and the broader culture surrounding it, the magic frontier did not disappear. Rather, like the nation itself, it simply redrew its borders. The relationship between frontier narratives and American boyhood remained potent, interacting in diverse and interesting ways in the new century's early decades.

Buffalo Bill did not disappear either, even after Cody's death in 1917. Rather, he continued to play a pivotal role in this relationship, finding new venues where the cherished wildness of the imagined frontier could be usefully balanced against encroaching visions of modernity. The themes of performance and play, already present in nineteenth-century frontier narratives, became increasingly prominent in early-twentieth-century cultures of American boyhood, while the specter of juvenile delinquency, looming in responses to the nineteenth-century dime novel and Mark Twain's *Adventures of Huckleberry Finn* alike, became an increasingly pressing social concern. This chapter traces these themes in the rise of character-building organizations such as the Boy Scouts of America (BSA) and in the way the dominant frontier narrative offered by Buffalo Bill's Wild West influenced the world of children's—notably boy's—toys. These two distinct strands converged in intriguing ways. For instance, the rifle, which had played such a prominent role in Buffalo Bill's Wild West, became a fixture both as a children's toy and a vehicle for character-building work with boys.

As he did throughout his career, Cody changed with the changing times; in fact, Cody was at the forefront of these changes. The closing years of the nineteenth century and the first decades of the twentieth saw Buffalo Bill move away from his role as Indian-killing scout and into the role of father figure. While the allure of Buffalo Bill remained as powerful as ever for boys, Cody was fully embraced as friend of and benefactor for the nation's "poor boys." In fact, as the friend of all American children and an idealized patriot, Cody presented himself less as a hard-edged killer and more as an affable ambassador for the frontier experience. Cody pitched this persona to American boys in several ways, most obviously through his show and its celebration of the American cowboy but also through his promotion of the frontier experience as a form of boy work and his rebranding of the frontier experience as a frame for children's play.

BUFFALO BILL, BOY WORKER

Throughout the first half of the twentieth century, organizational boy work molded the character of American children, shaping the boys of (largely) eastern middle-class families into hopeful visions of American manhood. The impetus to bring the boy back to nature helped spur the growth of youth scouting and camping in America, and the belief in the frontier as a space for shaping boys into men played a pivotal role in this movement, one that crystalized with the introduction of the Boy Scouts of America in 1910. Former Wild West cowboy Harry Webb boldly claimed that Cody "was instrumental in organizing the Boy Scouts of America," which is clearly an exaggeration.[4] Still, Cody directly and indirectly played a critical role in the growth of scouting in America, and certainly Buffalo Bill was a popular hero for the first generation of American boy scouts. There is likely more than a kernel of truth in Webb's insistence that boy scouts sent Buffalo Bill "thousands of letters," and that Cody "personally answered every one." What's more, Buffalo Bill's Wild West frequently entertained entire troops of scouts. On one such occasion, Webb recalls, Cody "guested two hundred Canadian Boy Scouts at his tables at one performance and voiced a glowing eulogy to the organization" (27).

By the time of his death in the first decade of the BSA's tenure, Cody had become an almost saintly figure, a silver-haired grandfather figure firmly established as the beloved hero to every American child. When he was buried, every grade school student in Denver was offered "a souvenir flower from the offerings" that made up the funeral bier, a souvenir fitting "to preserve the memory of Buffalo Bill in the minds of the thousands of school children who have made him their hero."[5] Over the previous fifty years, Cody had figured prominently as a hero to American boys and a symbol of the powerful connections between narratives of "civilizing" the frontier and American boyhood, presenting the West as an ideal space for developing white American boys into strong American men. Framing history as performance and entertainment as education, Cody and his Wild West did more than promote the vision of the West as the story of American progress; he framed that progress as a space of and for boyhood (figs. 13 and 14).

Kenneth Kidd identifies two dominant themes that govern varying discourses of American boyhood: boyology, which encompasses organizational boy work, and the feral tale, a host of literatures articulating boyhood through iterations of wildness. Examining popular boyhood literatures of the nineteenth century, Kidd argues that "feral tales for boys preserve and promote the scientific and imaginative conceits of major political projects such as British colonialism, urban American "child saving" and Native American assimilation."[6] Cody's use of the feral tale fits easily into Kidd's list of nineteenth-century projects. As noted previously, Buffalo Bill, whether on stage, page, or in the arena, simultaneously drew out and gave shape to the inner wildness of the American boy, coded as a white boy. As such, the frontier, if no longer viable as a physical place, remained crucial as a vehicle for developing these boys into the right kind of men, serving as a vital incubator for white American progress. The BSA stands out as an exemplar of boyology as Kidd describes it. Since its inception, the BSA has become a household name, but the rich history of American scouting remains more complex than commonly understood—and more deeply connected to American frontier mythology.

In fact, the BSA was far from the only American scouting organization active in the early twentieth century and certainly not the first character-building organization designed to organize and harness the wildness of boys. Born in England and raised in Canada, Ernest Seton was an established nature writer living in Connecticut when he founded the Woodcraft Indians in 1902. When a group of local youngsters repeatedly vandalized Seton's property, destroying his fences and making obscene pictures on his gate, Seton came up with a novel intervention. Rather than report the boys to the police, he issued an open invitation for local boys to spend the weekend camping on his property. Forty-two young boys responded to the call, and under Seton's supervision they spent the weekend playing, swimming, climbing trees, and tracking animals. Seton led the children in play and encouraged them in to participate in self-government, initiating a kind of tribal council.[7]

This distinctive mix between natural, or savage, play and tribal self-regulation was further defined in a series of articles Seton wrote for the *Ladies' Home Journal* under the heading "Ernest Thompson Seton's Boys," in May through November of 1902. Those articles fully articulated Seton's doctrine of Woodcraft, ultimately canonized in Seton's official manual for the Woodcraft Indians, *The Birch-Bark Roll* (1906). By that point, Seton's Woodcraft movement had moved from being a local experiment to a cultural phenomenon. Boy workers across the country followed Seton's examples, forming other "tribes" devoted to the practice of Woodcraft.

As Kent Baxter points out, Seton's Woodcraft Indians represented a response to widely held fears about juvenile delinquency in the early decades of the twentieth century. Seton was quite literal in describing children as savages, both more primitive and less corrupted than adults. In confronting the young vandals, Seton sought to harness their inner savagery rather than suppress it. His thinking was heavily influenced by G. Stanley Hall's theories of adolescence, and the rapid spread of the Woodcraft Indians movement tapped into a powerful cultural anxiety about this newly prominent life stage. At that same time, as Baxter puts it, this anxiety reveals panic about juvenile delinquency to be "more about the fear of adolescence than any actual rise in crime committed by teens."[8] Hall saw adolescence as a time of great peril but also great promise. Falling prey to their baser impulses, young people—especially boys—could become dangerous delinquents. With the proper adult guidance from men like Seton, these young boys could be developed into a new generation of superior American men.

Seton and Daniel Beard—both of whom later joined the BSA leadership—made extensive use of frontier rhetoric in providing this type of guidance. Seton's ideas of Woodcraft were essential in early iterations of the BSA's mandate, and Seton served as cofounder of the organization. Beard, who later replaced Seton in the BSA, initially founded the Sons of Daniel Boone in 1905. Both men used frontier mythology to construct idealized notions of white middle-class boyhood. While Seton sought to have his students emulate Indian life, Beard asked his young charges to model themselves after white pioneer scouts such as Daniel Boone and Kit Carson, and he devised a program in which, as Philip Deloria points out, these young pioneers were pitted in battle "against the Indian characters that Seton has used in organizing his tribes."[9] The two men had starkly different visions of the frontier, but both of their organizations were built on frontier narratives. In each of these narratives, Deloria argues, "campers played the primitive authentic against modernity's inauthenticity in order to devise a better modern" (102).

Beard and Seton had something else in common—a strong connection to William Cody. Seton and Cody were friends, and Beard made no secret of his admiration for Buffalo Bill and the importance of America's most famous scout to the BSA and its origins. This is not surprising, considering the Sons of Daniel Boone almost resembled a Wild West show on occasion. Rival scouting organizations, such as William Randolph

Hearst's American Boy Scouts, also looked to Buffalo Bill as inspiration. All told, the dynamic relationship between Buffalo Bill and the scouts enriches our understanding of how early American scouting organizations adopted nineteenth-century frontier rhetoric into an expansive vision of twentieth-century boyology, one that sought to develop American boys into the right kinds of American men.

The foundational rhetoric of Robert Baden-Powell's Boy Scouts owed a debt to Beard and, more directly, Seton. While Seton promoted his Woodcraft Indians in America, Baden-Powell was building his own scouting organization in Britain. A celebrated British Army officer, he was already an inspirational figure to British youth when he met Seton in 1906. Seton sought Baden-Powell out, eager to share ideas and recruit the former solider to help spread his philosophy of Woodcraft. He gave Baden-Powell a copy of *The Birch-Bark Roll*, and the two agreed to keep in touch and share ideas. Two years later, Baden-Powell published *Scouting for Boys: A Handbook for Instruction in Good Citizenship*. His Boy Scout movement was now well underway, and in 1910, Baden-Powell retired from military service and formed the Boy Scouts Association.[10]

Seton played a leading role in the early years of the BSA, alongside Beard, James West, and William Boyce, a publishing magnate who had been inspired to bring scouting to America after a business trip to London. The BSA's beginnings were chaotic, thanks in no small part to tensions among the group's leaders. Beard and Seton came to their leadership roles as competitors, while West, the BSA's first chief scout executive, clearly felt threatened by Seton. For his part, the Woodcraft founder remained bitter about his initial dealings with Baden-Powell, feeling as if his ideas had been stolen and distorted by the Boy Scout Association leader. This reaction was not unfounded. Baden-Powell's *Scouting for Boys* borrowed liberally from *The Birch-Bark Roll* to establish the Boy Scout system of ranks and merit awards, as well as much of the framework for its oaths and bylaws. Worst of all, Baden-Powell failed to give credit to Seton for his unwitting contributions.

That Buffalo Bill was a pivotal figure in the early days of scouting is not surprising. As we have seen, by the time the BSA was founded in 1910, Buffalo Bill was a pivotal figure in American culture and a fixture in the culture of boyhood. Baden-Powell saw Buffalo Bill's Wild West when it came to England in 1903 and, by some accounts, openly modeled the appearance of his scouts on the flamboyant showman, Buffalo Bill.

Whether fact or fiction, nearly all versions of Buffalo Bill—especially the version Cody and his colleagues promoted—invoked his upbringing in the Wild West, noting that he was educated on the plains and spent more of his childhood in the saddle than in the schoolhouse. Cody's autobiography reports that at ten years of age he worked on wagon trains for the firm of Russell, Majors, and Waddell, and it also offers fantastic claims about Cody serving as a Pony Express rider at fifteen and only slightly less inflated accounts of his time as a scout in the Union Army. In short, as discussed in previous chapters, the story of Buffalo Bill is the story of a boy reared into a successful vision of manhood in the contact zone of the frontier, where primitive and civilized met to form the distinctive American character.

Similar frontier rhetoric informed the early efforts of the BSA. In the first official BSA handbook (1911), then chief scout Seton waxes poetic about the powerful draw of the natural world and the stories of James Fenimore Cooper on young boys. For Seton, the allure of the frontier came from exposure both to the natural world and to the men who thrived in that setting. The modern scout will be "an expert in Life-craft as well as Wood-craft, for he is trained in the things of the heart as well as head and hand." For Seton, a deep love of nature was essential for this training.[11]

In this light, it is easy to see how Buffalo Bill served as a kind of patron saint, a model "boy scout" in the most literal sense, living proof that the kind of training Seton describes produced viable results. Beard was one of many BSA leaders to pay tribute to Buffalo Bill after Cody's passing in 1917. In a newspaper column entitled "The Friend of the American Boy," Beard recalls his early forays into scouting: "When I started the first society of boy scouts and tenderfeet," he reminisces, "I went to Washington by appointment with the President of the United States, to talk the scheme over him with unofficially." Both men lauded Cody as "the greatest scout in our western history," and the one man "whom all the boys love."[12] Indeed, after Cody's death, the BSA launched a prominent fund-raising effort to help establish Buffalo Bill's final resting place on Lookout Mountain in Colorado—calling on each scout to contribute a nickel apiece to the cause.

Frontier mythology inspired many late-nineteenth-century boy experts, who positioned nature as a potent antidote for the deleterious effects of modern urban life with its implied threat of immigrant "masses" from the lower classes. For both Beard and Seton, experiencing nature required the boy, as Deloria puts it, "to journey back in time to a simpler life, and then return, richer but unable to articulate what this pseudomystical encounter had been all about."[13] In this way, Beard and Seton imagined the frontier as a space where white middle-class boys encountered the primitive other, using notions of the primitive—albeit in different ways—to articulate a new model of enlightened manhood.

Cody shared these sentiments to some degree. He provided his own analysis of the problems confronting urban boys in a 1909 article from the *Bisbee Daily Review*, provocatively titled "American Boys Suffering from 'Ingrowing Spunk.'" According to Cody, boys are being coddled, having so much done for them that "the energy they would naturally employ in overcoming external difficulties" is instead directed "internally in polishing up their self-esteem."[14] He picked up on similar themes in a 1912 address to the BSA, noting that the modern boy is overly indulged, isolated from the simple life that breeds ingenuity and utility, all of which, he claims, results in physical and mental weakness.

These comments fall readily in line with the philosophies espoused by Beard and Seton, some of which other BSA leaders came to view with increasing wariness in the second half of the twentieth century. Seton's lingering resentment of Baden-Powell was never assuaged, and Seton was replaced in the BSA leadership in 1915. It was an ugly divorce that represented more than just a clash of personalities. By 1915, the BSA was moving away from the romance of the West and articulating a radically different relationship between man and nature, one steeped in scientific study and classification.[15]

Rather than reject urban society, Seton's successors in the BSA increasingly sought to prepare boys to prosper in an increasingly urban and corporatized American culture. While this shift from Seton and the romance of the American frontier seems to signify a shift away from the kind of frontier masculinity represented by Buffalo Bill, further scrutiny suggests otherwise. Buffalo Bill represented a type of frontier divergent from Seton's in notable ways, one that remained critical to the ideology of the BSA and offered a clear vision of the type of successful American manhood the organization came to embrace in the twentieth century.

While Buffalo Bill was no stranger to frontier romance, he viewed the West as a gateway to the future and not the past. In an address to the BSA, published as a newspaper article in 1912 or 1913, Cody offered a familiar antimodernist critique of urbanity and its discontents—specifically its tendency to render boys weak, nervous, and isolated. Cody praises the early scouting efforts of Beard and Seton, whom he describes as "a little ahead of the time." Praising the BSA, Cody notes that "its keynote is to make manly boys self-reliant." Describing the organization as a critical intervention for modern boys, he explains that it sets out "mentally, physically, and morally, to elevate the boy in *his own* estimation, as well as in the mind and heart of the people at large."[16]

For Cody, the key to frontier character building is self-reliance and self-control, and the importance of self-reliance is how it successfully prepares the individual to live with others and contribute to civil society. As Beard and Seton did, Cody imagined the frontier as a proving ground, a place that can develop the raw materials of boyhood into successful American manhood. For Cody, though, the process is hardly mystical. Rather, the hard lessons of frontier living are practical and clear. In his address to the BSA, Cody prizes the natural world for its ability to facilitate experiential learning and ultimately ties that learning directly to building character, specifically to becoming a "manly boy" and a better citizen. For Cody, the frontier work of lighting fires, reading the stars, sending smoke signals, or learning to track is not romantic indulgence but rather a form of practical training, one that helps a boy become "self-reliant, unselfish, helpful, ever keen to aid and assist others," all of which "makes the world happier and better for his having lived in it."

The process is explicitly communal and patriotic. As Cody explains in an interview in the *Bisbee Daily Review*, "every time an American boy GIVES A SQUARE DEAL he is giving a wave to the star spangled banner. Every time he TELLS THE TRUTH when it would be easier not to he is telling somebody that America is the best ever. And if a boy works hard and is on the level and helps the next fellow and behaves like a good sort generally he's SERVING HIS MOTHER COUNTRY IN JUST THE BEST WAY HE CAN."[17]

In short, the frontier breeds the romantic brand of American manhood embodied by iconic pioneer heroes from Natty Bumppo to Daniel Boone and, of course, Buffalo Bill. In Cody's estimation, though, these pioneer figures are most valuable as civilizing agents. Bumppo, as discussed earlier, was akin to the figure of the "vanishing Indian"—he leads settlers to the open land of the West to establish a civilization he has no place in. Buffalo Bill, by contrast, is both Indian scout and an avatar of civilization. In an address to English and Canadian scouts in Winnipeg on August 23, 1910, Scoutmaster Walker echoes these thoughts, holding up Cody as a role model specifically on this score. Cody is "a fitting example for the young of the land, his career had not been one of dare-devilry, but one of honest pursuit in the civilization of the great western country."[18]

This distinction between adventuring and civilizing can seem fuzzy, but it was critical for Cody, his public image, and his vision of scouting. Cody perceived the frontier as a space of development, a training ground where savage and civilized interacted to produce a more civilized manhood—a purely American vision of manhood. In fact, Cody attempted to launch his own school for this type of training in 1901, drawing up plans for the Cody Military College and International Academy of Rough Riders. An April 19, 1901, news article claims that the college would "train youths in military science, tactics, scouting, cavalry riding and rough riding." Meant to be located in Wyoming's Bighorn Basin, Cody's college promised to immerse students in "all the craft of frontier life." The object would be "to fit the students of the college for practical camp life and to be able to command a company of soldiers."[19] In an interview published in the *San Francisco Examiner*, Cody explains that he intended his students to "learn riding, marksmanship, scouting" and "to take care of himself on the prairie or in the mountains—if the occasion demands."[20]

The college never got off the ground, one of many failed business ventures dreamed up by the ambitious showman, and its rhetoric departs from the changing vision of the twentieth-century BSA in significant ways. Interestingly, Cody targeted a different age demographic than most early scouting movements, pitching his school to older youth and young adults. To some degree, Cody also sought to prepare his students to live and thrive in the wild, something BSA leaders became increasingly uninterested in during the first half of the twentieth century. Finally, Cody's emphasis on military training put him at odds with members of the BSA leadership disinclined to embrace a military model. This, however, demonstrates how deeply embedded Cody's frontier rhetoric was in the ideological foundation of the BSA.

Ultimately, as the BSA expanded and modernized, the organization moved away from the frontier rhetoric of early leaders like Beard and Seton. That rhetoric looked to the magic frontier Etulain describes, imagining this space as a vehicle for helping boys develop into successful men by immersing them in a state of transcendent primitivism. Buffalo Bill, on the other hand, endorsed a more enduring frontier narrative, one that made the frontier a kind of school, where wilderness skills were refined alongside democratic values, preparing boys to succeed in a modernizing society as a new breed of accomplished American man. This narrative remained central to the BSA mandate as it evolved in the second half of the twentieth century and beyond.

TOYS, GUNS, AND BOYS

While Buffalo Bill influenced early American scouting, he had an even more direct and sustained impact on the world of children's play. In fact, Cody's contributions to the American toy box go back to the second half of the nineteenth century. Current scholarship on toys and frontier mythology focuses largely on post–World War II America and the baby boom generation. For instance, Angela Keaton maintains that frontier play dominated postwar America, as the "urge for toy guns in American youth manifested itself in a 'cowboy craze.'"[21] Jay Mechling argues that for "baby boom boys born between 1946 and 1964, having a Daisy BB gun was the least of the socialization into the gun culture of the United States."[22] Citing TV and Hollywood westerns, Mechling describes how "lots of gun play" provided an immersive context for "the emergence of guns as props in the performance of masculinity" (193). This performance of masculinity, of course, was a performance of *white* masculinity, the John Wayne cowboy who, fighting black-hatted villains and vanquishing savage Indians, is a direct descendent of Buffalo Bill's Wild West. In essence, then, the games Mechling remembers playing as a boy had their roots in the games Buffalo Bill's young fans had played fifty years earlier.

"Cowboys and Indians" serves as a useful umbrella term for this kind of play, a game derived directly from reimagining the Indian Wars performed nightly in Buffalo Bill's Wild West. From the show's earliest days, these performances were connected to boys' play. One cigarette card from 1889 shows a rambunctious young boy with a lasso, the caption reading "Just See Me Lassoo The Dude." The flip side of the card contains a two-column list of "The Terrors of America and their doings," which included "Swimming," "Snowballing," and "Playing Buffalo Bill."[23] Similarly, an undated newspaper cartoon captioned "The Champion Lasso-Thrower of the Ward" (fig. 15) features three panels. In the first, a young boy with dark eyes, unruly dark hair, and a derby hat converted into a makeshift Indian headdress throws a lasso around an unsuspecting pedestrian, jerking him backward. In the second panel he prepares to try the same trick on a bicyclist. In the third panel the boy has succeeded but underestimated the power of the cyclist and his machine, as he is now lifted in the air and pulled away behind the bicycle. Like the cigarette card, the cartoon makes light of the child's mischievous play, while at the same time it renders the boy as primitive Indian, unprepared for the powerful reality of modern (read as white and civilized) technology.

In addition to this type of improvised play, Buffalo Bill toys were available for children as well. This fact alone is notable. As Gary Cross points out, the idea that children "needed specially manufactured objects" for play was fairly new before the beginning of the twentieth century.[24] In 1894, the McLoughlin Brothers produced a set of Buffalo Bill cutouts, which included three strips of figures. One strip featured Buffalo Bill on a horse in different poses, all holding or shooting a rifle or pistol; another featured Indian figures in full war dress, riding horses with rifles; and a third featured a team of horses leading the Deadwood coach from Buffalo Bill's Wild West.[25] Cut up and assembled, the figures could stand on their own and be posed however the user chose. The play scripts are clear, however. There are no animals to hunt—and hunting would be poor with a pistol—but there is a coach to protect and Indians for Buffalo Bill to do battle with. The Beinecke Library holds a similar set of cutouts, featuring nineteen Wild West play figures, including "seven Indian figures, six steers, five buffalos, and one cowboy." For these, the play scripts are slightly more ambiguous. The figures might be posed as hunters, and the cowboy is not holding a gun. Dressed for battle, however, the Indians do not look ready to hunt. In two of the cutouts, the Indian figure rides sideways, using the body of the horse for protection as he peers out menacingly at an adversary.[26]

Much like the postwar "cowboy craze" Keaton describes, early-twentieth-century forms of playing Buffalo Bill often involved gun play of a more lethal variety. In the late nineteenth and early twentieth centuries, newspapers reported numerous incidents of boys firing off real guns while playing Buffalo Bill. These accounts were notably less lighthearted than accounts of junior lasso champions, especially when play led to harm. The *New York Commercial Advertiser* reported an instance in which three boys accidentally shot a young lady standing at her window. One of the boys, aged thirteen, had been given new a new air rifle, and he invited two of his friends out to "play Buffalo Bill's Wild West in his yard." After shooting at a target for a while, and inspired by sharpshooters like Buffalo Bill and Annie Oakley, the boy with the gun was urged by his peers to "blow holes through neighboring windows." A young woman standing at one of those windows was hit above the right eye and badly injured.[27]

The air gun that injured this unfortunate young lady was not exactly a toy. Then again, it is not the kind of rifle Cody would take out to hunt buffalo either. In truth, the history of the toy gun remains ambiguous, troubling our understanding of the historical relationship between boys and guns in America. As of this writing, a comprehensive history of this object does not exist. Cross argues that toy weapons were not produced in large numbers before World War II, and he emphasizes that those that did exist served more as family parlor games than as "an invitation to war play."[28] He notes that global conflicts such as the Spanish-American War and World War I failed to have much impact on the American toy box. However, toy guns associated with Buffalo Bill's Wild West and the performance of "cowboys and Indians" were prevalent in the early twentieth century and suggest a different kind of war play.

Buffalo Bill used the rifle as a marketing tool from his earliest days as a performer. He, along with the other sharpshooters in Buffalo Bill's Wild West, had sponsorship agreements with different arms makers throughout the show's long tenure. This tradition can be traced back to

Cody's theater days; programs in the late 1870s often noted that Buffalo
Bill used only Winchester rifles. By the 1890s, Winchester ads were prevalent in show programs, and the 1898 program highlights a Columbian air
rifle described as "a source of great amusement for men and boys."[29] Toy
guns with Buffalo Bill's name and likeness were produced much earlier
than that. For instance, Ives, Blakeslee & Williams manufactured a cast-
iron toy gun engraved with "Buffalo Bill" in 1878 and a "Texas Jack" toy
pistol in 1886. A toy rifle billed as the "Buffalo Bill Gun" was advertised
in *The Farm and Fireside* on July 1, 1887, and a long-barrel Buffalo Bill toy
gun was put out by the J & E Stevens Company from 1890 into the 1950s.
This is hardly an exhaustive list, but it suggests the prominent place Buffalo Bill occupied in the world of children's play from the late nineteenth
century on. From the repeating rifle to the toy cap gun, these objects all
promoted a type of war play, the narrative of Indian conquest that was
the central theme of all Cody's frontier performances, most prominently
Buffalo Bill's Wild West.[30]

The physical object of the rifle linked toys, children's play, and organizational boy work together in the early twentieth century. Even as the
BSA grew away from the frontier narratives of men like Seton and Beard,
the kind of military training associated with the Cody Military College
remained a critical component of scouting and boy culture more broadly.
Through the rhetorical power of the rifle, Cody articulated frontier violence as a civilizing process. In promotional materials for Buffalo Bill's
Wild West, the rifle was viewed as a tool of progress, associated not with
the primitive but with the subjugation of the primitive. Programs for the
show prominently billed the rifle as an "aid to civilization," suggesting
that in learning to master the rifle, the frontiersman masters himself
and helps to build a strong foundation for successful civil society. One
news item in the July 1911 issue of *Boys' Life* gives dramatic play to this
narrative. Under the headline "Boy Scouts Capture Bandits," the story relates how a Canadian troop, armed with rifles, surrounded and subdued
bandits who had killed the local chief of police.[31]

Of course, incidents like that became increasingly rare in the
twentieth century. In fact, as Mechling notes, "there was a strong antimil-
itarist sentiment" among early BSA leadership.[32] Nevertheless, the BSA
kept the rifle in its repertoire long after scouts ceased to be tasked to

hunt down outlaws and bandits. In fact, the inclusion of marksmanship as a merit badge in the BSA's 1911 handbook is telling precisely in light of the organization's reluctance to be viewed as a paramilitary organization. Despite that disinclination, the BSA's founders recognized broader social pressure to ensure that boys were properly trained to shoot. The National Rifle Association (NRA) founded their youth programs in 1903, and Hearst's American Boy Scouts, a fierce early competitor of the BSA, was much more aggressive in their inclusion of guns. That militaristic zeal ultimately proved quite damaging after one of their scouts shot and killed a nine-year-old boy in New York City in 1912.[33] Still, the BSA continued to include marksmanship in their programs, viewing it as a valuable activity for fostering physical fitness, mental acuity, and civic spirit. In effect, they absorbed Cody's central message: mastering a rifle entailed both technical mastery and self-mastery, preparing the individual to become a better man and a better citizen.

Starting in the late nineteenth century, the emergence of lighter rifles for young users helped link ideologies of boyhood and narratives of the frontier in disparate ways. In 1885, Winchester introduced a single-shot .22 rifle; the gun was advertised at the Paris International Exhibition of that year. By 1887, gun historian Herbert Houze reports, the company was marketing an even lighter gun intentionally designed for youngsters, a small rifle with a twenty-one inch barrel intended for use by the NRA's youth programs. This single-shot rifle was considered too light, with "too short a pull for use by older children or adults," and in 1904 the company came out with an improved version, "which could be [used] with equal ease by children and adults." In the first year, according to Houze, they sold 3,321 units, and the company continued to actively court partnerships with school cadet programs and scouting organizations.[34]

In 1888, Daisy introduced its iconic all-metal air rifle to the market, an innovation that seems to have constituted a happy accident for the struggling company. Clarence Hamilton founded the Plymouth Iron Works in 1882 as a windmill company, but business floundered. Hamilton was having better luck producing wooden air guns on the side for his Plymouth Air Rifle Company. After a vote by the board nearly put the Plymouth Iron Works out of business, Hamilton showed general manager Lewis Hough a prototype for an iron air rifle. Nicknamed the

Daisy, the gun was produced at the windmill company and was meant as a giveaway to farmers who purchased a windmill. However, when Hough's nephew, Charles Bennett, went out as a salesman, he had much better luck selling the guns to farm boys for two dollars apiece. By 1895, the company had ceased manufacturing windmills and renamed itself the Daisy Manufacturing Company.[35]

Interestingly, the rifle carved out a prominent place for itself in children's culture as both tool and toy during the late nineteenth and early twentieth centuries. Mechling notes that the BSA did not target boys "raised in a hunting culture" and "familiar with guns and gun safety" in its early years.[36] These boys, it was assumed, already possessed the skills and discipline needed to use a rifle. At the same time, these same rural boys jumped at the opportunity to own a Daisy air rifle, which, while appropriate for some small-scale hunting, was clearly intended for more recreational usage.

By the early decades of the twentieth century, air rifles had become a staple of the boy's toy box, and advertisers built on the frontier narratives established by Cody and his partners. As Lisa Jacobson describes, advertising campaigns for air rifles both "dramatized anxieties about curtailed masculinity and the overfeminized home" and evoked "the cultural appeal of the savage boy."[37] Much as Cody had done in the Wild West arena and in ads for his Cody Military College, these ads positioned the frontier as a vital space for developing boys into men, while simultaneously lamenting its disappearance in the face of civilized modernity. Unable to access the open land of the frontier, the Progressive Era boy was urged to turn to the air rifle instead.

A 1913 Daisy ad reminds mothers that when their sons ask for an air rifle, it is "the upstanding American man in him asking for a chance to grow." The idea of the man already existent in the body, waiting to grow and being shaped by the materiality of the rifle, plays on familiar themes that can be traced back to the first performance of Buffalo Bill's Wild West, if not earlier. By the end of the Progressive Era, the rifle inflected the cultures of childhood using a consistent symbolic vocabulary. One narrative emphasized the child hunter and the value of marksmanship, as evident in the marksmanship programs developed by the BSA, the NRA, and the Winchester junior rifle corps. A second narrative emphasized the toy gun and the world of play, as seen in games like cowboys and Indians, even if many boy workers and air gun manufacturers sought to distance the skill of marksmanship from the world of play.[38]

These intertwined, if often contradictory, narratives reflect broader social and cultural trends in America. By the 1890s, the family farm and the need for the child hunter were greatly diminished. America was more urban, and the idea of guns in the city suggested multiple meanings, as a sampling of ads from a 1901 edition of *The Youth's Companion* shows. One Smith & Wesson ad warns against going unarmed in "business or pleasure."[39] The image of a middle-aged businessman putting a revolver in his valise suggests that respectable men take the necessary precautions to protect not only themselves but their wives and children (fig. 16). In the same issue, an advertisement for the Winchester Model 1900 rifle targets the boy reader directly, claiming that "for boys it is safer than most guns" and suggesting that the "rifle is just the thing to take on your summer vacation for fun and diversion" (368). While the Smith & Wesson ad gestures toward the growing danger of an increasingly urbanized America, the Winchester ad invokes the new culture of leisure and, with the young boy posed with his rifle in an open field, hearkens back to young marksmen like Johnny Baker, the child of nature hunting birds and squirrels in an idealized rural setting (fig. 17).

Some Progressive Era reformers saw any gun as a direct threat to children. In *The Spirit of Youth and the City Streets*, Jane Addams describes a confrontation between a group of boys that resulted in one boy shooting another dead—a story reminiscent of the one involving Hearst's well-armed scouts. The story, Addams notes, "could be duplicated almost every morning; what might be merely a boyish scrap is turned into a tragedy because some boy has a revolver."[40] In this fraught environment, the gun—in Addams's mind, a revolver in particular—provides no value as a character-building tool, a sentiment that became increasingly common in the twentieth century. As the century progressed, air rifles ceded prominence to guns that were clearly toys, responding to what Mechling describes as "a moral panic about adolescent boys, aggression, and gun violence."[41]

That moral panic also had its roots in early-twentieth-century frontier discourse and fears of juvenile delinquency. Progressive Era reformers such as Addams were increasingly concerned about juvenile delinquency and, as noted earlier, delinquent boys. As an autonomous juvenile justice system emerged in beginning of the twentieth century, a number of psychologists and sociologists attempted a more scientific study of adolescence and delinquency. Frederic Thrasher's work is notable in this regard. A member of the Chicago school of sociology, Thrasher is best known for *The Gang: A Study of 1,313 Gangs in Chicago* (1927). With section headings like "The Natural History of the Gang," Thrasher's book assumes a tone of scientific inquiry, building on developmental paradigms established by Hall and other boy workers. As Thrasher describes it, the boy is instinctually drawn to the gang, and the gang itself develops almost spontaneously, whenever and wherever boys congregate: "Every village has at least its boy gang," Thrasher notes, and these gangs are no different than their urban counterparts, "composed of those same footloose, prowling and predacious adolescents who herd and hang together after the manner of the undomesticated male everywhere."[42]

Boys and gangs form naturally, and Thrasher repeatedly notes that "gangs flourish on the frontier" (ix). Describing the parts of Chicago where gangs form most readily, Thrasher notes that "these regions of conflict are like a frontier; in others, like a 'no-man's land,' lawless, godless, wild" (6). Thrasher describes the urban frontier as an interstice, its physical location "pertaining to spaces that intervene between one thing and another." The gang, he writes, "may be regarded as an interstitial element in the framework of society, and gangland as an interstitial region in the layout of the city" (22).

In Thrasher's analysis, the vanishing frontier lived on, deeply embedded in the modern city. He describes gangland as a function of human ecology. As residential districts recede before the encroachments of business and industry, "the gang develops as one manifestation of the economic, moral, and cultural frontier which marks the interstice" (23). While conceptions of the urban frontier were not new in 1920s, Thrasher articulates a relationship between that frontier, boys, and gangs that would only grow more powerful in twentieth-century narratives of juvenile delinquency. The BSA and other scouting organizations rose to prominence by drawing on a similar rhetoric, positioning their character-building troops as an alternative to the juvenile gang, a place where the gang "instinct" Thrasher describes can be harnessed to develop cooperative teamwork and strong civic spirit. The rifle played an important role in this work. The successful boy learned to use the gun to suppress the senseless violence Addams abhors, rather than cause it, while learning self-reliance and discipline in the process.

PLAYING BUFFALO BILL

In the early twentieth century, playing cowboys and Indians was about more than guns. From Buffalo Bill cutouts to plastic sets of cowboys and Indians, this type of play was ubiquitous for American children throughout the century, and for many modern critics, the ramifications of the play scripts for these toys remain deeply problematic. Michael Yellow Bird speculates that most American boys growing up in the 1970s played cowboys and Indians, a group including "congressmen, police chiefs, religious clergy, and schoolteachers" and the other "folks that now run this country." As a result, Yellow Bird concludes, our leaders "killed a lot of Indians during their boyhood war games believing it was the right thing to do."[43]

Arlene Hirschfelder argues that the "cowboy-Indian motif is fraught for meaning with children," who are "programmed from many sources to see the cowboy as the hero and the good guy and the Indian as the bad guy." Echoing Yellow Bird's concern, she believes that children playing with these toys "reenact the violent and aggressive scenes they have seen or heard about, without having the slightest idea what was involved in the relationship between whites and Indians in the East and in the West."[44] Writing in the 1980s, Hirschfelder notes that this motif is institutionalized in American children's play through a variety of toys, including those popular plastic cowboy and Indian action figures posed in battle positions and with guns and tomahawks raised.[45]

Some forms of play are more forcefully scripted than others. Benjamin Hoy argues that board games have served as a potent delivery system for the dominant cultural narrative of civilizing the frontier. Frontier-related board games, Hoy asserts, cultivate "nostalgia to a scripted and manicured past." Reinforcing stereotypical representations of "cardboard Indians," these games offer generic misrepresentations of indigenous peoples that provide players with "a mixture of Indigenous tribes, fantasy, and a dash of historical flavor. They are one-dimensional representations, stamped onto cardboard, and shipped across the world."[46] Board games, Hoy points out, can reinforce specific narratives by "encouraging their participants to use them in specific, directed ways" (301). As such, these games have the potential to inscribe reductive histories of the American West and establish stereotypes such as the cardboard Indian into the way children understand and imagine the frontier through play.[47]

We know what these toys are, what they represent, and the history of that representation. But what did children make of them? To what extent did young children playing cowboys and Indians or Buffalo Bill in the early twentieth century assimilate narratives of colonization and white supremacy? How might they have incorporated these toys into play scripts of their own devising? These questions are difficult to answer and attempting to do so requires a nuanced consideration of how children play. The strong relationship between children and play is often taken for granted, but how children play, when they are allowed (and encouraged) to play, and what they play with is variable. In America, modern ideas of children's play and the notion of play as the natural vocation of the child can be traced to the second half of the nineteenth century. By that century's midpoint, Howard Chudacoff argues, "the playful rather than the sinful quality of childhood was winning acceptance, so that children's self-structured play was receiving a more widespread stamp of approval." Children, then, were given time and space to play, assuming their "play respected adult prerogatives for controlling the younger generation."[48]

As the relationship between childhood and play intensified, a strong market developed for children's playthings in America. While reformers and educators worried about the links between real guns and juvenile delinquency, toy marketers joined parents in seeking to guide—or at least profit from—boys playing cowboys and Indians. Lisa Jacobson's work focuses on efforts in the early decades of the twentieth century to cultivate a market of boy consumers as part of broader efforts to revitalize American masculinity. She argues that marketers targeted consumers with the prototype of the manly boy who emerged as a "miniature patriarch" within the white, middle-class family.[49] She notes the growing prominence of *American Boy* magazine, with five hundred thousand subscribers by 1910. In its appeals to advertisers and readers alike, the magazine promoted the primacy of "boy knowledge" and the idea that "the boy's consumer authority was equal, perhaps even superior, to his father's" (99). The ideal boy, she argues, was not one who resisted the urge to consume but one who made the right consumer choices, particularly those choices that valorized prevalent notions of masculinity. The same traits that made for a masculine man, "loyalty, enthusiasm, and decisiveness," made for a good consumer (109).

As Jacobson points out, Progressive Era marketers, like the second wave of BSA leadership, balanced the transition to new ideals of manhood, which involved relying less on "the autonomous self-made man" and more on "the corporate team player," with "a cultural yearning for 'new sources of male power and authority'" (110). Notably, the path to those new sources of power drew on a familiar formula—developing the boy by synthesizing elements of civilization and wildness. To develop a modern boy fit for the technological demands of the modern world, progressive marketers and educators sought to recover the playful freedom of imagined boyhood. As noted earlier, the air rifle emerged in the late nineteenth century as a vital symbol of boys' play. Jacobson notes that in the 1910s, air rifle ads filled *American Boy* and other magazines, delighting "in boyish exuberance and their parallel angst over imperiled masculinity" (111). These ads positioned manly boys outside with their air rifles in sharp contrast to sissified boys stuck in the house with their mothers.

Jacobson's analysis includes one notable ad for King air rifles that ably demonstrates this dynamic at work. In the ad, a "sissified" boy sits, apron-clad and shelling peas for his mother, as his friends congregate at the window, beckoning him to join them. "Come on out," one implores, holding out his weapon out for inspection, "we're going to Play Indian with my new King Air Rifle." Of course, there are no indigenous children in this image, and—unlike in Buffalo Bill's Wild West—this was likely the case in most child performances of cowboys and Indians in fields, backyards, and alleys all over America. That hardly refutes the fact that the Indians in the game were the "bad guys," whose role is only to be defeated and killed. But what does it mean to kill someone in play, to use a toy gun in simulating shooting and killing another person?

Applying Gregory Bateson's notion of the play frame to gun play, Mechling cautions against the easy interpretation that a child playing with a toy gun is simply rehearsing being an adult using a real gun to inflict violence: "Most adults" who watch boys play with guns "see the play in terms of real guns and real violence." This misses the point that "boys are shooting at each other in a play frame," a situation in which the two parties understand that their activity constitutes a form of play.[50] For Mechling, in construing gun play as a type of training for adult life, we buy into what Brian Sutton-Smith has described as the progress rhetoric of play, "the advocacy of the notion that animals and children, but not adults, adapt and develop through their play." This belief, Sutton-Smith notes, "is something that most Westerners cherish, but its relevance to play has been more assumed than demonstrated."[51]

Interestingly, Sutton-Smith traces the progress rhetoric of play back to Hall, recapitulation theory, and the synthesis of savage and civi-lized. For Hall and his peers, "a child's play proceeds through a series of increasingly complex and social stages," a development "believed to parallel the evolution of the species" (35). While Hall's theory of recapitulation has been discredited, Sutton-Smith argues that the idea that "children develop through their play, and their play is a map for their development," has only gained credence (36). Surprisingly, the question of what children think of play often remains an afterthought. Sutton-Smith notes that "child players themselves" tend to describe play as "having fun, being outdoors, being with friends, choosing freely, not working, pretending, enacting, fantasy, and drama, and playing games." These children, he points out, place "little or no emphasis on the kind of growth that adults have in mind with their progress rhetoric" (49).

Sutton-Smith's summary of what children value in play hearkens back to Ernest Seton's recollections of childhood, which he channeled in *Two Little Savages* (1903). Equal parts adventure story and instruction manual, the novel features two boys, Yan and Sam, who revel in playing outdoors, exploring the natural world, and living as "real" Indians did. They form their own small tribe and imitate the Indians as best they can, which includes building a tepee, fashioning their own bows and arrows, and making an Indian drum. By "playing Indian," they become more self-sufficient and better acclimated to the natural world.

Just as importantly, and unsurprisingly, the future BSA leader frames these memories of childhood revelry clearly in the rhetoric of progress. Seton places great emphasis on playing the right way—for instance, making a tepee just as the Indians did, using only the tools the Indians had at their disposal. While the boys engage in carefree fun, Seton strains to frame their activities as character-building play. Yan is hungry to learn as much as he can about the plants and animals he encounters, knowledge that helps develop his mind, body, and spirit. *Two Little Savages* narrates the boys' adventures in the woods while providing a model for its readers to emulate. Renowned American folk singer Pete Seeger used the book in precisely this way; as Seeger recalls, "I built a teepee and camped out in the cow pasture. I cooked my meals over a small fire in a teepee as I tried to replicate the life and experiences described in his stories."[52]

Seton's Yan reveled in a kind of "Indian play," and generations of boys, from those targeted by the King air rifle ad on, responded to a similar call. Were they drawn by the character-building attributes of these games that Seton lays out in *Two Little Savages*? It seems doubtful. Were they eager to relive the Indian Wars, rehashing the brutal murders of American colonization? Not directly, I suspect. More likely, Yan (and the young Seton) himself, enjoyed the freedom of wandering in the woods, fantasizing about the lives of indigenous peoples, and having the autonomy to actualize those fantasies in various forms. As Mechling suggests, even play that involves "cowboys" killing "Indians" is not necessarily about committing murder but rather engaging in a kind of fantasy.

Yet Michael Yellow Bird's concerns about toys as tools of colonization cannot not be easily dismissed. "As colonized peoples," he posits, many indigenous people "have internalized and adapted to the colonizer's dominant ideology," the ideology undergirding both Buffalo Bill's Wild West and the play of cowboys and Indians. This ideology encourages indigenous people to develop "a certain sense of denigration and personal contempt within our consciousness."[53] Yellow Bird describes his own youth, growing up in a community where the figure of the cowboy was valorized and indigenous people dressed as cowboys, noting that many men in his community "called each other 'cowboy,' and some would self-identify as an Indian cowboy" (41). These identity projects, he asserts, established a binary wherein the cowboy represented everything that was good and the Indian represented everything that was bad. For Yellow Bird, fighting back against this mentality, or "decolonizing" the mind, requires that indigenous people consciously "refuse to be little red plastic toy Indians participating in the racist American myths and policies of white colonial supremacy" (46).

Yellow Bird's analysis includes a fascinating anecdote concerning those little red and blue plastic toys. After buying a set of cowboy and Indian toys to use in a college class demonstration, he accidentally included them as gifts for children of a friend he visited for dinner. Distraught at accidently facilitating a type of play he disdains, Yellow Bird sat down to play with the children, hoping he could influence their conception and use of the plastic toys. After the children set the figures up to play, he asked them what they should do next, prompting the children by asking who the "good guys" and "bad guys" were. Avoiding the questions, the boys "pull out a brontosaurus and a T. Rex and began knocking down everybody, saying 'We have to kill them all'" (39).

The story raises some wonderful questions. Yellow Bird jokes that, when he was a child, his "play with toy cowboys and Indians would have ended much differently." Referring back to the master narrative of cowboys and Indians, he describes how "my cowboys would have heroically killed the dinosaurs and then the Indians" (39). What changed for this younger generation of children? The toys are as offensive as ever, painting indigenous people as timeless warrior Indians, and the play scripts of white conquest seem clear. However, the children felt no obligation to follow these scripts. They rejected Yellow Bird's suggestion of identifying good guys and bad guys. In fact, they introduced a new actor into the fray, the dinosaur, who quickly disposed of cowboy and Indian alike. Was this a conscious rejection of the master narrative Yellow Bird rightly decries? Does it constitute a kind of liberation from the play scripts prompted by years of Wild West shows, books, and movies? And what of the Buffalo Bill generations, the children of the late nineteenth and early twentieth centuries who were first encouraged to engage in this kind of play? To what degree did they understand or acquiesce to these play scripts of white conquest?

Robin Bernstein's revisiting of the famous Clark doll study helps reframe the relationship between children and these kinds of dominant play scripts. Kenneth and Mamie Clark designed the doll study in the 1940s, conducting a series of experiments with dolls and African American girls. The experiments used dolls that were identical except for color and asked subjects seven questions. One question asked subjects which doll they preferred to play with, and the majority of African American respondents picked the white doll. This result, along with the test as whole, purported to demonstrate the damaging impact of segregation on African American children and played a pivotal role in the 1954 Supreme Court decision *Brown v. Board of Education*. Revisiting the study, Bernstein describes how influential the Clarks' work was, persuasively cementing "the belief, which remains prominent today, that any black child who prefers white dolls is necessarily showing symptoms of individual and societal pathology: internalized racism."[54]

Bernstein's analysis of the Clark doll study is worth keeping in mind when thinking about children playing with a set of Buffalo Bill paper cutouts in 1910 or plastic cowboy and Indian action figures a hundred years later. As she notes, the study took place in a particular cultural moment, one in which advocates for African American rights like the Clarks hoped for "girls to embrace black dolls as signs and inculcators of self-respect" (228). The refusal of black dolls by African American girls was largely understood as a sign of their damaged self-esteem, their preference for the white dolls a symptom of the psychological damage done to them. However, Bernstein suggests that African American girls refused the black dolls because they refused "the scripts those dolls transmitted," which "can be understood as itself a sign and assertion of self-respect or at least self-protection" (229).

This analysis can be applied to Yellow Bird's refusal to play cowboys and Indians, which he describes as a tool of colonization and transmitter of a master narrative of white conquest over indigenous people. Since plastic cowboy and Indian figures transmit undesirable play scripts, Yellow Bird rejects the toys. In fact, we might be tempted to view both Yellow Bird's rejection of the toys and his young playmates' engagement with them as acts of resistance, as individuals exerting agency by authoring their own play scripts. The full dimensions of this kind of agency remain complex, however. Ultimately, Bernstein reminds us, "people are able to resist scripting because they have agency, but agency can also, even simultaneously, emerge *through* scripting. Resistance and scripting are not incompatible; they are often mutually constitutive" (240).

It is difficult to offer a decisive assessment of how this collaborative scripting worked for the many children playing cowboys and Indians in the late nineteenth and early twentieth centuries. The master narrative of white supremacy scripted by the tropes and toys involved in playing cowboy and Indians is clear, but not enough is known about the children playing with Buffalo Bill cutouts in the 1890s or a King air rifle some twenty years later. What's more, while toy makers and character builders alike worked to create strong links between the American frontier and white boyhood, this kind of play surely included a broader range of children, including indigenous people, and it is difficult to draw firm conclusions about how the agency of these marginalized groups worked within the dominant play scripts of cowboys and Indians.

Christine Bold has established a precedent for this kind of specu-lation in her analysis of Beadle & Adams dime novels featuring the Mohawk woman Go-won-go, a real-life actress sensationalized in a series of novels written by Prentiss Ingraham. Bold asks whether indigenous people read dime novels. Clearly, the answer is yes, and Bold argues that these novels might have served as "affirmations of cultural survival and self-determination."[55] Bold is aware of the racist depictions of indigenous people in nineteenth-century dime novels, including the Go-won-go books. Still, she argues that this legacy of racism should not blind us to the long history of indigenous people interacting with popular cultural forms, such as Wild West shows and dime novels, and the potential for those forms to be "richly re-Indigenised and reread as sites in which nuggets of traditional practices were nurtured and adapted within com-mercial frameworks, secrets, and codes hid in plain sight, communities were strengthened, and Indigenous expressive culture innovated and expanded" (138).

These same acts of innovation and expansion almost certainly took place when child spectators and fans of Buffalo Bill's Wild West played cowboys and Indians. As noted in chapter 4, the child performers and spectators alike became increasingly diverse in the late nineteenth and early twentieth centuries. While the show's master narrative framed a conflict of civilized whites and savage Indians, the roster of performers featured a more international bent, matching the growing number of immigrants in the audience. In fact, what is most notable about the game of cowboys and Indians is its reductive frame, how it distills the American experience into a simple conflict between good guys (white cowboys) and bad guys (Indians).

As Bernstein suggests, children surely understood these scripts and, like the children in the Clark doll study, understood the power dynamics within this frame. Children playing cowboys and Indians in the first half of the twentieth century learned the sham history of Buffalo Bill's Wild West, while having the opportunity to refashion that historical narrative as they saw fit. These acts of interpretation can be multifaceted. Echoing Philip Deloria's observations on the nuances of "playing Indian," Michelle Raheja points out the dominant narrative of white conquest and Indian subjugation conjoins two "twin desires that seek to simultaneously celebrate Native American cultures by domesticating them for mass consumption and, in a more literal form of consumption, embody in European Americans the desire to be Native American."[56]

Playing Buffalo Bill activates the interplay of these twin desires. If cowboys and Indians is the game Cody gave the world, the reductive nature of this particular play frame is one of its defining features. The ability of that reductive frame to enable diverse forms of children's play is another. In this way, the play scripts Buffalo Bill offered children of the twentieth century kept the nineteenth century's magic frontier very much alive, and the powerful impressions left behind by Buffalo Bill's Wild West shaped how children actively imagined the past and future and how they played.

Elisha Brooks's recollections of his prairie childhood provide a striking example of this process at work. Brooks's memoir, *A Pioneer Mother of California*, recounts his journey from Michigan to California, traveling with his four siblings and intrepid mother. Brooks describes meeting people along the way who spread "harrowing stories of blood-curdling horrors," all of which revolved around the central theme that "the plains were alive with Indians on the war path."[57] When the family actually encounters indigenous people, Brooks is struck by his experience with friendly group of Crow Indians who travel with the family for a spell. Brooks describes the procession in detail:

Red men in rich robes of bear and panther skins decked out with fringe and feathers; red men without robes or feathers, and unwashed; favorite and actually handsome squaws in elegant mantles of bird skins, tattooed and adorned with beads; unlovely squaws in scanty rags and no beads, and unwashed; papooses rolled in highly ornamental blankets; papooses without a rag, and unwashed; ponies hidden under monumental burdens; packs of dogs creeping under wonderful loads; and, bringing up the rear, an old ox team with six wild, ragged children and a woman once called white, and sometimes unwashed. We were a Wild West Show. (25)

Tellingly, Brooks describes the experience as a Wild West show; there were no Wild West shows in 1852, when this encounter took place, but presumably the author became familiar with them later. More notably, these shows made such a powerful impression on him that they colored his recollection of an actual encounter with indigenous people, prompting him to imagine the richly dressed Indians, the ragged children, and a woman "once called white" proceeding along with his family such that "we" comprised a Wild West show.

This, then, is the true legacy of Buffalo Bill, along with the host of other writers, performers, and educators who helped enshrine frontier mythology in the culture of American boyhood during the late nineteenth and early twentieth centuries. By Cody's death in 1917, the idea of cowboys and Indians worked through the American imagination in varied registers, a process that continued throughout the first half of the twentieth century. Cowboys and Indians was history distilled into myth, repackaged as Hollywood entertainment and as a child's game adults used to smooth over the messy contradictions of the past and imagine a brighter future. It was, as Michael Yellow Bird suggests, a rehearsal of the genocidal themes of white conquest and the annihilation of indigenous people—an open wound that has long gone untreated.

Notably, though, Cowboys and Indians was a game that children themselves played, a loose set of structures they arranged and rearranged to make sense of their world in ways far more complex and diffuse than is often assumed. Preserving the frontier as a timeless space of boyhood, this kind of play made sure the dominant narrative of Buffalo Bill's Wild West was ensconced in American children's culture. At the same time, the act of play offered countless opportunities for children to revisit and reform this narrative in ways that defy easy categorization. As in Brooks's memoir, it became a tool to shape individual stories, for individuals to interact with restrictive play scripts in ways that were variable and profound. Ultimately, these acts of play reveal children both absorbing the frontier myth handed down by Cody and others, and using that material to help produce and define notions of identity—national, gender, racial, and otherwise—that had a lasting impact on American culture and society throughout the twentieth century.

CONCLUSION

In 1917, Buffalo Bill's death was front-page news nationwide. Over a hundred years later, the internationally acclaimed showman's star has dimmed considerably. Indeed, for many, the name of the iconic frontier hero inspires only the briefest glimmer of recognition. Of course, much has changed in America during the past century, and it is not surprising to find that accounts of the history of the West have too. Historians of the West have worked diligently to counter Frederick Jackson Turner's distorted vision of the "free" or "open" frontier with the lesser-known histories of the diverse people who actually lived there and the complicated history of the landscape transformed by western migration. Likewise, the power dynamics undergirding Cody's performance of frontier history have been rightfully challenged for their promotion of white male power at the expense of just about everyone else. Nevertheless, the mythology of the frontier continues to play a powerful role in shaping American identity, existing in different forms that feature new variations on the familiar Western hero. For instance, when Gene Roddenberry's *Star Trek* television series debuted in 1966, Captain Kirk—rugged, white, and very masculine—took viewers out of our solar system "where no man has gone before."

As the William Shatner monologue introducing each episode of the original *Star Trek* series reminds viewers, space is (or was) "the final frontier." Roddenberry, a veteran TV writer and former head writer for *Have Gun—Will Travel*, conceived of *Star Trek* as a variation on traditional Western motifs, and the ascendance of *Star Trek* and *Star Wars* in American popular culture during the second half of the twentieth century largely serves to reinscribe the central tenets of frontier mythology in new formats. Certainly, the idea of the rugged frontier hero has not faded from the American consciousness. One need look no further than the

189

successful campaigns of Presidents Ronald Reagan, a former Hollywood actor known for appearing in Westerns, and George W. Bush, who followed closely in the footsteps of Teddy Roosevelt, eschewing his eastern roots to present himself in the public view as an authentic western man out working on his ranch in Crawford, Texas. Despite the best efforts of hardworking historians of the West, the mythology of the frontier has proven remarkably durable.[1]

That mythology continues to exert a strong influence on American cultures of childhood as well. That influence can be seen in any number of contemporary toys, books, and films. In chapter 5, I argue that Buffalo Bill's most lasting impact was on children's play, and Pixar's *Toy Story* films offer a useful lens to examine that impact. This popular film series demonstrates how frontier themes continue to play a prominent role in children's culture and narratives of boyhood, while simultaneously offering a playful reflection on the changing fortunes of the cowboy in the American toy box. The films feature an ensemble cast of American toys, but the star attractions are Buzz Lightyear and Sheriff Woody, archetypal astronaut and cowboy heroes. Ultimately, the *Toy Story* movies flesh out longstanding connections between American frontier mythology and idealized American boyhood, while re-enshrining the "old-fashioned" pull-string toy Sheriff Woody as a classic toy and an iconic figure of boyhood.[2]

The *Toy Story* films continue a long tradition of children's books and films that entertain the notion of toys coming to life. The films' representation of the seemingly inanimate toys as living things with a range of thoughts and feelings easily identifiable to any human viewer opens fertile ground for varied interrogations of ownership, identity, posthumanism, and more. Notably, the films work to promote a familiar representation of white middle-class childhood as the ideal form of childhood. In the films, the toy characters live with their benevolent boy owner Andy, and where the toys live is as important as how they live. As Lewis Roberts claims, "Andy's suburban middle-class home is romanticized as a sanctuary from the violence and uncertainty of the outside world."[3] As a white middle-class boy in a leafy suburb, Andy represents the same vision of ideal American boyhood writers and character builders had in mind in the late nineteenth century.

The films also employ pathological visions of masculinity and boy-hood to juxtapose with Andy. *Toy Story* offers Sid, a violent, destructive child whose reckless toy play stands in direct opposition to Andy's respon-sible stewardship. In this way, Roberts points out, Sid represents a kind of anti-Romantic child, whose appetite for wanton destruction prompts a kind of play that involves mutilating and disfiguring his toys. The juxta-position of Sid and Andy is reminiscent of the disparate visions of proper and improper boyhood promoted by nineteenth-century depictions of boyhood in frontier literature and performance. In familiar fashion, the *Toy Story* films home in on the thin line between autonomy and deviance. Sid, after all, is a powerful figure who operates free of any consistent adult control or supervision. Just as dime novel hero Deadwood Dick's freedom from adult authority is intertwined with the threat he poses to the social order as a murderer and bandit, Sid's autonomy is tied to the sadism he visits upon his toys, reminding viewers he is the proverbial "bad kid." Andy, of course, is the "good kid," representing a vision of boyhood—and a degree of social control—that adults desire. For Rob-erts, the act of "romanticizing childhood is a way to control childhood, to box it up as a sacred space of innocence" (425).

When the movie was released in 1995, *Toy Story* offered viewers a full realization of this sacralized childhood, a time and space completely separated from adulthood and locked in timeless innocence. This ideal represents broad social approval of the "useless" child Viviana Zelizer describes, a model that Progressive Era reformers argued for in early-twentieth-century disputes about child labor. Indeed, by the 1990s, Andy and his idyllic suburban home present a nostalgic look back at this ideal of childhood and domesticity—an ideal the film suggests might be threatened by looming forces in the contemporary world such as crass commercialism, bleak urbanity, and the dissolution of the family unit. As Alan Ackerman argues, Andy and his toys convey "the rareness of (and nostalgia for) the 1950s nuclear family," with Buzz and especially Woody symbolizing "the embattled position of the benevo-lent white patriarch."[4] In this way, the film targets adult viewers as much as—or perhaps more than—child viewers. As Roberts explains, adults "watching *Toy Story* are reminded of toys they owned as children."[5] These acts of remembrance are tied to sanctified acts of consumption, both the consumption of the film itself and the subsequent purchase of *Toy Story*–related products such as Woody books, action figures, and lunch boxes.

This nostalgia for ideal childhood remains deeply intertwined with nostalgia for the frontier—the imagined frontier performed in Buffalo Bill's Wild West, inscribed in the pages of Wister's *The Virginian*, and immortalized in a spate of Western TV shows such as *Bonanza* and *Gunsmoke*. Woody, of course, is meant to be a product of that cultural landscape. In fact, his discovery of his "other life" with the Roundup Gang and as star of a 1950s television show drives the plot of *Toy Story 2*. While *Toy Story*'s plot largely concerns Buzz Lightyear's struggles to come to terms with the fact that he is a toy and not a space ranger, *Toy Story 2* focuses on Woody's struggle to negotiate different versions of himself. Ultimately, he must choose between being Andy's cherished toy or the star attraction of an exhibition in a toy museum.

Toy Story 2 expands the roster of Western characters, most notably through the introduction of toy cowgirl Jessie. Jessie's inclusion seems to disrupt the strictly gendered vision of the *Toy Story* films and of the mythic West as a hypermasculine space. After all, as Jane Tompkins argues, the classic Western is "the antithesis of the cult of domesticity that dominated Victorian culture," and the archetypal Western hero's purpose is to replace representations of domestic tranquility with the solitary figure of the Western hero.[6] Woody's relationship with Jessie and his sense of loyalty to the rest of the Roundup Gang do suggest Woody is a different kind of frontier hero. At the same time, *Toy Story 2*'s vivacious cowgirl is something of a red herring, and the film's dominant frontier narrative is less progressive than it seems. Rather, it props up longstanding ideations of the West as a space of white male supremacy.

Much like the archetypal Hollywood Western, *Toy Story 2*'s plot derives from Woody's threatened obsolescence, and its central conflict is resolved through reestablishing the sheriff's manly vitality. In the process, the film engages in precisely the kind of identity project Tompkins discerns in the classic Hollywood Western. Reworking this narrative in the new genre of the animated children's movie, *Toy Story 2* demonstrates both the durability and versatility of the American frontier myth and how deeply invested it is with narratives of white male potency.

As this book has demonstrated, the Western hero occupies a prominent place in American cultural memory. That hero signifies white masculinity and reinforces narratives of white American supremacy. As film started to supplant literature, and the rugged Indian scout of the nineteenth century gave way to the stoic and solitary cowboy of the twentieth, these narratives remained intact. In fact, their focus on masculinity became even more singular. Nineteenth-century Wild West shows were huge touring spectacles featuring international casts, and early-twentieth-century Western films continued to dramatize the settling of the West and the conflict between white men and Indians. The Hollywood Western eventually shifted its focus to a different set of conflicts. As Tompkins explains, everything else recedes to the background in these movies aside from the Western male hero. The typical Western movie rarely makes room for significant Indian characters, nor does it dwell too long on frontier domesticity—the solitary figure of the white male hero dominates the frame. In one way, this is familiar territory, and the hero Tompkins describes can be traced straight back to Cooper's Natty Bumppo, the Indian scout caught between two worlds. Unlike Bumppo, though, this new hero does not appear as a "white Indian" or a creature of nature. Rather, he has mastered both Indian and nature. More importantly, he does not lack the ability to join the civilized world; rather, he wants no part of that world or the civilizing forces forever seeking to fence him in.

In many ways, Pixar's Sheriff Woody represents a different kind of animal. He does not live alone but rather with a ragtag community of toys, and his adventures typically revolve around threats to disrupt or destroy that community. Woody is not exactly a John Wayne or Clint Eastwood character either, violent men with deadly guns and little use for words. Woody does not even have a gun but rather wears an empty holster. His natty attire, easy demeanor, and status as a sheriff put him more in the company of singing cowboys like Gene Autry or Roy Rogers. In fact, *Toy Story* functions as a kind of wry metanarrative, commenting on how Woody's old West is eclipsed by that final frontier, space, and his status as hero is threatened by the ascent of swaggering spaceman Buzz Lightyear.

The *Toy Story* films openly reconfigure the grizzled alpha male of the Hollywood Western into the kinder, gentler Sheriff Woody. "Fear of losing his identity drives a man west," Tompkins writes, describing the protagonist of Louis L'Amour's 1958 novel *Radigan* (47). Woody, by contrast, associates identity with community. As Ken Gillam and Shannon Wooden argue, there is a trend in Pixar films that "consistently promotes a new model of masculinity, one that matures into acceptance of its more traditionally 'feminine' aspects." Describing how this "New Man" model functions in Pixar films, Gillam and Wooden note that male heroes, including Buzz and Woody, "all strive for an alpha-male identity," all "face emasculating failures," all "find themselves in large part through what Eve Sedgwick refers to as 'homosocial desire' and . . . finally, they all "achieve (and teach) a kinder, gentler understanding of what it means to be a man."[7]

Gillam and Wooden trace this pattern through the plot in *Toy Story*, showing Woody's emasculation upon Buzz's arrival, then Buzz's emasculation upon being captured by the malevolent Sid (at one point, he is dressed up in women's clothing for a tea party), followed by Buzz and Woody's bonding through their shared desire for the surprisingly racy Little Bo-Peep and, more importantly, their homosocial desire to bond with Andy, their boy owner. This last element of the films is one of their most notable features. And while it is not my focus here, scholars have examined the *Toy Story* movies as a reflection on slavery and ownership, an aspect of the films that could benefit from further scrutiny.[8]

Ultimately, Gillam and Wooden contend, Woody triumphs not through violence and aggression but through his "newfound ability to give and receive care."[9] I find this argument largely convincing. Still, the movies' formulation of Woody's masculinity does little to subvert readings of the West as a masculine space; they simply remap the contours of that space. Woody may be a new man, but he continues to live, prosper, and dominate in a man's world, where other characters, including female companions such as Jessie and Little Bo-Peep, remain relegated to secondary roles or sidekick status. Nowhere is this clearer than in *Toy Story 2*.

As the film begins, Woody busily prepares to go to cowboy camp with Andy. Just before they head out, Woody, who is wearing with age, tears an arm, and Andy decides to leave him behind, putting the broken toy up on a high shelf in his room. This is the place where toys go to die or, more specifically, to gather dust and fade from view, presaging the fact that one day Andy will move on and leave Woody behind—a fear shown vividly in a nightmare the good sheriff has of Andy closing the lid of a garbage can on him, leaving him to waste away in a pile of broken toys. As Andy's mom tells him when Woody rips his arm, "Toys don't last forever." This haunting proclamation serves as the movie's central theme, and the source of Woody's identity crisis, which is the crux of *Toy Story 2*. Ultimately, Woody is given the chance to live forever, not as a child's plaything but as a prized collector's item. The nefarious toy collector Al—another example of failed masculinity—steals Woody from his suburban paradise with Andy to complete his collection of Woody's Roundup Gang for a lucrative sale to a Japanese museum. Realizing his importance as a collector's item, Woody is forced to choose between the life he has always known with Andy and the life he could lead as the "star attraction" of the museum exhibit.

In the course of his decision, Woody explores not only his own mortality, as it were, but also the strength of his bond with Andy and his status as a child's toy. This status lies at the core of Woody's ethos and justifies his leadership status among the toys in Andy's room. The plot of the first *Toy Story* film revolves around Buzz Lightyear's delusion on this score, and Woody is instrumental in helping Buzz realize that he is, in fact, a toy, and that being Andy's toy offers him the greatest possible form of fulfillment and purpose. In one of the more evocative scenes from *Toy Story 2*, Jessie offers a compelling counternarrative to Woody's affirmation of life as a child's toy, relating the sad story of how she ended up in Al's possession. As revealed in a wordless flashback set to "When She Loved Me," sung by Sarah McLachlan, the viewer learns that Jessie once belonged to Emily and that their relationship was just as fulfilling as the one enjoyed by Woody and Andy. Emily, however, grew up and grew out of that relationship, ultimately leaving Jessie and her other childhood toys by the side of the road in a box for donation.

"How long will it last, Woody?" asks Stinky Pete the Prospector, another member of the Roundup Gang, after Jessie relates her sad story. Pete warns Woody that Andy will eventually abandon him as Emily abandoned Jessie, and he promises that in the museum he can "live forever." Woody confronts a hard choice: temporary glory with Andy or eternal life behind glass. For a time, Woody is seduced by the prospects of the latter. By the film's end, of course, Woody does not have to make that choice. He and the viewer realize that Andy will never abandon him the way Emily abandoned Jessie. In fact, the juxtaposition between Woody and Jessie highlights not only the masculinized nature of the imagined West, but the deeply gendered nature of development on and through the frontier. Andy will grow up, but frontier boyhood is time-less, and Woody, as a boyhood hero and unlike Jessie, already has access to eternity.

Whether Woody qualifies as one of Tompkins's new men or not, *Toy Story 2* nevertheless echoes her vision of the frontier as a masculine space, with one important clarification. Frontier masculinity remains linked to boyhood, a place where boys play at being men and, after they are grown, men play at being boys, reveling in the golden hew of nostalgia. At the film's end, Woody is rescued from Al and restored to his idyllic life with Andy and Buzz. "Life's only worth living if you're loved by a kid," Buzz reminds Woody, but that life lasts longer for a boy and his toys, bound together by homosocial desire. Characters like Jessie and Little Bo-Peep can tag along for the ride, but they will always be peripheral figures. "When it all ends, I'll have old Buzz Lightyear to keep me company," Woody remarks in the film's final scene, clapping Buzz on the shoulder as the two stand apart from the group, staring out the window—to infin-ity and beyond, as Buzz's catchphrase proclaims.

In the full scope of the first three films, this picture is incomplete, of course. In *Toy Story 3*, released eleven years after its predecessor, the day Woody feared has come to pass. Andy is leaving for college and, as the Prospector predicted in the previous film, he does not plan to take all of his toys with him. He does, however, plan to take Woody. The twist, at the film's end, is that Woody chooses not to go with Andy but rather to stay with Bonnie, a younger child Andy has chosen to give his toys to. In choosing Bonnie, as Roberts notes, Andy is bestowing upon her the responsibility of taking care of the toys as he did, an act that reinforces the status of the toys as objects and charges Bonnie with preserving not only the toys but the ideal of Romantic Childhood. As Roberts points out, in order for "childhood innocence to endure as an ideal, not only must the toys not be abandoned," they must be played with and played with properly.[10]

Woody's role in the exchange between Andy and Bonnie is particularly intriguing. While Andy chooses to give the bulk of the toys to Bonnie, Woody chooses to include himself in the gift; Andy intends to bring
Woody to college with him, but the sheriff sneaks out to join the box of
toys set aside for Bonnie instead. This ending offers an intriguing twist
to the valorization of frontier nostalgia and male homosocial play that
dominates the first two films. Woody's choice to stay with his community
of toys, reassessing his identity as Andy's plaything, and the prospect of
Woody and Buzz becoming subjects of new play narratives authored by
a young girl open up space for future analysis of contemporary connections between play, frontier narratives, and girlhood—not to mention
the relationship between American frontier mythology and contemporary iterations of Romantic childhood.

There remains plenty of room for exploring the impact of Buffalo Bill
on children's culture as well. Cody's life and career straddled two centuries. Even after his death, his adventures were recast in books and films,
maintaining a vivid presence in the culture of boyhood. For instance, *The
Adventures of Buffalo Bill*, adapted from Cody's autobiography, was first
published in 1904 by Harper & Row as part of the Harper's Young People
series and was reprinted several times in the decades that followed—one
of several repackagings of Buffalo Bill's story. In the foreword to a 1965
edition of the book, an uncredited author describes Cody as "the last of
those intrepid pathfinders who gave their lives to the taming of the West,"
a process that only finished when "the young and vigorous life of the
Pacific States had been linked up for all time with the older civilization
of the Atlantic seaboard."[11] As this book demonstrates, this collision of
young and old is a long-running theme in the creation myth of America,
one as present in Turner's frontier thesis as it is in the iconic figure of
Buffalo Bill or the timeless play of Sheriff Woody. In the second half of
the nineteenth century, the endurance of this rhetoric gestures to the dynamic interplay between the frontier and boyhood in shaping American
notions of race, gender, and national identity. Attached to Cody in a 1965
book for boys, this language reminds us of the powerful resonance of this
frontier myth, now deeply embedded in American cultural memory.

Ideally, this project will provide a springboard to future research
that explores this promising, if largely unmapped, terrain. I especially

look forward to work that explores links between American frontier mythology and childhood in transnational settings. Since the 2005 publication of Robert Rydell and Rob Kroes's *Buffalo Bill in Bologna: The Americanization of the World, 1869–1922*, there has been a surge of interest in the global impact of mass culture enterprises such as Buffalo Bill's Wild West. In recent years, interesting work has been produced on the transnational influence of Buffalo Bill specifically and American frontier mythology more broadly. In addition to Buffalo Bill's Wild West, frontier dime novels, Hollywood films, and American television shows all circulated internationally, and these cultural products certainly had sizable child audiences and contributed to youth cultures in various regional and national contexts. The full extent of the influence of American frontier mythology on disparate notions of childhood and the lives of actual children remains largely unknown. I trust that will not be the case for long.[12]

NOTES

INTRODUCTION

1. See Thomas Fuller's "Go West, Young Man!—An Elusive Slogan," for an examination of who may have, and who clearly did not, utter these famous words.
2. For a comprehensive history of westward migration, see Robert V. Hine and John Mack Faragher's *The American West: A New Interpretive History*. For a look at how notions of the frontier worked their way through American culture in the twentieth century, see Patricia Limerick's "The Adventures of the Frontier in the Twentieth Century."
3. Turner, "Significance of the Frontier in American History." Throughout this book, parenthetical numbers or number spans in the text refer to pages in the work cited in the previous note.

     For representations of America as "young," see Thomas Paine's *The American Crisis*, sections VII and VIII, in Paine, *The Writings of Thomas Paine*. In section VII, he warns Britain they will lose any war with the colonies, noting that America "is like a young heir coming to large improvable estate," and Britain is "like an old man whose chances are over, and his estate mortgaged for half its worth. For an analysis of Thomas Jefferson's and others' early focus on westward expansion, see book 1 of Henry Nash Smith's *Virgin Land: The American West as Symbol and Myth*.
4. Lawrence, *Studies in Classic American Literature*, 60. Historians have long debated Turner's theory as history, as well as his status as a historian of the West. For an overview, see John Mack Faragher's introduction and commentaries in Turner's *Rereading Frederick Jackson Turner: "The Significance of the Frontier in American History" and Other Essays*. In "Becoming West: Toward a New Meaning for Western History," William Cronon, George Miles, and Jay Gitlin discuss the staying power of frontier mythology in the face of criticism of Turner's work as history. "For many historians," they write, "the western past has lost its fascination because there seems to be nothing new or important to say about it. For many ordinary Americans, on the other hand, the western past has lost none of its excitement— for much of the same reason. It is so well known, so reassuringly familiar, that it feels like home" (5).
5. Lewis, *American Adam*, 5.
6. See Love, *Life and Adventures of Nat Love*, and Micheaux, *The Conquest*.
7. Quoted in Pizer, "Hamlin Garland in the *Standard*," 403.
8. MacNeil, *Emergence of the American Frontier Hero*, 68.
9. Smith, *Virgin Land*, 114.
10. See Gail Bederman's *Manliness and Civilization*, especially chapter 1, "Remaking Manhood through Race and 'Civilization.'"
11. Mintz, *Huck's Raft*, 76.
12. Higonnet, *Pictures of Innocence*, 9. Higonnet's work provides a summary of Romantic Childhood's historical trajectory in Western Europe.

13. Philippe Ariès's *Centuries of Childhood: A Social History of Family Life* is a foundational text in the history of childhood. Ariès's contention that parents in the Middle Ages did not revere children or conceive of childhood as a privileged life stage became a call to arms to historians of childhood. Ariès has had his share of critics, and Nicholas Orme offers a staunch rebuke to Ariès in *Medieval Children*. The work of scholars such as Higonnet, who looks at changing visual representations of childhood in Europe and America, demonstrates that ideas of childhood have changed dramatically in the last few centuries. In the last half century, those changes—and the soundness of contemporary ideals of childhood—have been scrutinized by practitioners in the emergent field of childhood studies. Much of this work grew out of the sociological study of childhood, and *Theorizing Childhood* by Allison James, Chris Jenks, and Alan Prout provides a solid introduction to the field.

14. See Zelizer, *Pricing the Priceless Child: The Changing Social Value of Children*. Karen Sánchez-Eppler's *Dependent States: The Child's Part in Nineteenth-Century American Culture* also provides a thorough and trenchant analysis of how ideas of social class contributed to changing American notions of childhood in the nineteenth century.

15. Mintz, *Huck's Raft*, 82.

16. Rotundo, *American Manhood*, 30.

17. Turner, "Significance of the Frontier in American History."

18. Hofstadter, *Progressive Historians*, 151.

19. DeLuzio, *Female Adolescence*, 64.

20. In chapter 3 of *Manliness and Civilization*, Bederman explains how Hall used racial recapitulation to construct a developmental model linking individual human growth with evolutionary progress. In short, Hall uses recapitulation theory to describe all children as primitives with access to a primitive strength lacking in men. As they grew, he surmises, boys could develop this primitive strength. At the same time, a boy's ability to become civilized is limited by the history of his race. Racial recapitulation thus offered a tidy explanation for how non-white boys could possess "primitive strength," but only white boys could grow into men synthesizing the primitive and civilized to maximum effect.

21. Hall, *Youth*, 6, 4.

22. Marten, *America's Corporal*, 165.

23. Garland, *Boy Life on the Prairie*, 8.

CHAPTER 1

1. For a history of the Boy Book, see Marcia Jacobson's *Being a Boy Again: Autobiography and the American Boy Book*. For additional analysis of the genre, including connections to nineteenth-century character-building, see chapter 2 of Kenneth Kidd's *Making American Boys: Boyology and the Feral Tale*.

2. Aldrich, *Story of a Bad Boy*, 1.

3. Macleod, *Building Character in the American Boy*, 54. I use the term *Anglo-Saxon* in keeping with nineteenth-century rhetorical projects that projected the Anglo-Saxon as racially superior, even in comparison to other "white" races. Reginald

Horsman's *Race and Manifest Destiny: The Origins of American Racial Anglo-Saxonism* remains a foundational piece of scholarship on this topic, establishing how Anglo-Saxonism shaped racist ideologies in America during the nineteenth century and beyond.

4. Aldrich, *Story of a Bad Boy*, 4.

5. Richard White notes the rich symbolism in both men's presence at the Columbian Exposition, analyzing their distinctive visions of the frontier and/as American history. See his "Frederick Jackson and Buffalo Bill," in *The Frontier in American Culture: An Exhibition at the Newberry Library*. In addition, chapter 2 of Richard Slotkin's *Gunfighter Nation: The Myth of the Frontier in Twentieth Century America* sets the history of Buffalo Bill's Wild West in ideological opposition to the White City at the Columbian Exposition. For more of Cody's promotional rhetoric, see the 1887 program *Buffalo Bill's Wild West and Congress of Rough Riders of the World*, though this language is standard in programs for the show.

6. Slotkin, *Fatal Environment*, 55.

7. White, "Frederick Jackson Turner and Buffalo Bill," 11.

8. For more on dime novels and "Indian-hating" in the context of developing ideas of American nationalism, see Alexander Saxton's *The Rise and Fall of the White Republic: Class Politics and Mass Culture in Nineteenth-Century America*, 322–41.

9. Jacobson, *Being a Boy Again*, 11.

10. Macleod, *Building Character in the American Boy*, 52.

11. Kidd, *Making American Boys*, 79.

12. For more on Hall and his influence, see chapters 3 and 5 in Gail Bederman's *Manliness and Civilization: A Cultural History of Gender and Race in the United States, 1880–1917*.

13. Quoted in Jacobson, *Being a Boy Again*, 2. See Mary Ryan's *Cradle of the Middle Class: The Family in Oneida County, New York, 1790–1865*, chapter 4, for an analysis of the American middle-class family in the northeast during the second half of the nineteenth century. See Steven Mintz and Susan Kellog's *Domestic Revolutions: A Social History of American Family Life*, chapter 6, for an account of perceived threats to this family structure and the subsequent development of the companionate family beginning at the turn of the century.

14. Jacobson, *Being a Boy Again*, 99.

15. Rotundo, *American Manhood*, 35.

16. Macleod, *Building Character in the American Boy*, 52.

17. Kidd, *Making American Boys*, 36; "Boy Life in a Massachusetts Town Thirty Years Ago," in *Proceedings of the American Antiquarian Society*, 1890.

18. West, *Growing Up with the Country*, 74.

19. Garland, *Boy Life on the Prairie*, 21.

20. West, *Growing Up with the Country*, 16.

21. Garland, *Boy Life on the Prairie*, 67.

22. Jacobson, *Being a Boy Again*, 102.

23. Garland, *Boy Life on the Prairie*, 311.

24. Pizer, "Hamlin Garland in the *Standard*," 403–4.

25. Pizer, *Hamlin Garland, Prairie Radical*, xv.

26. Clemens and Howells, *Mark Twain-Howells Letters*, 112.

27. Slotkin, *Fatal Environment*, 521.

28. See Armon and Blair's explanatory notes to Twain, *Huck Finn and Tom Sawyer among the Indians and Other Unfinished Stories*, 271–72.

29. Krause, "Mark Twain's Image of the American West," 44–45.

30. Coulombe, *Mark Twain and the American West*, 48.

31. See Armon and Blair's explanatory notes to Twain, *Huck Finn and Tom Sawyer among the Indians and Other Unfinished Stories*, 33.

32. Hall, *Adolescence*, xi.

33. Twain, *Adventures of Huckleberry Finn*, 26.

34. Howells, "Review of *The Adventures of Tom Sawyer*," 21.

35. Fielder, *Love and Death in the American Novel*, 282, 279.

36. Twain, *Adventures of Huckleberry Finn*, 136.

37. Kidd, *Making American Boys*, 55.

38. Twain, *Adventures of Huckleberry Finn*, 250.

39. For more on Tom Sawyer and emergent middle-class ideals, see Mark Decker's "From Bad Boys to Good Managers: Twain, Aldrich, and the Creation of a Middle-Class Ideal." Decker argues that Twain and Aldrich used the Boy Book to argue that boyhood mischief prepared middle-class boys for the kind of new managerial roles offered by the late-nineteenth-century American economy.

40. For more on Huck and juvenile delinquency, see Steven Mailloux's *Rhetorical Power*, 110–29. The theme is taken up more recently by Andrew Levy in *Huck Finn's America: Mark Twain and the Era That Shaped His Masterpiece*.

41. Twain, *Huck Finn and Tom Sawyer among the Indians*, 40.

42. Harris, "Mark Twain's Response to the Native American," 35.

43. Twain, *Huck Finn and Tom Sawyer among the Indians*, 41.

44. Michelle Ann Abate's "'Bury My Heart in Recent History': Mark Twain's "Hellfire Hotchkiss," the Massacre at Wounded Knee, and the Dime Novel Western" discusses Twain's fondness for the dime novel and his desire to write one.

45. Russell, *Lives and Legends of Buffalo Bill*, 403.

46. Warren, *Buffalo Bill's America*, 235.

47. Cody, *Life of Hon. William F. Cody*, 19.

48. For a historical overview of the Kansas-Missouri border wars, see Anne Hyde's *Empires, Nations, and Families: A History of the North American West, 1800–1860*, 475–84.

49. Cody, *Life of Hon. William F. Cody*, 49.

50. Quoted in Christianson's introduction to Cody, *The Life of Hon. William F. Cody*, xxvi.

51. Leonard and Goodman, *Buffalo Bill*, 9.

52. Cody, *Life of Hon. William F. Cody*, 470.

53. Clemens and Howells, *Mark Twain-Howells Letters*, 92.

CHAPTER 2

1. The best source of information on the case is Joan Jacobs Brumberg's *Kansas Charley: The Boy Murderer*. Brumberg examines Miller's life and execution for

the murder of the two youths in detail, paying careful attention to the social conditions surrounding his life and the political debate spurred by his death.

2. Bederman, *Manliness and Civilization*, 11.

3. Quoted in Bederman, *Manliness and Civilization*, 92. For more on G. Stanley Hall's efforts to develop white boys into a better class of white men, see Bederman, chapter 3; chapter 5 assesses Roosevelt's construction of the frontier as a proving ground for white manhood and American progress. For more on Hall and recapitulation theory, see Jon Savage's *Teenage: The Prehistory of Youth Culture, 1875–1945*, chapter 5.

4. Lears, *Rebirth of a Nation*, 36.

5. Bederman, *Manliness and Civilization*, 171.

6. Hallwas, *Dime Novel Desperadoes*, 31.

7. Brace, *Dangerous Classes of New York*, 27.

8. Ashby, *Saving the Waifs*. 39. For more on the orphan trains, see Stephen O'Connor's *Orphan Trains: The Story of Charles Loring Brace and the Children He Saved and Failed*, Marilyn Irvin Holt's *The Orphan Trains: Placing Out in America*, and John Myers's *Child Protection in America: Past, Present, and Future*. The Myers book contains damning commentary from L. P. Alden, principal of the State Public School for Children in Coldwater, Michigan, written about the program in 1880. Alden notes, "I think that Mr. Brace has done a great thing for the city of New York in relieving it of so many incipient criminals, for which that city could well afford to erect him a monument. From all the testimony, however, that has reached me, it seems quite improbable that the West, where these children are sent, feel so grateful that it will contribute much towards its erection" (225).

9. Brumberg, *Kansas Charley*, 48.

10. For more on dime novels and young readers, see Stephen Mailloux's *Rhetorical Power* and Dawn Keetley's "The Injuries of Reading: Jesse Pomeroy and the Dire Effects of Dime Novels," a detailed examination of infamous boy "serial killer" Jesse Pomeroy.

11. Kett's *Rites of Passage: Adolescence in America, 1790 to the Present* traces adolescence and its precursors back to late eighteenth-century America. Kent Baxter's *The Modern Age: Turn-of-the-Century American Culture and the Invention of Adolescence* focuses on the end of the nineteenth and beginning of the twentieth centuries as a key turning point in the history of American adolescence. For more on dime novels and early adolescence, see Ryan Anderson's *Frank Merriwell and the Fiction of All-American Boyhood: The Progressive Era Creation of the Schoolboy Sports Story*, Lorinda Cohoon's *Serialized Citizenships: Periodicals, Books, and American Boys, 1840–1911*, and Paul Ringel's *Commercializing Childhood: Children's Magazines, Urban Gentility, and the Ideal of the Child Consumer in the United States, 1823–1918*.

12. See, for instance, chapter 8 of *The Adventures of Tom Sawyer*, in which Tom declares himself the Black Avenger of the Spanish Main, the titular character in a Ned Buntline dime novel. Throughout this novel and *Adventures of Huckleberry Finn*, there are numerous incidents where Tom imagines himself as a type of dime novel hero and/or play-acts scenarios clearly inspired by sensational fiction.

13. In *Mechanic Accents*, Denning cautions that early criticism of sensational literature by scholars like Daryl Jones and Henry Nash Smith "tends to reify that genre, and, though giving an account of its internal relations, lose a sense of its relations to other genres" (76). He argues that framing dime novels about Jesse James or Buffalo Bill as Westerns obscures the broader themes running through the bulk of sensational literature, whether they are factory girl romances or stories of heroic mechanics. For more on dime westerns, see Bill Brown's "Reading the West: Cultural and Historical Background." See Marcus Klein's *Easterns, Westerns, and Private Eyes: American Matters, 1870–1900* for more on how class tensions and racial anxieties work to implicate various forms of sensational literature in broader cultural trends in nineteenth-century America.

14. Bold, *Frontier Club*, 2.

15. Worden, *Masculine Style*, 40.

16. In *Masculine Style*, Worden argues that the subversive power of the dime novel works as a counternarrative to the wholesale reorganizing of late-nineteenth-century American masculinity by cultural elites as described by scholars such as Gail Bederman. He suggests, not convincingly to my mind, that Bederman overestimates the power of patriarchal structures that men such as Teddy Roosevelt worked to enshrine at the end of the nineteenth century and the early decades of the twentieth century.

17. Dean, "Calamities of Convention," 40.

18. Worden, *Masculine Style*, 33.

19. Johnson, *Black Masculinity and the Frontier Myth*, 99, 102. There is scant research about marginalized groups as dime novel readers. Bold's "Did Indigenous People Read Dime Novels? Re-indigenizing the Western at the Turn of the Twentieth Century" represents an important step in addressing this gap in scholarship. As Bold suggests, dime novels had a wide readership, and more attention needs to be paid to the marginalized readers of these texts.

20. De Certeau, *Practice of Everyday Life*, xvii.

21. Ringel, *Commercializing Childhood*, 102.

22. Mintz, *Huck's Raft*, 185; Ringel, *Commercializing Childhood*, 11.

23. Denning, *Mechanic Accents*, 30.

24. Letter to Frank O'Brien, Jan 1, 1915. Manuscript Collection 354, University of Delaware Library Special Collections. In one letter, Harbaugh makes this bold claim: "I met Ned Buntline once in Baltimore when he was on the stage in the 'old days' with Buffalo Bill and 'Texas Jack.' But those stories can't hold a candle to the Beadle 'Dimes.'"

25. Harbaugh, "A Christmas Sentiment," 1921. Manuscript Collection 354, University of Delaware Library Special Collections.

26. Manning, letter to Frank O'Brien, April 14, 1897. Manuscript Collection 354, University of Delaware Library Special Collections. Hall defined the adolescent years as between fourteen and twenty-four. Intriguingly, Edward Wheeler may also have been an adolescent when he began publishing sensational fiction for Beadle & Adams. As Albert Johannsen notes, while there's a lack of good

NOTES TO CHAPTER 2

biographical information on Wheeler, he may well have been in his teens or early twenties when he published his first novel in 1877. For more, see Albert Johannsen's *The House of Beadle & Adams and its Dime and Nickel Novels: The Story of a Vanished Literature*.

27. Johannsen, *House of Beadle & Adams*, chapter 11.
28. Harbaugh, *Judge Lynch, Jr.*, 2.
29. Stone, *Innocent Eye*, 99.
30. Sumner, "What Our Boys Are Reading," 681.
31. Apol, "Tamings and Ordeals," 63.
32. Alcott, *Eight Cousins*, chapter 17.
33. For more on Alcott's perceived attack on Optic, and the latter's (very public) response, see Arthur Young's "Banish the Books: Horatio Alger Jr., the Censors, the Libraries, and the Readers, 1870–1910," 424–25.
34. Denning, *Mechanic Accents*, 50.
35. Comstock is best known for his war on women's reproductive rights and his efforts to censor "obscene" materials about abortion and contraception. Nicola Beisel offers a thorough analysis of Comstock's moral crusade against women's rights (and their bodies) in *Imperiled Innocents: Anthony Comstock and Family Reproduction in Victorian America*. Comstock was also concerned with the pernicious effect of dime novels on boys, a topic he expounds upon in *Traps for the Young* (1883). Beisel discusses Comstock's triangulation of boys, dime novels, and delinquency on pages 64–66.
36. Chamberlain, "'Wise Censorship,'" 191.
37. Macleod, *Building Character in the American Boy*, 55.
38. Savage, *Teenage*, 36.
39. Kett, *Rites of Passage*, 128–29.
40. Chudacoff, *How Old Are You?* 22.
41. Kett, "Reflections on the History of Adolescence," 357.
42. DeLuzio, *Female Adolescence in American Scientific Thought*, 64.
43. Anderson, *Frank Merriwell*, xvi.
44. Chinn, *Inventing Modern Adolescence*, 84.
45. Kett, *Rites of Passage*, 140.
46. Ringel, *Commercializing Childhood*, 150.
47. Anderson, *Frank Merriwell*, xxii.
48. Moore, *Cow Boys and Cattle Men*, 43.
49. Smith, *Virgin Land*, 102.
50. Quoted in Mailloux, *Rhetorical Power*, 120.
51. Johannsen, *House of Beadle & Adams*, chapter 11.
52. Jones, *The Dime Novel Western*, 81.
53. Smith, *Virgin Land*, 119.
54. Worden, *Masculine Style*, 29.
55. See Bold, *Selling the Wild West*.
56. Wheeler, *Deadwood Dick*, 280.
57. Worden, *Masculine Style*, 26.

58. Wheeler, *Deadwood Dick*, 287.

59. Wheeler, *Double Daggers*, 2.

60. Worden, *Masculine Style*, 28.

61. Wheeler, *Deadwood Dick*, 273.

62. Worden, *Masculine Style*, 38.

63. Wheeler, *Double Daggers*, 16.

64. Wheeler, *Deadwood Dick*, 13.

65. Wheeler, *Black Hills Jezebel*, 2.

66. Ingraham, *Gold Plume*, 3. University of Delaware Library, Special Collections, Manuscript Collection 354.

67. Parille, *Boys at Home*, 91. A number of scholars highlight self-mastery and self-restraint as key to the transition from boyhood to manhood in late-nineteenth-century America. For more on this, see E. Anthony Rotundo's *American Manhood: Transformations in Masculinity from the Revolution to the Modern Era*, chapters 1–3. In "Middle-Class Men and the Solace of Fraternal Ritual," Mark Carnes examines how fraternal societies helped nineteenth-century youth negotiate the transition from boyhood to manhood.

68. Stone, *Innocent Eye*, 103.

69. Wheeler, *Deadwood Dick*, 353.

70. Wheeler, *Double Daggers*, 2.

71. Whitaker, *Dick Darling*, 2.

72. Wheeler, *Double Daggers*, 2.

73. Shaheen, "Endless Frontiers," 21–22.

74. Lewis, *American Adam*, 5.

75. Turner, "Significance of the Frontier," chapter 1.

76. Wheeler, *Wild Ivan*, 2.

77. Badger, *Roving Joe*, 1.

78. Wheeler, *Wild Ivan*, 11.

79. Wheeler, *Deadwood Dick's Dream*, 2.

80. Taylor, *A Strange Story*, 2.

81. Interestingly, Buffalo Bill's friends and coworkers also received this treatment, with dime novels devoted to fantastic adventures and exploits that have been wholly fabricated. For instance, Cody's pal Frank Powell, who took on the name of White Beaver, often appears in Beadle & Adams dime novels about the young Buffalo Bill. The young Powell plays a starring role in Ingraham's *Fancy Frank's Drop*.

82. Anderson, *Frank Merriwell*, xxii.

CHAPTER 3

1. Russell, *Lives and Legends of Buffalo Bill*, 379.

2. "Affected with the Buffalo Bill Measles," *Atchison Daily Globe*, October 27, 1887, 3.

3. *New York American and Mercury*, Aug 19, 1893. William Frederick Cody/Buffalo Bill Papers (WH72).

4. Buffalo Bill and Doc Carver shared billing on the program for the inaugural season of the show, Wild West: Rocky Mountain and Prairie Exhibition. After

parting with Carver, the show became known as Buffalo Bill's Wild West. It retained that name, with "the Congress of Rough Riders of the World" added on in later years.

5. Warren, *Buffalo Bill's America*, 264.

6. Reddin, *Wild West Shows*, 63.

7. Warren, *Buffalo Bill's America*, 216–17.

8. Newspaper accounts of boys and girls playing Buffalo Bill proliferated with increasing frequency in the late nineteenth and early twentieth centuries. See, for instance, "Domestic News: An Imitator of Buffalo Bill," in the *San Francisco Bulletin*, October 7, 1884, or "Playing Buffalo Bill," in the *Philadelphia Inquirer*, July 11, 1887. This subject is covered in some depth in chapter 5 of this book.

9. Kolodny, *Lay of the Land*, 136.

10. Ashby, *Saving the Waifs*, 80.

11. Altherr, "Let 'Er Rip," 81. For more on Barnum and frontier spectacle, see Neil Harris's *Humbug: The Art of P. T. Barnum* (66). Paul Reddin's *Wild West Shows* offers an in-depth analysis of Catlin's career and his significance as a progenitor of the late-nineteenth-century explosion of frontier spectacle (see chapters 1 and 2). Joy Kasson's *Buffalo Bill's Wild West: Celebrity, Memory, and Popular History* (67–68; 84–85) and L. G. Moses's *Wild West Shows and the Images of American Indians, 1883–1933* (14–19) address Catlin's connection to Wild West shows.

12. Leslie, "At the Fair." William F. Cody Collection (MS06).

13. Sagala, *Buffalo Bill on Stage*, 79.

14. Aveling, *An American Journey*, 150.

15. Paris, "Through the Looking Glass," 107.

16. "Buffalo Bill is Coming: A Chance for the Children to See This Hero of Romance and Reality," *Worcester Sunday Spy*, May 30, 1897. NewsBank/Readex, Database: America's Historical Newspapers.

17. Levine, *Highbrow/Lowbrow*, 37.

18. Sagala, *Buffalo Bill on Stage*, 194. For an overview of the show's creation and early history see Joy Kasson's *Buffalo Bill's Wild West* (chapter 1), Reddin's *Wild West Shows* (chapter 3), and Warren's *Buffalo Bill's America* (chapter 9).

19. Nathan Salsbury Papers (YCAL MSS17).

20. Cody and Salsbury had a prosperous but contentious relationship. The Nathan Salsbury Collection at Yale's Beinecke Library contains many hostile letters from Salsbury to Cody. In addition, the collection has drafts of Salsbury's memoir, in which he muses that when the book was finished, "I intend on dubbing it, Sixteen Years in Hell with Buffalo Bill." Despite personal differences, their working relationship served as a foundation for the show's most profitable years, from 1884 to 1902. By 1895, Cody and Salsbury began partnering with James Bailey. According to Warren's *Buffalo Bill's America*, a sideshow was added to Buffalo Bill's Wild West at this time (230). The sideshow became a fixture of the show after Salsbury's death, and Cody was forced to forge new partnerships with Bailey and others.

21. Salsbury, "The Origin of the Wild West Show," Nathan Salsbury Papers (YCAL MSS17).

22. "A Notable Man," 1878, William F. Cody Collection (MS06).
23. "Grand Opera House—'The Knights of the Plains.'" William F. Cody Collection (MS06).
24. "Fire Arms on the Stage: The Shooting of a Boy in the Gallery of a Baltimore Theater by Buffalo Bill," 1878, MS071. In *Performing the American Frontier, 1870–1906,* Roger Hall discusses the "explosion" of frontier drama between 1872 and 1876. He argues that Cody and actor Frank Mayo's Davy Crockett "defined the poles of sentiment and fierce action that influenced every succeeding border drama" (74). In Hall's analysis, Cody's violent, action-filled plays were the preferred fare for working-class male audiences (see 49–87).
25. Russell, *Lives and Legends of Buffalo Bill,* 272.
26. Like much of Buffalo Bill's history, the duel with Yellow Hand is controversial and has been since it was first reported. Over the years, reports surfaced containing wildly different claims, ranging from a full endorsement of Cody's story to the claim that he didn't kill Yellow Hand at all. Warren's *Buffalo Bill's America* offers an even-handed assessment of the incident, concluding that (if nothing else) Cody did kill Yellow Hand (118–20).
27. Warren, *Buffalo Bill's America,* 118.
28. Kasson, *Buffalo Bill's Wild West,* 136.
29. *Springfield Republican,* 1882, MS06.
30. "Amusements," *The Public Ledger,* December 23, 1875. NewsBank/Readex, Database: America's Historical Newspapers.
31. "The Wild West," *Chicago Tribune,* October 18, 1883. NewsBank/Readex, Database: America's Historical Newspapers.
32. Quoted in Deahl, "A History of Buffalo Bill's Wild West Show, 1883–1913," 33.
33. Buffalo Bill's Wild West and Congress of Rough Riders of the World, 1884 program, 22. William F. Cody Collection (MS06).
34. "Playing Buffalo Bill," *The Philadelphia Inquirer,* July 11, 1887. NewsBank/Readex, Database: America's Historical Newspapers.
35. The newspaper stories of children playing vary in scope and tone. For a light-hearted account of boys at play, see "New Wild West Show: How Seventh Avenue Youngsters Imitate Buffalo Bill and His Tribes of Indians," August 28, 1894, Nate Salsbury Scrapbooks (NSS). Even examples of children injured while playing Buffalo Bill varied in tone, with earlier accounts tending to be more anxious. For examples, see "Played Wild West," in the *New York Commercial Advertiser,* August 29, 1894, Nate Salsbury Scrapbooks (NSS), which worriedly recounts the story of a young woman shot by two boys playing Buffalo Bill, and "Little George Rhoads Receives Gash in Head Which Removes Him from the Warpath," in the *Urbana Daily Courier,* August 7, 1909. NewsBank/Readex, Database: America's Historical Newspapers, which is surprisingly playful in its description of a boy falling on a hatchet.
36. Wallis, *Real Wild West,* 267.
37. Ingraham, *Adventures of Buffalo Bill from Boyhood to Manhood,* 3. McCracken Research Library. Buffalo Bill Center of the West.

38. Cody, *The Adventures of Buffalo Bill*, 34.
39. Life on the Plains & Wild West Combination, 1883 program. William Frederick Cody/Buffalo Bill Papers (WH72).
40. Quoted in Nolan, "The Roundup," November 1963, 102. William F. Cody Collection (MS06).
41. "We Are Coming! The World's Champion Trio: Buffalo Bill, Doctor Carver, Captain Bogardus," 1883. William F. Cody Collection (MS06).
42. Rennert, *100 Posters*, 5.
43. Martin, "Grandest and Most Cosmopolitan Object Teacher," 96. Richard Slotkin's *Gunfighter Nation: The Myth of the Frontier in Twentieth-Century America* discusses Turner and frontier mythology through the rhetoric of development (16–21). More recently, Karen Jones and John Wills's *The American West: Competing Visions* reevaluates Turner's thesis through the lens of development, both in his time and ours, and its relationship to nineteenth-century germ theory.
44. Buffalo Bill's Wild West, 1885 program, 5. William Frederick Cody/Buffalo Bill Papers (WH72).
45. *Pomeroy's Democrat*, July 18, 1886. Nate Salsbury Scrapbooks (NSS).
46. Buffalo Bill's Wild West and Congress of Rough Riders of the World, 1887 program, 11. William F. Cody Collection (MS06).
47. Cody and Salsbury eventually toured all over the United States and traveled to many parts of Europe. In later years, especially after Salsbury died, Cody toured relentlessly, often because of his declining financial situation. The Buffalo Bill Museum and Grave's website provides a comprehensive of list of every place Cody went, titled "Did Buffalo Bill Visit Your Town?"
48. *Pomeroy's Democrat*, July 18, 1886. Nate Salsbury Scrapbooks (NSS).
49. Martin, "Grandest and Most Cosmopolitan Object Teacher," 102.
50. MacKaye, letter to Nate Salsbury, November 8, 1876. Nathan Salsbury Papers (YCAL MSS17).
51. Warren, *Buffalo Bill's America*, 264.
52. Deahl, "A History of Buffalo Bill's Wild West Show," 60.
53. Field, interview with John Burke, *Kate Field's Washington*, July 19, 1893. William Frederick Cody/Buffalo Bill Papers (WH72).
54. *A Peep at Buffalo Bill's Wild West*, 1887. William F. Cody Collection (MS06).
55. In *The W. F. Cody Buffalo Bill Collectors Guide with Values*, James Wojtowicz includes a section on "Toys & Other Juvenile Delights," featuring toy guns, board games, and more. There are many nineteenth-century descriptions of Buffalo Bill toys in newspapers. For instance, see "Christmas Toys: Plenty of Them This Year for the Youth of Any Age," in the *Wheeling Sunday Register*, December 14, 1890, which recommends a set of Buffalo Bill action figures. The *Brooklyn Eagle*, December 16, 1894, contains an ad of Buffalo Bill "Box Sets" for sale. Also, see "Dan Beard's New Ideas for Boys," in the *Ladies Home Journal*, November 19, 1899, wherein Beard guides readers in constructing their own Wild West cutout figures.
56. Sánchez-Eppler, *Dependent States*, 819.
57. Quoted in Russell, *The Lives and Legends of Buffalo Bill*, 305.

58. Buffalo Bill's Wild West, 1884 program, 25. William F. Cody Collection (MS06).

59. Moore, *Cow Boys and Cattle Men*, 5.

60. Aveling, *An American Journey*, 155.

61. Moore, *Cow Boys and Cattle Men*, 210. In the introduction to *The Frontier Club: Popular Western and Cultural Power, 1880–1924*, Christine Bold provides an in-depth analysis of the Johnson County War as a symbol of frontier class conflict, and its mediation through fiction. For more on class differences and frontier mythology in the late nineteenth century, see Slotkin's *Gunfighter Nation*, chapter 5.

62. Bederman, *Manliness and Civilization*, 195.

63. Bold, *Frontier Club*, 92.

64. Buffalo Bill's Wild West, 1887 program, 2. William F. Cody Collection (MS06). The "whiting" of the cowboy clearly contradicts the historical record. See Jacqueline Moore's *Cow boys and Cattle men: Class and Masculinities on the Texas Frontier* (134–40) for an analysis of contentious race relations among nineteenth-century cowboys. Also see John Ravage's *Black Pioneers: Images of the Black Experience on the North American Frontier*, chapter 6, for an overview of black cowboys and an intriguing set of accompanying images.

65. Buffalo Bill's Wild West, 1893 program, 27. William F. Cody Collection (MS06).

66. Buffalo Bill's Wild West, 1902 program, 20. William F. Cody Collection (MS06).

67. Warren, *Buffalo Bill's America*, 421.

68. Buffalo Bill's Wild West, 1893 program, 3. William F. Cody Collection (MS06).

69. Buffalo Bill's Wild West, 1902 program, 24. William F. Cody Collection (MS06).

70. *Daily Inter-Ocean*, July 23, 1893. Nate Salsbury Scrapbooks (NSS).

71. "Indians at Erastina," *New York Times*, June 26, 1886.

72. "The Greatest Summer Show," *New York Times*, September 9, 1894.

73. *Bison Courier*, 2. William F. Cody Collection (MS06). The *Bison Courier* was a show publication, similar to a program, but published and distributed separately.

74. *Daily Inter Ocean*, December 22, 1893. NewsBank/Readex, Database: America's Historical Newspapers.

75. *Daily Inter Ocean*, July 28, 1893. Nate Salsbury Scrapbooks (NSS).

76. Marden, "Book Dedication." William F. Cody Collection (MS06). The connection between Cody and Marden, a popular artist of success-story books like *Pushing to the Front* (1894), was more than coincidental. In the late nineteenth century, Buffalo Bill became a fixture of literature advocating the rhetoric of the self-made man, especially in pedagogical texts urging boys to work hard and live respectably. For instance, John Habberton's *Poor Boy's Chances* (1900) featured a biography of Cody emphasizing how his commendable work ethic and sterling character earned him a place in the "full list of poor boys who have become successful men."

CHAPTER 4

1. For an in-depth comparison of the two men, see Richard White's "Frederick Jackson Turner and Buffalo Bill."

2. Gubar, "Entertaining Children of All Ages," 3.

3. Lott, *Love and Theft*, 110.

4. Baker, MS06. For more on Baker's parents and their willingness to let him travel with Cody but not allow him to be formally adopted by the showman, see Don Russell's *Lives and Legends of Buffalo Bill*, 207.

5. "Education and Amusement," William F. Cody Collection (MS06). Most of the show's programs featured an extensive biography of Baker, as they did all for all featured performers. This promotional write-up was distributed separately. John Burke authored many of these, and his work as publicist for Buffalo Bill's Wild West played a considerable role in the show's success. For more, see chapter 4 of Joe Dobrow's *Pioneers of Promotion: How Press Agents for Buffalo Bill, P. T. Barnum, and the World's Columbian Exposition Created Modern Marketing*.

6. William F. Cody Collection (MS06).

7. *Anaconda Standard*. William F. Cody Collection (MS06).

8. Pawnee Bill's Historic Wild West, 1904 program. William F. Cody Collection (MS06).

9. Kasper, *Annie Oakley*, 61.

10. On expectations of girlhood, see Lynne Vallone's *Disciplines of Virtue: Girls' Culture in the Eighteenth and Nineteenth Centuries*, 114–24. On Lillian Smith and ethnicity, see Laura Browder's *Slippery Characters: Ethnic Impersonators and American Identities*. For more on Smith, see Julia Bricklin's *America's Best Female Sharpshooter: The Rise and Fall of Lillian Frances Smith*.

11. Jordan, *Cowgirls*, xxi.

12. Marra, "Taming America as Actress," 57.

13. "Calamity Jane Gone over the Divide," *Omaha World Herald*, August 8, 1903. NewsBank/Readex, Database: America's Historical Newspapers.

14. Browder, *Slippery Characters*, 66. In *America's Best Female Sharpshooter: The Rise and Fall of Lillian Frances Smith*, Julia Bricklin complicates Browder's description of how Smith left the show, the full reasons for which remain unclear. Bricklin discusses Smith's first marriage, its dissolution, and her departure from Buffalo Bill's Wild West in chapter 3.

15. Burke, "Education and Amusement—How they go Hand in Hand," July15, 1895. William Frederick Cody/Buffalo Bill Papers (WH72).

16. Deloria, *Indians in Unexpected Places*, 65.

17. O'Kieffe, *Western Story*, 112–13.

18. Quoted in Moses, *Wild West Shows*, 48–49.

19. O'Kieffe, *Western Story*, 145.

20. See "A Band of Seventy Indians: Will Give a Concert at Plymouth Church Tonight." *Brooklyn Eagle*. April 15, 1894. Brooklyn Newsstand: New York Public Library. For more on Carlisle and other Indian schools see David Wallace Adams's *Education for Extinction: American Indians and the Boarding School Experience, 1875–1928*.

21. "Indian Children's Ways: How the Little Braves and Squaws Play at Ambrose Park," *New York Recorder*, June 24, 1894. NewsBank/Readex, Database: America's Historical Newspapers.

22. Gallop, *Buffalo Bill's British Wild West*, 133.
23. Deloria, *Indians in Unexpected Places*, 64. While Buffalo Bill's Wild West billed Johnny Burke No Neck as the sole survivor of Wounded Knee, scholars dispute this account. For instance, Sam Maddra's *Hostiles? The Lakota Ghost Dance and Buffalo Bill's Wild West* describes the fate of another infant girl survivor. Ultimately, Johnny's real background remains grounds for speculation.
24. Sully, *Studies of Childhood*, 4–5.
25. Darwin, "A Biographical Sketch of an Infant."
26. Castañeda, *Figurations*, 21.
27. Quoted in Shuttleworth, *Mind of the Child*, 40.
28. Hall, *Youth*, 74. The idea of "ontogeny recapitulates phylogeny," the notion that the development of a single body recapitulates the development of its species, provided a critical foundation for Hall's theories of development. See Stephen Jay Gould's *Ontogeny and Phylogeny* for a cultural history of Haeckel and recapitulation theory.
29. Bank, "Archiving Culture," 43.
30. Quoted in Hassrick, et al., *Buffalo Bill and the Wild West*, 49–50.
31. Warren, *Buffalo Bill's America*, 358.
32. Maddox, "Politics, Performance and Indian Identity," 9.
33. Kasson, *Buffalo Bill's Wild West*, 212.
34. McNenly, *Native Performers in Wild West Shows*, 85.
35. Simmel, *On Individuality and Social Forms*, 295.
36. "Behind the Scenes: Inner Life of the Wild West Show," *The Times Democrat*, October 27, 1900. NewsBank/Readex, Database: America's Historical Newspapers.
37. Griswold, *Renaissance Revivals*, 6.
38. Warren, *Buffalo Bill's America*, 402–5.
39. For more on Rose Nelson, see Beverly Cox and Martin Jacobs's "Remembering Princess Blue Waters."
40. For an analysis of indigenous dress in photos from the show, see McNenly's *Native Performers in Wild West Shows: From Buffalo Bill to Euro Disney*, 90–99.
41. Warren, *Buffalo Bill's America*, 407.
42. Standing Bear, *My People the Sioux*, 266.
43. While it's not clear just what he did, Bennie Irving was a featured performer for portions of the Buffalo Bill's Wild West Show's 1890 tour of Europe. The Italian program lists him as "Il piu piccolo cow-boy del mondo." See also James Wojtowicz's *The W. F. Cody Buffalo Bill Collectors Guide with Values*, 19, which reports a similar billing for Irving in the 1890 German program.
44. Warren, *Buffalo Bill's America*, 404–7.
45. See Cox and Jacobs, "Remembering Princess Blue Waters."
46. Standing Bear, *My People the Sioux*, 141.
47. The books are interesting in their attribution, as well as for being variations on one another published in the same year by the same publisher. *Boy Acrobat* is attributed to George Hamid Jr. and *Circus* is attributed to George Hamid, but "as told to his son George Hamid Jr." In both books, the son tells the father's story.

48. Hamid, *Boy Acrobat*, 62.
49. Hamid, *Circus*, 40.
50. Bernstein, *Racial Innocence*, 14. Bernstein's idea of the repertoire is, at least in part, a response to Diana Taylor's *The Archive and the Repertoire: Performing Cultural Memory in the Americas*.
51. "American Icons: Buffalo Bill's Wild West," *Studio 360*. Marirose Nelson's reflections are part of a broader meditation on Buffalo Bill's Wild West that is worth listening to or reading in full.
52. "Girls See the Wild West," *New York Sun*, May 20, 1894. NewsBank/Readex, Database: America's Historical Newspapers.
53. "Gazed Upon Poor Lo!" *Boston Daily Globe*, May 24, 1897. NewsBank/Readex, Database: America's Historical Newspapers.
54. White, "'Through Their Eyes,'" 46. Alison Fields's "Circuits of Spectacle: The Miller Brothers' 101 Ranch Real Wild West" makes similar conjectures regarding a photograph of an Indian boy holding a revolver up at a photographer.
55. "Indians at Erastina," *New York Times*, June 26, 1886.
56. Buffalo Bill's Wild West, 1899 program, 10.
57. *Buffalo Bill: Showman of the West*, A&E video.
58. McGoff, "When Buffalo Bill's 'Red Injuns' Took Chances on 'Poled Ponies.'" *Brooklyn Daily Eagle*, August 5, 1945. Brooklyn Newsstand, New York Public Library.
59. Bernstein, *Racial Innocence*, 29.
60. Quoted in White, "'Through Their Eyes,'" 46.
61. Buffalo Bill's Wild West, 1891 program, 10.
62. Shuttleworth, *Mind of the Child*, 267.
63. Quoted in Grey, "Zane Grey Adds the Finishing Touch," 323.

CHAPTER 5

1. Etulain, *Telling Western Stories*, 77.
2. Tompkins, *West of Everything*, 45. This claim by Tompkins folds into her larger analysis of the twentieth-century response to women's entering the public sphere.
3. Bold, *Selling the Wild West*, 43.
4. Webb, "Buffalo Bill, Saint or Devil?" 27. Webb's reminiscences were solicited by Edward Le Blank of *Real West* magazine, June 1982. William F. Cody Collection (MS06).
5. "All Nation Grieves with the Family in Death of Col. Cody." William F. Cody Collection (MS06).
6. Kidd, *Making American Boys*, 88. See also David Macleod's *Building Character in the American Boy: The Boy Scouts, YMCA, and Their Forerunners, 1870–1920* for an overview of organizational boy work in the nineteenth century.
7. There are several biographies of Seton available. For a more extended examination of Seton's younger years, see Betty Keller's *Black Wolf: The Life of Ernest Thompson Seton*. David Witt covers some of the same material in his biography, paying particular attention to Seton's early efforts as a painter. Witt's book also

contains some fine color prints of a few of Seton's paintings. Kent Baxter covers the genesis of the Woodcraft Indians in some depth in chapter 3 of *The Modern Age: Turn-of-the-Century American Culture and the Invention of Adolescence.*

8. Baxter, *Modern Age,* 97.

9. Deloria, *Playing Indian,* 97. Chapter 4 of *Playing Indian* provides a thorough examination of Beard and Seton and their use of frontier iconography.

10. Ben Jordan's *Modern Manhood and the Boy Scouts of America: Citizenship, Race, and the Environment, 1910–1930* sets the standard for histories of the Boy Scouts of America. For more on Powell and the Boy Scouts, see Robert MacDonald's *Sons of the Empire: The Frontier and the Boy Scout Movement, 1890–1918.* David Macleod's *Building Character in the American Boy* provides an overview of character-building organizations, including the Woodcraft Indians and the Boy Scouts, and the cultural context that helped them thrive.

11. *Boy Scouts Handbook,* xiii. The first BSA handbook, printed in 1910, bore Seton's stamp even more clearly than this one, sometimes thought of as the first "official" handbook. Seton wove the history of his ideas of Woodcraft seamlessly into the history of the BSA in the 1910 edition, an effect that was diminished by the wider release of the 1911 handbook.

12. Beard, "Buffalo Bill, The Friend of the American Boy," March 1917. William F. Cody Collection (MS06).

13. Deloria, *Playing Indian,* 102.

14. "American Boys Suffering From 'Ingrowing Spunk,'" *Bisbee Daily Review,* December 30, 1909. William F. Cody Collection (MS06).

15. On the eve of World War I, Seton increasingly came under fire from BSA leaders and other critics for his pacifist leanings, his lack of American citizenship, and Grace Gallatin Seton's prominence as a suffragette. Much of Seton's messy divorce from the BSA played out in public, and James West repeatedly attacked Seton's character and his qualifications for teaching American boys how to be good citizens.

16. William F. Cody Collection (MS06).

17. "American Boys Suffering From 'Ingrowing Spunk,'" *Bisbee Daily Review,* December 30, 1909. William F. Cody Collection (MS06).

18. "Boy Scouts See Wild-West Show," *The Winnipeg Telegram,* August 23, 1910. William F. Cody Collection (MS06). Cooper's novel *The Prairie* best demonstrates Bumppo's inability to live in the civilized world. While the novel is the third of the five Leatherstocking novels Cooper wrote, it features the end point of the series chronologically, with the then octogenarian hero dying at the book's end. Plagued by the sound of trees being felled, the scout has fled his eastern home, travelled around the country, and settled in the desolate prairie (which Cooper never saw with his own eyes). Once he helps a group of settlers survive their encounter with Indians—and one another—Bumppo dies, having nowhere else to go.

19. "Rough Riding School to Brace Up Men About Town," April 19, 1901. William F. Cody Collection (MS06).

20. William F. Cody Collection (MS06).

21. Keaton, "Backyard Desperadoes," 182.
22. Mechling, "Gun Play," 192.
23. Wojtowicz, *The W. F. Cody Buffalo Bill Collectors Guide With Values*, 191.
24. Cross, *Kid's Stuff*, 11.
25. Wojtowicz, *The W. F. Cody Buffalo Bill Collectors Guide With Values*, 189.
26. Western Americana Collection, Beinecke Rare Book and Manuscript Library, Yale University.
27. "Played Wild West," *New York Commercial Advertiser*, Aug. 29, 1894. NewsBank/Readex, Database: America's Historical Newspapers.
28. Cross, *Kids Stuff*, 66.
29. An 1876 program for the Buffalo Bill Combination notes, "the celebrated Winchester Repeating Rifles are the ones used by Mr. Cody (Buffalo Bill), both on the plains and the stage." William F. Cody Collection (MS06).
30. Images of advertisements for most of these toys appear in James Wojtowicz's *The W. F. Cody Buffalo Bill Collector's Guide with Values*. That this book remains one of the best sources of information on this subject demonstrates that collectors have paid far more attention to these objects than scholars.
31. "Boy Scouts Capture Bandits," *Boys' Life*, 29.
32. Mechling, "Boy Scouts," 9.
33. Palmer, "The Gun-Loving Boy Scouts," Palmer provides a full recounting of the deadly encounter between the armed American Boy Scout and his victim, and he also includes links to two newspaper articles published at the time of the shooting.
34. Houze, "To the Dreams of Youth," 63, manuscript draft. Herbert Houze Collection (MS344).
35. Cass Hough's *It's a Daisy!* and Joe Murfin's *Daisy: It All Starts Here* are institutional histories written by company insiders; both books provide a useful history of the air rifle and the company that created it.
36. Mechling, "Boy Scouts," 9.
37. Jacobson, *Raising Consumers*, 112.
38. During a 2015 phone call, Joe Murfin, Daisy's vice-president of publicity, repeatedly told me he was uncomfortable associating Daisy air rifles with the idea of play and suggested using the term "recreational uses."
39. *The Youth's Companion*, July 18, 1901. Boston, MA, 363.
40. Addams, *The Spirit of Youth*, chapter 4.
41. Mechling, "Boy Scouts," 6.
42. Thrasher, *The Gang*, ix. For more on the history of juvenile justice in the United States, see Anthony Platt's *The Child Savers: The Invention of Delinquency* and Eric Schneider's *In the Web of Class: Delinquents and Reformers in Boston, 1810s–1930s*. Platt's account is theoretical, suggesting a radical reappraisal of Progressive Era reformers and the institutions they created. Schneider offers a detailed account of juvenile justice institutions in the United States, from public reformatories and asylums to the first juvenile courts.
43. Yellow Bird, "Cowboys and Indians," 43.

44. Hirschfelder, "Still Playing Cowboys and Indians," 164.
45. As of this writing, these toys remain readily available for purchase in the United States. For instance, several different sets of these toys can be purchased on Amazon.com, including Kidsco's twenty-pack of plastic cowboys and Indian figures. In this set, the red Indians and brown cowboys are all dressed for battle, and the copy notes the figures are "very detailed" presenting "Indians with primitive weapons and Cowboys with rifles and pistols."
46. Hoy, "Cardboard Indians," 303.
47. Video games also offer a distinctive type of scripted play. Katharine Slater's "Who Gets to Die of Dysentery: Ideology, Geography, and *The Oregon Trail*" explores this phenomenon and provides an insightful analysis of how the choices offered—and not offered—to players of *The Oregon Trail* may encourage scripted play.
48. Chudacoff, "History of Children's Play," 104.
49. Jacobson, *Raising Consumers*, 97.
50. Mechling, "Gun Play," 203–4.
51. Sutton-Smith, *Ambiguity of Play*, 9.
52. Seeger's quote comes from his preface to Knox, *The Storyteller*, xi.
53. Yellow Bird, "Cowboys and Indians," 45.
54. Bernstein, *Racial Innocence*, 197. For more on the Clark doll study, see Kiri Davis's short 2005 documentary, *A Girl Like Me*.
55. Bold, "Did Indians Read Dime Novels?" 151.
56. Raheja, *Reservation Reelism*, 37.
57. Brooks, *A Pioneer Mother of California*, 15.

CONCLUSION

1. For more on Roddenberry and the genesis of *Star Trek*, see the Smithsonian's "An Oral History of 'Star Trek.'" Ronald Reagan appeared in many Hollywood Westerns and served as the host of the television show *Death Valley Days* from 1964 to 1965, just prior to launching his career in politics. News stories about Bush's working vacations on the ranch were commonplace during his presidency. In one *Washington Post* article, Lisa Rein describes how the then president's "idea of paradise is to hop in his white Ford pickup truck in jeans and work boots, drive to a stand of cedars, and whack the trees to the ground."
2. At the time of this writing, a fourth *Toy Story* film had just been released in American theaters. That film—along with any future sequels—is not included in this analysis.
3. Roberts, "'It's a Dangerous World Out There for a Toy,'" 417. For more on toys that come to life, see Lois Kuznets's *When Toys Come to Life: Narratives of Animation, Metamorphosis, and Development*.
4. Ackerman, "The Spirit of Toys," 904.
5. Roberts, "'It's a Dangerous World Out There for a Toy,'" 425.
6. Tompkins, *West of Everything*, 39.
7. Gillam and Wooden, "Post-Princess Models of Gender," 3.

8. For an analysis of master-slave play in dolls, see Robin Bernstein's *Racial Innocence*. On the *Toy Story* films in particular, see Gina Camodeca's "Uncle Tom's Cabin: The Politics of Ownership in Disney's *Toy Story*."

9. Gillam and Wooden, "Post-Princess Models of Gender," 6.

10. Roberts, "'It's a Dangerous World Out There for a Toy,'" 433.

11. Cody, *Adventures of Buffalo Bill*, vii.

12. In recent years, there has been some wonderful scholarship on the transnational impact of American frontier culture. For instance, see Emily Burns's *Transnational Frontiers: The American West in France* and Ch. Didier Gondola's *Tropical Cowboys: Westerns, Violence, and Masculinity in Kinshasa*.

BIBLIOGRAPHY

ARCHIVAL SOURCES

William Frederick Cody/Buffalo Bill Papers (WH72). Western History Collection,
Denver Public Library, Denver, Colorado.
Nate Salsbury Scrapbooks (NSS)
McCracken Research Library. Buffalo Bill Center of the West, Cody, Wyoming.
Buffalo Bill Scrapbooks
William F. Cody Collection (MS06)
Herbert Houze Collection (MS344)
Vincent Mercaldo Collection (MS071)
Special Collections, University of Delaware Library.
Manuscript Collection 354
Western Americana Collection. Beinecke Rare Book and Manuscript Library, Yale
University Library.
Nathan Salsbury Papers (YCAL MSS17)

NEWSPAPERS

Anaconda Standard
Atchison Daily Globe
Bisbee Daily Review
Bison Courier
Boston Daily Globe
Brooklyn Eagle
Chicago Tribune
Columbus Enquirer
Daily Inter Ocean
Illinois State Journal
Kansas City Times
Kate Field's Washington
New Hampshire Recorder
New York Journal
New York American and Mercury
New York Commercial Advertiser
New York Recorder
New York Sun
New York Times
New York Tribune
Philadelphia Inquirer
Omaha World Herald
Pomeroy's Democrat
Public Ledger
San Francisco Bulletin

Springfield Republican
Times Democrat
Urbana Daily Courier
Wheeling Sunday Register
Winnipeg Telegram
Worcester Sunday Spy

BOOKS AND ARTICLES

Abate, Michelle Ann. "'Bury My Heart in Recent History': Mark Twain's 'Hellfire Hotchkiss,' the Massacre at Wounded Knee, and the Dime Novel Western." *American Literary Realism* 42, no. 2 (Winter 2010): 114–28.

Ackerman, Alan. "The Spirit of Toys: Resurrection and Redemption in *Toy Story* and *Toy Story 2*." *University of Toronto Quarterly* 74, no. 4 (Fall 2005): 895–912.

Adams, David Wallace. *Education for Extinction: American Indians and the Boarding School Experience, 1875–1928*. Lawrence: University Press of Kansas, 1995.

Addams, Jane. *The Spirit of Youth and the City Streets*. New York: Macmillan Company, 1909. https://www.gutenberg.org/ebooks/16221.

Alcott, Louisa May. *Eight Cousins*. Boston: Roberts Brothers, 1887. https://www.gutenberg.org/ebooks/2726.

Aldrich, Thomas Bailey. *The Story of a Bad Boy*. In *Our Young Folks: An Illustrated Magazine for Boys and Girls*, January 1869. American Periodicals Series Online.

Alger Jr., Horatio. *Julius, The Street Boy, or Out West*. Chicago: M. A. Donohue & Company, 1890.

———. *Ragged Dick*. Edited by Hildegard Hoeller. New York: W. W. Norton, 2007.

Altherr, Thomas. "Let 'Er Rip: Popular Culture Images of the American West in Wild West Shows, Rodeos, and Rendezvous." In *Wanted Dead or Alive: The American West in Popular Culture*, edited by Richard Aquila, 73–104. Champaign: University of Illinois Press, 1998.

"American Icons: Buffalo Bill's Wild West." *Studio 360*. November 5, 2010. Transcript.

Anderson, Ryan. *Frank Merriwell and the Fiction of All-American Boyhood: The Progressive Era Creation of the Schoolboy Sports Story*. Fayetteville: University of Arkansas Press, 2015.

Apol, Laura. "Tamings and Ordeals: Depictions of Female and Male Coming of Age in the West in Turn-of-the-Century *Youth's Companion* Serials." *The Lion and the Unicorn* 24, no. 1 (January 2000): 61–80.

Ariès, Philippe. *Centuries of Childhood: A Social History of Family Life*. Trans. Robert Baldick. New York: Random House, 1962.

Ashby, LeRoy. *Saving the Waifs: Reformers and Dependent Children, 1890–1917*. Philadelphia: Temple University Press, 1985.

Aveling, Edward. *An American Journey*. New York: Lovell, Gestefeld and Co., 1892.

Bank, Rosemarie K. "Archiving Culture: Performance and American Museums in the Earlier Nineteenth Century." In *Performing America: Cultural Nationalism in American Theater*, edited by Jeffrey Mason and J. Ellen Gainor, 37–51. Ann Arbor: University of Michigan Press, 2001.

Baxter, Kent. *The Modern Age: Turn-of-the-Century American Culture and the Invention of Adolescence*. Tuscaloosa: University of Alabama Press, 2008.

Bederman, Gail. *Manliness and Civilization: A Cultural History of Gender and Race in the United States, 1880–1917*. Chicago: University of Chicago Press, 1995.

Beisel, Nicola. *Imperiled Innocents: Anthony Comstock and Family Reproduction in Victorian America*. Princeton: Princeton University Press, 1997.

Bernstein, Robin. *Racial Innocence: Performing American Childhood from Slavery to Civil Rights*. New York: New York University Press, 2011.

Bold, Christine. "Did Indigenous People Read Dime Novels? Re-indigenizing the Western at the Turn of the Twentieth Century." In *New Directions in Popular Fiction: Genre, Distribution, Reproduction*, edited by Ken Gelder, 135–56. London: Palgrave Macmillan, 2016.

———. *The Frontier Club: Popular Westerns and Cultural Power, 1880–1924*. Oxford: Oxford University Press, 2013.

———. *Selling the Wild West: Popular Western Fiction, 1860–1960*. Bloomington: Indiana University Press, 1987.

"Boy Scouts Capture Bandits," *Boys' Life Magazine*, July 11, 1911.

Boy Scouts Handbook. New York: Doubleday, Page & Company, 1911.

Brace, Charles Loring. *The Dangerous Classes of New York and Twenty Years' Work among Them*. New York: Wynkoop & Hallenbeck, 1872. https://openlibrary.org/books /OL13557403M/The_dangerous_classes_of_New_York_and_twenty_years' _work_among_them.

Bricklin, Julia. *America's Best Female Sharpshooter: The Rise and Fall of Lillian Frances Smith*. Norman: University of Oklahoma Press, 2017.

Brooks, Elisha. *A Pioneer Mother of California*. San Francisco: Harr Wagner, 1922.

Browder, Laura. *Slippery Characters: Ethnic Impersonators and American Identities*. Chapel Hill: University of North Carolina Press, 2000.

Brown, Bill. "Reading the West: Cultural and Historical Background." In *Reading the West: An Anthology of Dime Westerns*, edited by Bill Brown, 1–40. Boston: Bedford St. Martin's, 1997.

Brumberg, Joan Jacobs. *Kansas Charley, The Story of a Nineteenth-Century Boy Murderer*. New York: Penguin, 2003.

Burns, Emily C. *Transnational Frontiers: The American West in France*. Norman: University of Oklahoma Press, 2018.

Camodeca, Gina. "Uncle Tom's Cabin: The Politics of Ownership in Disney's *Toy Story*." *Studies in Popular Culture* 25, no. 2 (October 2003): 51–63.

Carnes, Mark C. "Middle-Class Men and the Solace of Fraternal Ritual." In *Meanings for Manhood: Constructions of Masculinity in Victorian America*, edited by Mark C. Carnes and Clyde Griffen, 37–52. Chicago: University of Chicago Press, 1990.

Castañeda, Claudia. *Figurations: Child, Bodies, Worlds*. Durham: Duke University Press, 2002.

Chamberlain, Kathleen. "'Wise Censorship': Cultural Authority and the Scorning of Juvenile Series Books, 1890–1940." In *Scorned Literature: Essays on the History and Criticism of Popular Mass-Produced Fiction in America*, edited by Lydia

Cushman Schurman and Deidre Johnson, 187–212. Westport, CT: Greenwood Press, 1992.

Chinn, Sarah E. *Inventing Modern Adolescence: The Children of Immigrants in Turn-of-the-Century America.* New Brunswick, NJ: Rutgers University Press, 2009.

Chudacoff, Howard P. "The History of Children's Play in the United States." In *The Oxford Handbook of the Development of Play,* edited by Anthony D. Pellegrini, 101–9. Oxford: Oxford University Press, 2011.

———. *How Old Are You? Age Consciousness in American Culture.* Princeton: Princeton University Press, 1989.

Clemens, Samuel L., and William D. Howells. *Mark Twain–Howells Letters: The Correspondence of Samuel L. Clemens and William D. Howells, 1872–1910.* Edited by Henry Nash Smith and William M. Gibson. Cambridge, MA: Belknap Press of Harvard University Press, 1960.

Cody, William F. *The Adventures of Buffalo Bill.* New York: Bonanza Books, 1965.

———. *The Life of Hon. William F. Cody, Known as Buffalo Bill.* Edited by Frank Christianson. Lincoln: University of Nebraska Press, 2011.

Cohoon, Lorinda B. *Serialized Citizenships: Periodical, Books, and American Boys, 1840–1911.* Lanham, MD: Scarecrow Press, 2006.

Coulombe, Joseph, L. *Mark Twain and the American West.* Columbia: University of Missouri Press, 2003.

Cox, Beverly, and Martin Jacobs. "Remembering Princess Blue Waters." *Native Peoples Magazine* 18, no.1 (January/February 2005): 26.

Cronon, William, George Miles, and Jay Gitlin. "Becoming West: Toward a New Meaning for Western History." In *Under an Open Sky: Rethinking America's Western Past,* edited by William Cronon, George Miles, and Jay Gitlin, 3–27. New York: W. W. Norton & Company, 1992.

Cross, Gary. *Kids' Stuff: Toys and the Changing World of American Childhood.* Cambridge, MA: Harvard University Press, 1997.

Darwin, Charles, "A Biographical Sketch of an Infant." *Mind* 2 (1877): 285–94. Classics in the History of Psychology. https://psychclassics.yorku.ca/Darwin/infant.htm.

Davis, Kiri, dir. *A Girl Like Me.* Reel Works Teen Filmmaking, 2015.

Deahl, William Evans, Jr. "A History of Buffalo Bill's Wild West Show, 1883–1913." PhD diss., Southern Illinois University, 1974.

Dean, Janet. "Calamities of Convention in a Dime Novel Western." In *Scorned Literature: Essays on the History and Criticism of Popular Mass-Produced Fiction in America,* edited by Lydia Cushman Schurman and Deidre Johnson, 37–50. Westport, CT: Greenwood Press, 1992.

De Certeau, Michel. *The Practice of Everyday Life.* Translated by Steven Rendall. Berkeley: University of California Press, 2011.

Decker, Mark, "From Bad Boys to Good Managers: Twain, Aldrich, and the Creation of a Middle-Class Ideal." *Children's Literature Quarterly* 42, no. 3 (Fall 2017): 267–84.

Deloria, Philip J. *Indians in Unexpected Places.* Lawrence: University Press of Kansas, 2004.

———. *Playing Indian*. New Haven, CT: Yale University Press, 2004.

DeLuzio, Crista. *Female Adolescence in American Scientific Thought, 1830–1930*. Baltimore: Johns Hopkins University Press, 2007.

Denning, Michael. *Mechanic Accents: Dime Novels and Working-Class Culture in America*. London: Verso, 1998.

Dobrow, Joe. *Pioneers of Promotion: How Press Agents for Buffalo Bill, P. T. Barnum, and the World's Columbian Exposition Created Modern Marketing*. Norman: University of Oklahoma Press, 2018.

Etulain, Richard W. *Telling Western Stories: From Buffalo Bill to Larry McMurtry*. Albuquerque: University of New Mexico Press, 1999.

Fiedler, Leslie A. *Love and Death in the American Novel*. New York: Criterion Books, 1960.

Fields, Alison, "Circuits of Spectacle: The Miller Brothers' 101 Ranch Real Wild West." *American Indian Quarterly* 36, no. 4. (Fall 2012): 443–64.

Ford, John, dir. *The Man Who Shot Liberty Valance*. Paramount Pictures, 1962.

Fuller, Thomas. "Go West, Young Man!—An Elusive Slogan." *Indiana Magazine of History* 100, no. 3 (September 2004): 232–42.

Gallop, Alan. *Buffalo Bill's British Wild West*. Thrupp, UK: Sutton, 2001.

Garland, Hamlin. *Boy Life on the Prairie*. New York: Frederick Ungar, 1959.

———. "Mr. Howells's Latest Novels." In *The War of the Critics over William Dean Howells*, edited by Edwin H. Cady and David L. Frazier. Evanston, IL: Row, Peterson, and Company, 1962.

Gillam, Ken, and Shannon R. Wooden, "Post-Princess Models of Gender: The New Man in Disney/Pixar." *Journal of Popular Film and Television* 36, no. 1 (April 2008): 2–8.

Gondola, Didier Ch. *Tropical Cowboys: Westerns, Violence, and Masculinity in Kinshasa*. Bloomington: Indiana University Press, 2016.

Gould, Stephen Jay. *Ontogeny and Phylogeny*. Cambridge, MA: Belknap Press of Harvard University Press, 1977.

Grey, Zane. "Zane Grey Adds the Finishing Touch to the Story by Telling of the Last Days of the Last of the Great Scouts." In Helen Cody Wetmore's *Last of the Great Scouts: Buffalo Bill*, 321–33. New York: Grosset and Dunlop, 1918.

Griswold, Wendy. *Renaissance Revivals: City Comedy and Revenge Tragedy in the London Theatre, 1576–1980*. Chicago: University of Chicago Press, 1986.

Gubar, Marah. "Entertaining Children of All Ages: Nineteenth-Century Popular Theater as Children's Theater," *American Quarterly* 66, no. 1 (March 2014): 1–34.

Habberton, John, *Poor Boy's Chances*. Philadelphia: Henry Altemus Company, 1900.

Hall, G. Stanley. *Adolescence: Its Psychology and its Relations to Physiology, Anthropology, Sociology, Sex, Crime, Religion, and Education*. New York: D. Appleton and Company, 1906.

———. *Youth: Its Education, Regimen, and Hygiene*. New York: D. Appleton and Company, 1906.

Hall, Roger A. *Performing the American Frontier, 1870–1906*. Cambridge: Cambridge University Press, 2001.

Hallwas, John E. *Dime Novel Desperadoes: The Notorious Maxwell Brothers.* Champaign: University of Illinois Press, 2008.

Hamid, George, as told to his son George Hamid, Jr. *Circus.* New York: NY Sterling, 1956.

Hamid, George, Jr. *Boy Acrobat.* New York: NY Sterling, 1956.

Harbaugh. T. C. *Judge Lynch, Jr.; or the Boy Vigilante.* Beadle & Adams Half Dime Library 6, no. 139, March 23, 1880. Van Pelt Library, University of Pennsylvania. Microfilm.

Harris, Bill, dir. *Buffalo Bill: Showman of the West.* 1995; New York: A&E Home Video. 2004. DVD.

Harris, Helen L. "Mark Twain's Response to the Native American." *American Literature* 46, no. 4 (January 1975): 495–505.

Harris, Neil. *Humbug: The Art of P. T. Barnum.* Chicago: University of Chicago Press, 1973.

Hassrick, Peter, Richard Slotkin, Vine Deloria Jr., Howard Lamar, William Judson, and Leslie Fiedler. *Buffalo Bill and the Wild West.* Brooklyn: Brooklyn Museum, 1981.

Higonnet, Anne. *Pictures of Innocence: The History and Crisis of Ideal Childhood.* New York: Thames and Hudson, 1996.

Hine, Robert V., and John Mack Faragher. *The American West: A New Interpretive History.* New Haven, CT: Yale University Press, 2000.

Hirschfelder, Arlene, "Still Playing Cowboys and Indians after All These Years?" In *American Indian Stereotypes in the Word of Children,* edited by Arlene Hirschfelder, Paulette Fairbanks Molin, and Yvonne Wakim, 137–220. Lanham, MD: Scarecrow Press, 1999.

Hofstadter, Richard. *The Progressive Historians: Turner, Beard, Parrington.* New York: Alfred A. Knopf, 1968.

Holt, Marilyn Irvin. *The Orphan Trains: Placing Out in America.* Lincoln: University of Nebraska Press, 1992.

Horsman, Reginald. *Race and Manifest Destiny: The Origins of American Racial Anglo-Saxonism.* Cambridge, MA: Harvard University Press, 1981.

Hough, Cass S. *It's a Daisy!* 30th anniversary ed. Rogers, AZ: Daisy Corporation, 2006.

Howells, William Dean. "Review of *The Adventures of Tom Sawyer.*" In *Critical Essays on the Adventures of Tom Sawyer,* edited by Gary Scharnhorst, 21–34. New York: G. K. Hall, 1993.

Hoy, Benjamin. "Cardboard Indians: Playing History in the American West." *Western Historical Quarterly* 49, no. 3 (Autumn 2018): 299–324.

Hyde, Anne F. *Empires, Nations, and Families: A New History of the North American West, 1800–1860.* Lincoln: University of Nebraska Press, 2011.

Jacobson, Lisa. *Raising Consumers: Children and the American Mass Market in the Early Twentieth Century.* New York: Columbia University Press, 2004.

Jacobson, Marcia. *Being a Boy Again: Autobiography and the American Boy Book.* Tuscaloosa: University of Alabama Press, 1994.

James, Allison, Chris Jenks, and Alan Prout. *Theorizing Childhood.* Cambridge, UK: Polity Press, 1998.

Johannsen, Albert. *The House of Beadle & Adams and its Dime and Nickel Novels: The Story of a Vanished Literature.* Norman: University of Oklahoma Press, 1950. The Beadle & Adams Dime Novel Digitization Project, Northern Illinois University Libraries. https://www.ulib.niu.edu/badndp/contents2.html.

Johnson, Michael K. *Black Masculinity and the Frontier Myth in American Literature.* Norman: University of Oklahoma Press, 2004.

Jones, Daryl. *The Dime Novel Western.* Madison, WI: Popular Press, 1978.

Jones, Karen R. and Wills, John. *The American West: Competing Visions.* Edinburgh, UK: Edinburgh University Press, 2009.

Jordan, Benjamin René. *Modern Manhood and the Boy Scouts of America: Citizenship, Race, and the Environment, 1910–1930.* Chapel Hill: University of North Carolina Press, 2016.

Jordan, Teresa. *Cowgirls: Women of the American West.* Lincoln, NE: Bison Books, 1992.

Kasper, Shirl. *Annie Oakley.* Norman: University of Oklahoma Press, 1992.

Kasson, Joy S. *Buffalo Bill's Wild West: Celebrity, Memory, and Popular History.* New York: Hill and Wang, 2000.

Keaton, Angela F. "Backyard Desperadoes: American Attitudes concerning Toy Guns in the Early Cold War Era." *Journal of American Culture* 33, no. 3 (September 2010): 183–86.

Keetley, Dawn. "The Injuries of Reading: Jesse Pomeroy and the Dire Effects of Dime Novels." *Journal of American Studies* 47, no. 3 (August 2013): 673–97.

Keller, Betty. *Black Wolf: The Life of Ernest Thompson Seton.* New York: HarperCollins, 1985.

Kett, Joseph F. "Reflections on the History of Adolescence in America." *History of the Family* 8, no. 3 (January 2003): 355–73.

———. *Rites of Passage: Adolescence in America, 1790 to the Present.* New York: Basic Books, 1977.

Key, Ellen. *The Century of the Child.* New York: G. P. Putnam's Sons, 1909.

Kidd, Kenneth B. *Making American Boys: Boyology and the Feral Tale.* Minneapolis: University of Minnesota Press, 2004.

Klein, Marcus. *Easterns, Westerns, and Private Eyes: American Matters, 1870–1900.* Madison: University of Wisconsin Press, 1994.

Kolodny, Annette. *The Lay of the Land: Metaphor as Experience and History in American Life and Letters.* Chapel Hill: University of North Carolina Press, 1975.

Knox, Leila Moss. *The Storyteller: My Years with Ernest Thompson Seton.* Minneapolis: Langdon Street Press, 2015.

Krause, Sydney J. "Mark Twain's Image of the American West: Land of Marvels and Malevolence." In *Samuel L. Clemens: A Mysterious Stranger,* edited by Hans Borchers and Daniel E. Williams, 35–54. Frankfurt: Peter Lang, 1986.

Kuznets, Lois Rostow. *When Toys Come to Life: Narratives of Animation, Metamorphosis, and Development.* New Haven, CT: Yale University Press, 1994.

Lasseter, John, dir. *Toy Story.* Walt Disney Pictures/Pixar Animation Studios, 1995.

Lasseter, John, dir. *Toy Story 2.* Walt Disney Pictures/Pixar Animation Studios, 1999.

Lawrence, D. H. *Studies in Classic American Literature.* London: Penguin Books, 1923.

Lears, Jackson. *Rebirth of a Nation: The Making of Modern America, 1877–1920*. New York: HarperCollins, 2009.

Leonard, Elizabeth Jane, and Julia Cody Goodman. *Buffalo Bill: King of the Old West: A Biography of William F. Cody*. Edited by James William Hoffman. New York: Library Publishers, 1955.

Levine, Lawrence W. *Highbrow/Lowbrow: The Emergence of Cultural Hierarchy in America*. Cambridge, MA: Harvard University Press, 1988.

Levy, Andrew. *Huck Finn's America: Mark Twain and the Era That Shaped his Masterpiece*. New York: Simon & Schuster, 2015.

Lewis, R. W. B. *The American Adam: Innocence, Tragedy, and Tradition in the Nineteenth Century*. Chicago: University of Chicago Press, 1955.

Limerick, Patricia Nelson. "The Adventures of the Frontier in the Twentieth Century." In *The Frontier in American Culture: An Exhibition at the Newberry Library, August 26, 1994–January 7, 1995*, edited by James R. Grossman, 67–102. Berkeley: University of California Press, 1994.

Lott, Eric. *Love and Theft: Blackface Minstrelsy and the American Working Class*. New York: Oxford University Press, 1993.

Love, Nat. *The Life and Adventures of Nat Love*. Lincoln: University of Nebraska Press, 1995.

MacDonald, Robert H. *Sons of the Empire: The Frontier and the Boy Scout Movement, 1890–1918*. Toronto: University of Toronto Press, 1993.

Macleod, David I. *Building Character in the American Boy: The Boy Scouts, YMCA, and Their Forerunners, 1870–1920*. Madison: University of Wisconsin Press, 1983.

MacNeil, Denise Mary. *The Emergence of the American Frontier Hero, 1682–1826: Gender, Action, and Emotion*. New York: Palgrave Macmillan, 2009.

Maddox, Lucy. "Politics, Performance, and Indian Identity." *American Studies International* 40, no. 2 (June 2002): 7–36.

Maddra, Sam A. *Hostiles? The Lakota Ghost Dance and Buffalo Bill's Wild West*. Norman: University of Oklahoma Press, 2006.

Mailloux, Steven. *Rhetorical Power*. Ithaca, NY: Cornell University Press, 1989.

Manning, William. "Letter to Frank O'Brien, April 14, 1897." Manuscript Collection 354, University of Delaware Library Special Collections.

Marra, Kim. "Taming America as Actress: Augustin Daly, Ada Rehan, and the Discourse of Imperial Frontier Conquest." In *Performing American Culture*, edited by Jeffrey D. Mason and J. Ellen Gainor, 52–72. Ann Arbor: University of Michigan Press, 1999.

Marten, James. *America's Corporal: James Tanner in War and Peace*. Athens: University of Georgia Press, 2014.

Martin, Jonathan D. "The Grandest and Most Cosmopolitan Object Teacher: *Buffalo Bill's Wild West* and the Politics of American Identity, 1883–1899." *Radical History Review* 66 (Fall 1996): 93–123.

McGoff, Parker (Paddy). When Buffalo Bill's 'Red Injuns' Took Chances on 'Poled Ponies." *The Brooklyn Eagle*, August 5, 1945. Brooklyn Newsstand.

McNenly, Linda Scarangella. *Native Performers in Wild West Shows: From Buffalo Bill to Euro Disney*. Norman: University of Oklahoma Press, 2012.

Mechling, Jay, "Boy Scouts, the National Rifle Association, and the Domestication of Rifle Shooting." *American Studies* 53, no. 1 (2014): 5–26.

———. "Gun Play." *American Journal of Play* 1, no. 2 (Fall 2008): 192–209.

Micheaux, Oscar. *The Conquest: The Story of a Negro Pioneer.* College Park, MD: McGrath, 1969.

Mintz, Steven. *Huck's Raft: A History of American Childhood.* Cambridge, MA: Harvard University Press, 2004.

Mintz, Steven, and Susan Kellog. *Domestic Revolutions: A Social History of American Family Life.* New York: The Free Press, 1988.

Moore, Jacqueline M. *Cow Boys and Cattle Men: Class and Masculinities on the Texas Frontier, 1865–1900.* New York: New York University Press, 2010.

Moses, L. G. *Wild West Shows and the Images of American Indians, 1883–1933.* Albuquerque: University of New Mexico Press, 1999.

Murfin, Joe C. *Daisy: It All Starts Here: Celebrating 135 Years as the Company the Teaches America to Shoot, 1886–2011.* Rogers, AR: Daisy Outdoor Products, 2011.

Myers, John E. B. *Child Protection in America: Past, Present, and Future.* Oxford: Oxford University Press, 2006.

O'Connor. Stephen. *Orphan Trains: The Story of Charles Loring Brace and the Children He Saved and Failed.* Boston: Houghton Mifflin, 2001.

O'Kieffe, Charley. *Western Story: The Recollections of Charley O'Kieffe, 1884–1898.* Lincoln: University of Nebraska Press, 1974.

"An Oral History of Star Trek." Interviews by Edward Gross and Mark A. Altman. *Smithsonian*, May 2016. https://www.smithsonianmag.com/arts-culture/oral -history-star-trek-180958779/.

Orme, Nicholas. *Medieval Children.* New Haven, CT: Yale University Press, 2001.

Paine, Thomas. *The Writings of Thomas Paine, Volume 1 (1774–1779): The American Crisis.* Edited by Moncure Daniel Conway. New York: G. P. Putnam's Sons, 1894. http://www.gutenberg.org/ebooks/3741.

Palmer, Alex, "The Gun-Loving Boy Scouts of the Early 20th Century." *Mental Floss*, February 1, 2016. https://mentalfloss.com/article/74545/gun-loving-boy-scouts -early-20th-century.

Parille, Ken. *Boys at Home: Discipline, Masculinity, and "the Boy-Problem" in Nineteenth Century American Literature.* Knoxville: University of Tennessee Press, 2009.

Paris, Leslie. "Through the Looking Glass: Ages, Stages, and Historical Analysis." *Journal of the History of Childhood and Youth* 1, no. 1 (Winter, 2008): 106–13.

Pizer, Donald. "Hamlin Garland in the *Standard*." *American Literature* 26, no. 3 (November 1954): 401–15.

Pizer, Donald, ed. *Hamlin Garland, Prairie Radical: Writings from the 1890s.* Urbana: University of Illinois Press, 2010.

Platt, Anthony M. *The Child Savers: The Invention of Delinquency.* Expanded 40th Anniversary Edition. New Brunswick, NJ: Rutgers University Press, 2009.

Raheja, Michelle H. *Reservation Reelism: Redfacing, Visual Sovereignty, and Representations of Native Americans in Film.* Lincoln: University of Nebraska Press, 2010.

Ravage, John W. *Black Pioneers: Images of the Black Experience on the North American Frontier.* Salt Lake City: University of Utah Press, 2008.

Reddin, Paul. *Wild West Shows*. Champaign: University of Illinois Press, 1999.

Rein, Lisa. "Down on the Ranch, President Wages War on the Underbrush." *Washington Post*, December 31, 2005.

Rennert, Jack. *100 Posters of Buffalo Bill's Wild West*. New York: Darien House, 1976.

Ringel, Paul B. *Commercializing Childhood: Children's Magazines, Urban Gentility, and the Ideal of the Child Consumer in the United States, 1823–1918*. Amherst: University of Massachusetts Press, 2015.

Roberts, Lewis. "'It's a Dangerous World Out There for a Toy': Identity Crisis and Commodity Culture in the *Toy Story* Movies." *Children's Literature Association Quarterly* 42, no. 4 (Winter 2017): 417–37.

Rotundo, E. Anthony. *American Manhood: Transformations in Masculinity from the Revolution to the Modern Era*. New York: Basic Books, 1993.

Russell, Don. *The Lives and Legends of Buffalo Bill*. Norman: University of Oklahoma Press, 1960.

Ryan, Mary P. *Cradle of the Middle Class: The Family in Oneida County, New York, 1790–1865*. Cambridge: Cambridge University Press, 1981.

Rydell, Robert W, and Rob Kroes. *Buffalo Bill in Bologna: The Americanization of the World, 1869–1922*. Chicago: University of Chicago Press, 2005.

Sagala, Sandra. *Buffalo Bill on Stage*. Albuquerque: University of New Mexico Press, 2008.

Sánchez-Eppler, Karen. *Dependent States: The Child's Part in Nineteenth-Century American Culture*. Chicago: University of Chicago Press, 2005.

Savage, Jon. *Teenage: The Prehistory of Youth Culture, 1875–1945*. London: Penguin, 2007.

Saxton, Alexander. *The Rise and Fall of the White Republic: Class Politics and Mass Culture in Nineteenth-Century America*. London: Verso, 1990.

Schneider, Eric C. *In the Web of Class: Delinquents and Reformers in Boston, 1810s–1930s*. New York: New York University Press, 1992.

Seton, Ernest. *Two Little Savages: Being the Adventures of Two Boys Who Lived as Indians and What They Learned*. New York: Dover, 1962.

Shaheen, Aaron. "Endless Frontiers and Emancipation from History: Horatio Alger's Reconstruction of Place and Time in Ragged Dick." *Children's Literature* 33 (2005): 20–40.

Shuttleworth, Sally. *The Mind of the Child: Child Development in Literature, Science, and Medicine, 1840–1900*. Oxford: Oxford University Press, 2010.

Simmel, Georg. *On Individuality and Social Forms*. Edited by Donald N. Levine. Chicago: University of Chicago Press, 1971.

Slater, Katharine. "Who Gets to Die of Dysentery? Ideology, Geography, and *The Oregon Trail*." *Children's Literature Association Quarterly* 42, no. 4 (Winter 2017): 374–95.

Slotkin, Richard. *The Fatal Environment: The Myth of the Frontier in the Age of Industrialization, 1800–1890*. New York: Atheneum, 1985.

———. *Gunfighter Nation: The Myth of the Frontier in Twentieth-Century America*. New York: Atheneum, 1992.

Smith, Henry Nash. *Virgin Land: The American West as Symbol and Myth*. New York: Vintage Books, 1957.

Spencer, Herbert. *A System of Synthetic Philosophy—First Principles.* Vol. 1. Redditch, UK: Read Books, 2008.

Standing Bear, Luther. *My People the Sioux.* Lincoln: University of Nebraska Press, 1975.

Stone, Albert E. *The Innocent Eye: Childhood in Mark Twain's Imagination.* Hamden, CT: Archon Books, 1970.

Sully, James. *Studies of Childhood.* Latham, MD: University Publications of America, 1977.

Sumner, William Graham. "What Our Boys Are Reading." *Scribner's Monthly,* March 1, 1878.

Sutton-Smith, Brian. *The Ambiguity of Play.* Cambridge, MA: Harvard University Press, 1997.

Taylor, Diana. *The Archive and the Repertoire: Performing Cultural Memory in the Americas.* Durham: Duke University Press, 2003.

Thrasher, Frederic M. *The Gang: A Study of 1,313 Gangs in Chicago.* Chicago: University of Chicago Press, 1927.

Tompkins, Jane. *West of Everything: The Inner Life of Westerns.* Oxford: Oxford University Press, 1992.

Turner, Frederick Jackson. *Rereading Frederick Jackson Turner: "The Significance of the Frontier in American History" and Other Essays.* Commentary by John Mack Faragher. New Haven, CT: Yale University Press, 1994.

———. "The Significance of the Frontier in American History." *Report of the American Historical Association* (1893). University of Virginia. http://xroads.virginia.edu/~hyper/turner/chapter1.html#text1.

Twain, Mark. *Adventures of Huckleberry Finn.* Edited by Thomas Cooley. New York: W. W. Norton & Company, 1999.

———. *The Adventures of Tom Sawyer.* New York: Harper & Brothers, 1920.

———. *Huck Finn and Tom Sawyer among the Indians and Other Unfinished Stories.* Edited by Dahlia Armon and Walter Blair. Berkeley: University of California Press, 1989.

Unkrich, Lee, dir. *Toy Story 3.* Walt Disney Pictures/Pixar Animation Studios, 2010.

Vallone, Lynne. *Disciplines of Virtue: Girls' Culture in the Eighteenth and Nineteenth Centuries.* New Haven, CT: Yale University Press, 1995.

Wallis, Michael. *The Real Wild West: The 101 Ranch and the Creation of the American West.* New York: St. Martin's Press, 1999.

Warren, Louis S. *Buffalo Bill's America: William Cody and the Wild West Show.* New York: Alfred A. Knopf, 2005.

West, Elliott. *Growing Up with the Country: Childhood in the Far Western Frontier.* Albuquerque: University of New Mexico Press, 1989.

Wheeler, Edward L. *The Black Hills Jezebel; or, Deadwood Dick's Ward.* Beadle & Adams Half Dime Library 8, no. 201. May 31, 1881.

———. *Deadwood Dick, The Prince of the Road; or, The Black Rider of the Black Hills.* In *Reading the West: An Anthology of Dime Westerns.* Edited by Bill Brown. Boston: Bedford Books, 1997.

——. *Deadwood Dick's Dream, or The Rivals of the Road.* Beadle & Adams Half Dime Library 8 no. 195. August 19, 1881.

——. *The Double Daggers, or, Deadwood Dick's Defiance.* Beadle & Adams Half Dime Library 20, no. 4. February 6, 1884. Microfilm.

——. *Wild Ivan, the Boy Claude Duval, or the Brotherhood of Death.* Beadle & Adams Half Dime Library 35, no. 14. April 16, 1884. Microfilm.

Whitaker, Frederick. *Dick Darling, the Pony Express Rider.* Beadle & Adams Half Dime Library 3, no. 6, May 21, 1878. https://dimenovels.lib.niu.edu/islandora/object /dimenovels:129483.

White, Kathryn. "'Through Their Eyes': Buffalo Bill's Wild West as a Drawing Table for American Identity," *Constructing the Past* 7, no. 1 (2006): 35–50.

White, Richard. "Frederick Jackson Turner and Buffalo Bill" In *The Frontier in American Culture: An Exhibition at the Newberry Library, August 26, 1994–January 7, 1995.* Edited by James R. Grossman, 7–65. Berkeley: University of California Press, 1994.

Witt, David L. *Ernest Thompson Seton: The Life and Legacy of an Artist and Conservationist.* Layton, UT: Gibbs Smith, 2010.

Wojtowicz, James W. *The W. F. Cody Buffalo Bill Collectors Guide with Values.* Paducah, KY: Collector Books, 1998.

Worden, Daniel. *Masculine Style: The American West and Literary Modernism.* New York: Palgrave Macmillan, 2011.

Yellow Bird, Michael, "Cowboys and Indians: Toys of Genocide: Icons of American Colonialism" *Wicazo Sa Review* 19, no. 2 (Fall 2004): 33–48.

Young, Arthur. "Banish the Books: Horatio Alger Jr., the Censors, the Libraries, and the Readers, 1870–1910." *Children's Literature Association Quarterly* 38, No. 4. (Winter 2013): 420–34.

The Youth's Companion. Boston, MA. July 18, 1901.

Zelizer, Viviana A. *Pricing the Priceless Child: The Changing Social Value of Children.* Princeton: Princeton University Press, 1985.

INDEX

www.ingramcontent.com/pod-product-compliance
Lightning Source LLC
Chambersburg PA
CBHW021356090426
42742CB00009B/882